MAKING CONNECTIONS

MAKING CONNECTIONS

The Relational Worlds
of Adolescent Girls
at Emma Willard School

EDITED BY

Carol Gilligan, Nona P. Lyons,
and Trudy J. Hanmer

Harvard University Press
Cambridge, Massachusetts
London, England
1990

This book is printed on acid-free paper, and its binding materials
have been chosen for strength and durability.

Library of Congress Cataloging-in-Publication Data

Making connections : the relational worlds of adolescent girls at Emma
    Willard School / edited by Carol Gilligan, Nona P. Lyons, and Trudy
    J. Hanmer.
        p. cm.
    Includes bibliographical references.
    ISBN 0-674-54040-9 (alk. paper). — ISBN 0-674-54041-7 (pbk. :
alk. paper)
    1. Teenage girls—New York (State)—Troy—Attitudes—Case studies.
    2. Teenage girls—New York (State)—Troy—Psychology—Case studies.
    3. Teenage girls—Education—New York (State)—Troy—Case studies.
    4. Emma Willard School (Troy, N.Y.) I. Gilligan, Carol, 1936—   .
    II. Lyons, Nona. III. Hanmer, Trudy J. IV. Emma Willard School
    (Troy, N.Y.)
    [HQ798.M296   1990]   90-30819
    305.2'35'08352—dc20   CIP

Permissions

The two poems quoted in the preface are "Obsolete Geography," reprinted
from *The Land of Look Behind,* by Michelle Cliff, published by Firebrand
Books (Ithaca, New York) in 1985; and "Time-Travel," reprinted from
Satan Says, by Sharon Olds, by permission of the University of Pittsburgh
Press, © 1980 by Sharon Olds.

Designed by Romeo Enriquez.

For Robert C. Parker

Acknowledgments

Robert C. Parker, principal of Emma Willard School from 1979 to 1986, gave vision, commitment, and energy to this project. Without him it would never have been undertaken. His memory has served as a guiding force in the preparation of this volume.

We wish also to thank Scott McVay and Valerie Peed of the Geraldine R. Dodge Foundation for their support of the project. In addition, we want to acknowledge the Trustees of Emma Willard School, especially President Jameson A. Baxter, for their leadership, foresight, and financial contributions.

Without the work—the energy, the dedication, and the insights—of women students at the Harvard Graduate School of Education and also Suzie Benack of Union College, this research could not have been undertaken. We are grateful for the contributions and the colleagueship of Jane Attanucci, Susan Cook, Dorothy Danaher, Margie Lippard, Valerie Johnson, Kay Johnston, Kate O'Connell, Susan Pollak, Sharon Rich, Jane Saltonstall, Judy Salzman, Lisa Smulyan, Catherine Steiner-Adair, and Janie Ward. Our special thanks to Sharry Langdale, who collaborated in planning the project and in conducting the research.

In the execution of any work as extensive as this, there are always those people whose names do not appear on the title page but whose efforts are invaluable in seeing the project through to completion. Our thanks in this case go to Liz Westbrook and Cheryl Ackner at Emma Willard and Carole Lee and Markie Trottenberg at Harvard.

Finally, we want to acknowledge the teachers and staff at Emma Willard who collaborated on this project. But, most of all, we thank the students of Emma Willard School for their willingness to join in this exploration of girls' lives.

Carol Gilligan
Nona P. Lyons
Trudy J. Hanmer
June 1989

Contributors

Elizabeth Bernstein worked with Carol Gilligan at the Harvard Graduate School of Education while pursuing her doctorate. She is currently a third-year student in the clinical psychology doctoral program at Boston University.

Kathleen Holland Bollerud used the data from the Emma Willard study for the pilot project for her dissertation on gender differences in adolescents. She received her doctorate from the Harvard Graduate School of Education in 1987. She is currently director of psychology at Beech Hill Hospital in Dublin, New Hampshire. Her special area of interest is the treatment of substance abusers who have experienced physical or sexual abuse.

Lyn Mikel Brown is an instructor at the Harvard Graduate School of Education and a research associate at the Center for the Study of Gender, Education, and Human Development. She is currently directing a four-year longitudinal study of girls' development with Carol Gilligan in collaboration with Laurel School in Shaker Heights, Ohio. Lyn's particular interests focus on girls' narratives of relationships and the development of a relational, reader-response method for analyzing interview texts.

Susan Boynton Christopherson is a doctoral candidate at the Harvard Graduate School of Education. Her special interest is adolescent females from alcoholic families. She is currently a clinical intern at Tufts University.

Emily Schultz Frank is a doctoral candidate in counseling and consulting psychology at the Harvard Graduate School of Education. Her dissertation topic is "The Role of Shame and Guilt in Eating Disorders." She is currently an intern in clinical child psychology at Tufts New England Medical Center.

Carol Gilligan is the author of *In a Different Voice: Psychological Theory and Women's Development* and is Professor of Education at Harvard University. Along with former principal Robert C. Parker, she initiated the Dodge Study at Emma Willard School. Her current project is: "Strengthening healthy resistance and courage in girls."

Trudy J. Hanmer has been associate principal of Emma Willard School since 1981. She served as the site coordinator for the project between 1981 and 1985.

Nona P. Lyons was the principal researcher and coordinator of the research team for the Dodge Study at Emma Willard. She currently teaches at the Harvard Graduate School of Education. Her research interests continue to focus on examining conflict and decision-making in a variety of settings. Her current work includes a project examining the ethical and epistemological dimensions of teachers' work and development, for which she received a Spencer Fellowship, and a study of decision-making and conflict negotiation of men and women managers and administrators.

Janet Mendelsohn is currently a documentary filmmaker whose most recent work is *Figure in a Landscape: A Conversation with J. B. Jackson*. She has been a doctoral candidate in counseling and consulting psychology at the Harvard Graduate School of Education. While there, her interests centered on issues of women's development.

Sharon Rich served as an interviewer and researcher throughout the Dodge Study. She received her doctorate in education from Harvard University in 1986 and before that had taught in a public high school for several years. She received a master of arts in teaching from the University of Chicago in 1978. Currently Sharon is a financial planner teaching women about money management and is the mother of an infant daughter.

Annie G. Rogers received her doctorate from Washington University in educational and counselling psychology in 1987. She is currently Lecturer on Education and a research associate in human development and psychology at Harvard University Graduate School of Education. Her thesis research was a validity study of ego development and moral voice.

Jane Forbes Saltonstall served as an interviewer for the Dodge Study for two years. She received her Ed.D. from the Harvard Graduate School of Education. Her dissertation focused on learning about learning through the experience of adult women students. Her special interest is the interaction between the two modes of moral development and ways of learning, curriculum and pedagogy. She is a research associate in a study of community college presidents.

Judith P. Salzman served as an interviewer and researcher throughout the Dodge Study. She received her doctorate from Harvard University and is currently a clinical intern in psychology at Boston Evening Medical Clinic, where she works with older adolescents and young adults. She has continued her research on ambivalent attachment.

Catherine Steiner-Adair was a psychologist at Phillips Academy in Andover, Massachusetts, before earning her doctorate at Harvard in the

Counselling and Consulting Psychology program. She is currently in private practice at Middlesex Family Associates, in Lexington, Massachusetts. In addition she is a research associate at the Center for the Study of Gender, Education, and Human Development.

Lori Stern is a doctoral candidate in counselling and consulting psychology at Harvard University and is a Clinical Fellow in Psychology at Massachusetts General Hospital and Harvard Medical School. Her research interests are in female development, object relations theory, and clinical practice.

Janie Victoria Ward is an assistant professor of education and human services at Simmons College. In addition she is a research associate at Harvard Graduate School of Education. Her research interests include the development of racial identity and the development of morality in children of color. She completed her doctorate in human development at Harvard Graduate School of Education in 1986.

Note to the Harvard Edition

This collection of essays was originally published by Emma Willard School and records the study of girls' psychological development conducted at the school between 1981 and 1984. In writing a prologue and preface to these essays and appending as an epilogue part of a recent paper suggesting a musical language for psychology, I have placed the study at Emma Willard within the context of continuing research on psychological theory and women's development. Specifically, I have introduced a thesis drawn from studies involving younger girls and girls living in different settings, and in doing so, framed these essays on the relational worlds of adolescent girls at Emma Willard with evidence that the time between ages eleven and sixteen is an especially critical one in girls' lives and that the crisis is one of relationship.

The study at Emma Willard (a day and boarding high school for girls) was the first in a series of studies designed to connect a psychology of women with girls' voices. These studies, which constitute the Harvard Project on the Psychology of Women and the Development of Girls, have involved listening to girls in Boys' and Girls' Clubs in three Boston neighborhoods, in an urban public high school, in an independent coeducational high school (roughly comparable to Emma Willard), and at Laurel School in Cleveland, where a five-year longitudinal study of girls ages six to eighteen was conducted between 1985 and 1989. This sustained attention to girls' psychological development following the Emma Willard study was made possible by grants from the Lilly Endowment, the Rockefeller Foundation, the Joseph S. Klingenstein Foundation, the Cleveland Foundation, and the George Gund Foundation. Edith Phelps, Janie Ward, Jill Taylor, Betty Bardige, and Kay Johnston contributed in major ways to this work, particularly in the studies of urban youth. Sharry Langdale amplified the voices of eleven-year-old girls within the ongoing project by conducting a series of interviews with girls of that age, supported by a grant from Marilyn Hoffman. The Harvard-Laurel project was directed by Lyn Mikel Brown, and in contrasting the voices of eleven- and sixteen-year-old girls, I have drawn centrally on her work as well as the work of Annie Rogers.

Carol Gilligan
February 14, 1990
Cambridge, Massachusetts

Prologue

In the fall of 1981, I went to Emma Willard School to speak with the students about what was to become known as "the Dodge Study." It was the beginning of school, and as I drove, first west across Massachusetts and then north into New York, the New England landscape yielded to the more somber tones of red brick buildings, iron fences, tall pines. I thought of Dreiser's novel, *An American Tragedy*; I thought of childhood summers spent in the Adirondacks—Loon Lake, Tupper Lake. Then, suddenly, I was in Troy.

The school is surrounded by walls, set up on a hill, apart from the town, from Rensselaer Polytechnic Institute which is down and across the road, from the river, from the valley, from boys. The buildings extend the atmosphere of seclusion; they are mostly gothic—elegant against the late September sky, a cloisters enclosing a greensward, grass carefully tended and crossed diagonally by paths. The rule is that only the seniors may walk on the central triangle of grass. The dormitory buildings with their dining halls are named Sage and Kellas; there is a new library and studios—airy spaces for artwork and dance. An old vision of young women returns. I have come to begin a study of adolescence—to think about what "development" means for girls coming of age in the late twentieth century.

I talk about the study briefly in the morning assembly—white walls playing against the dark woods of stairs and stage, brown-backed chairs filled with girls wearing navy blue sweaters, some reds and greens, plaid skirts or grey, and the faculty seated among them—women and men. I explain the hopes with which I have come. I speak of collaboration—we will labor together to begin to fill in a startling omission: the absence of girls from the major studies of adolescence. It was this absence which sparked the collaboration between Emma Willard School, the Harvard Graduate School of Education, and the Geraldine Rockefeller Dodge Foundation—a tristate liaison devoted to the exploration of girls' development and girls' education. As the 1980 *Handbook of Adolescent Psychology* wryly observed: "Adolescent girls have simply not been much studied."

The students listened with the restlessness, the distraction of adolescents. My question was not their question, they had other things on their minds. I finished my presentation and asked for questions. A student, to my left, about midway back, raised her hand: "What could you possibly learn," she asked, "by studying us?"

Like perfect pitch, her question caught the tradition in which she was living. How many others in effect had asked: what could you possibly learn by studying girls? And yet now that tradition was ending. Clearly girls at Emma Willard are not representative of girls in general. I was interested, however, in adolescence—the time when, in Erik Erikson's terms, the intersection between life-history and history becomes acute, the time when what Hannah Arendt calls "the urge toward self-display" becomes pressing—the human impulse "to respond by showing to the overwhelming effect of being shown." In one of Virginia Woolf's stories, a character asks, "When the self speaks to the self, who is speaking?" and answers, "the entombed soul, the spirit driven in . . . the self that took the veil and left the world—a coward perhaps, yet somehow beautiful." Innocently, artfully, under a placid surface of self-deprecation, my questioner in the morning assembly had touched upon the heart of the matter. In learning to think in the terms of the disciplines and thus to bring her thoughts and feelings into line with the traditions of Western culture, was she also learning to dismiss her own experience, so that it seemed implausible that someone would learn something of value by listening to her?

Women educated in the Western tradition, when writing novels of education, tend to begin their novels not in infancy or early childhood (as in *David Copperfield* or *Tom Jones* or *A Portrait of the Artist*), but at the edge of adolescence with a girl of eight or nine or ten. Jane Eyre, for example, is ten at the beginning of Charlotte Bronte's novel, and she declares herself "a resister" at the start. Her resistance is demonstrated by her refusal to say that she loves Aunt Reed when she does not. Similarly Claudia, the nine-year-old narrator of Toni Morrison's novel, *The Bluest Eye*, refuses to align her perceptions with or justify the conventions that rule the society around her—the conventions that would have her, a black girl, love a white Shirley Temple doll. Claudia knows the difference between love that is genuine ("Love, thick and dark as Alaga syrup . . . I could smell it—taste it . . . everywhere in that house") and "fraudulent love," the idealized love that is, she observes, "the best hiding place" for cruelty and violence.

I listened to these resisters in women's fiction, these girls who speak about what they are hearing and seeing, who know what they are feeling and thinking and will not make false protestations of love, and I heard the voices of eleven- and twelve-year-old girls in my studies. Like Amy, who does not change her mind when she is asked repeatedly whether a man should steal or let his wife die; who says, over and over, that stealing is not a good way to solve the problem. Or Tanya, who when told by a camp director that her homesick cousin cannot call his parents because it was against the rules, says, "Sorry, but he's only seven" and "people are more important than rules." Like Claudia, Tanya describes the world of human feelings, including her own, with the eye of a fine naturalist. The clarity of her perception is startling as she, distinguishing her own feelings from those of her cousin, lays out the difference between feeling another person's feelings (empathy) and responding to another person's feelings with feelings of one's own. "It wasn't my feeling, my cousin's," she explains. "I wasn't feeling what he was feeling, but I did have a little empathy, but not that much. . . . But he was very miserable, and I almost felt like he did in a way, so I did go up [to the camp director] because I felt miserable having him feel miserable."

At the edge of adolescence, in a class studying holocaust and human behavior, a third of the girls take evidence of violence at face value, writing journal entries recording their feelings and taking feelings as grounds for knowing what is going on. Like Tanya, they respond to the feelings of others with feelings of their own. Like Claudia in Morrison's novel, these girls do not justify violence or question their feelings—they do not ask why or whether it happened; instead they ask: how does this happen, and how can they or someone else stop it. Another twelve-year-old in a different setting, when asked to complete a sentence beginning "Rules are—," writes, "Rules are—supposed to be the guidelines of life and the way to live it, but I can't say frankly that I'm convinced of that."

Traditional descriptions of women as "unruly" thus raise the question: whose rules? In novels of education written by women, the astute and outspoken and clear-eyed resister often gets lost in a sudden disjunction or chasm as she approaches adolescence, as if the world that she knows from experience in childhood suddenly comes to an end and divides from the world she is to enter as a young woman, a world that is governed by different rules. How to bridge this chasm or cross this disjunction becomes the question explored in the novels. And the novelists' suggestion that a girl's education hinges on the strength of her knowledge and the fate of her resistance finds an echo in women poets' description of a journey to retrieve their twelve-year-old self—a journey linked with the recovery of voice and therefore with psychological survival.

Perhaps adolescence is an especially critical time in women's development because it poses a problem of connection that is not easily resolved. As the river of a girl's life flows into the sea of Western culture, she is in danger of drowning or disappearing. To take on the problem of appearance, which is the problem of her development, and to connect her life with history on a cultural scale, she must enter—and by entering disrupt—a tradition in which "human" has for the most part meant male. Thus a struggle often breaks out in girls' lives at the edge of adolescence, and the fate of this struggle becomes key to girls' development and to Western civilization.

In the course of the journey that began with the study at Emma Willard, I wondered: are girls the wooden horse in the story about human development—the story in which an earlier Troy plays so large a part? I began to suspect that inside the question "What could you possibly learn by studying us?" there was another question: "What would happen if what was inside of us were to enter the world?" Was the question a test? Was I going to listen to girls' thoughts and feelings?: Would I take seriously what girls themselves, and also the world in general, said was not worth listening to—like girls' descriptions of their relationships with others or girls' perceptions of the human social world? Are girls, in fact, capable, as women's novels suggest, of distinguishing genuine from fraudulent love?

Once, at a time when I was asking women to solve moral problems that men had framed, like the dilemma whose premises eleven-year-old Amy called into question, a woman—a college graduate—looked at me and said, "Would you like to know what I think or would you like to know what I *really* think?" thus conveying that she had learned to think in a way that differed from the way she really thought. Increasingly, I suspected that this learning takes place during adolescence, the time when girls come up against the wall of Western culture. Listening to Amy at fifteen become deeply confused as she answers the question which she resisted so steadfastly at eleven; listening to the interviewer—a woman —respond to Amy's saying that the situation is unreal and that she has "a lot of trouble buying that story" by telling Amy that "You have to make a lot of assumptions;" listening to Tanya at fifteen explain how she signed "love" to a letter she had written to someone whom she did not love, I heard evidence suggesting that girls' development in adolescence may hinge on their resisting not the loss of innocence but the loss of knowledge. And I became interested in the ability of girls to resist this loss.

The essays in this volume then are part of a process that they also describe: of changing a tradition by including girls' voices, of listening to girls and asking again about the meaning of self, relationship, and morality—concepts central to any psychology of human development. For obvious reasons, the studies here are not intended as definitive statements about girls or relationships or development or adolescence. Instead, they are offered in a spirit of celebration, to honor the 175th anniversary of a school founded by a woman who took action on behalf of girls' education. Each essay originated with a question that arose or became clarified in the experience of the research. No attempt has been made to unify these essays or to arrive at a central thesis, beyond the common intention to listen for the ways in which girls orchestrate themes of connection and separation and concerns about care and justice in speaking about themselves, about their relationships, and about experiences of conflict. Brought together, these essays become a collage of sorts; a series of impressions gathered at a particular time and place from a variety of angles; a series of exercises en route to a new psychology of adolescence and of women; an elaborate counterpoint of connections between a group of women who have chosen to work in the fields of pyschology and education and adolescent girls who are living in a relatively isolated setting, in an atmosphere of privilege and promise, in an intensely female community housed in the architecture of high Western culture.

Preface

Teaching Shakespeare's Sister: Notes from the Underground of Female Adolescence

CAROL GILLIGAN

Editors' Note: *This preface was read in somewhat different versions at the American Association for Higher Education Conference: "Highest Calling: Teaching to Rebuild the Nation," on March 11, 1988, in Washington, D.C., and as one of two lectures on love and resistance, given as the Heinz Werner Lectures on November 18, 1988, at Clark University.*

At Harvard last year, a Women's Studies program began in the college, after much deliberation. Women's Studies is old news by now, but it continues to raise the question: What are the experiences of girls coming of age in a culture that contains the need for Women's Studies? The absence of women from the curriculum that poses a problem in education also creates a problem in girls' development, a problem that girls encounter in the course of their education. As the swirl of controversy currently attests, secondary and higher education constitute an initiation into Western culture, leading students into the ways of seeing and listening and speaking that over the centuries have created both Western civilization and the need for Women's Studies. To see the absence of women as a significant omission means to change civilization, to reform the disciplines, and thereby to change higher education. Thus if women students—half the university population—experience their perceptions or their questions as disruptive, it may be because, in fact, they are so.

It was in graduate school, one woman said—a recent graduate student—that she learned the meaning of "the disciplines." In graduate school she had to put aside her questions about political science (her chosen field) and learn what were the right questions or the questions she should ask if she wanted to become a good political scientist. So she developed the following practice: she would sit at her desk writing her thoughts about Hannah Arendt (whose work she had read over the summer) on little slips of paper, which she would then stuff into the drawer, thus leaving the top of the desk clear for Locke and Mill and Rousseau. Hannah Arendt, she was told, wrote well and was interesting, but she was not a real political scientist. The graduate student secretly feared that she was not either. In teaching such women students, the question arises: What does one teach them?

I will begin with Shakespeare, who turned at the beginning of his last play to the question of a daughter's education. Miranda, witnessing the terrible scene of storm and shipwreck that opens *The Tempest*, cries out that she cannot bear to see such suffering. "Had I been any god of power," she says, she would have taken action to stop it. At which point Prospero decides that it is time for her education. "Pluck my magic garment from me," he tells her, "Ope thine ear,/ Obey, and be attentive." But first he asks whether she remembers a time before they came to the island. "Tis far off," Miranda says, "And rather like a dream than an assurance . . . [but] Had I not/ Four, or five women once that tended me?" More, Prospero says, "but how is it that this lives in thy mind?"

In short, Miranda's questions—Why all the suffering? and Where are the women?—are essentially irrelevant to the story that Prospero proceeds to tell: of court intrigue; of betrayal by his brother who forged an alliance with the King of Naples and took over his kingdom; about her mother, who, Prospero explains, "was a piece of virtue," her virtue manifest in her assurance that Miranda was, in fact, his daughter, from whom he, Prospero, drew comfort in the dark time of exile and sea voyage that brought them, father and daughter, to this strange island with its mixture of old world and new.

Miranda listens to her father's tale of pain and suffering, high intrigue, and heroic adventure. Clearly moved by his story, she thanks him for so tutoring her. "And now," she says, returning to her question, "For still 'tis beating in my mind,—your reason/ For raising this sea storm?" Prospero's answer is *The Tempest*—the play—that great musical drama, that pageant of Western civilization, bringing to Miranda in the end honor, riches, marriage, and her father's blessing. Yet the costs of this education also are clear. In the last scene, Miranda, playing at chess with her husband, Ferdinand, says that "for a score of kingdoms," she would be willing to call false play fair. The drownings of the opening storm turn out to have been a mirage or illusion; what has been drowned or drowned out in the *The Tempest* is the opening voice of Miranda.

In 1928, Virginia Woolf wrote about being shut out of this world— shut out literally from its great universities, unable to go into the libraries and see how they did it: how Milton created his manuscript, what words he crossed out, what corrections he made. But also shut out of the creative process that issued forth with the plays of Shakespeare. And to examine this question, Woolf creates the character not of Prospero's daughter but of Shakespeare's sister, whom she calls Judith Shakespeare—the poet who "died young and never wrote a word." She lies buried, Woolf tells us, at the crossroads—the place where Oedipus killed his father, "where the omnibuses now stop, outside the Elephant and Castle." But it was Woolf's belief that underneath this seemingly ordinary surface of daily life, "this poet who never wrote a word and was buried at the crossroads still lives . . . and needs only the opportunity to walk among us in the flesh." This opportunity, she enjoins her reader, "is now coming within your power to give her." The year was 1928.

In my class last fall on clinical interviewing, I asked the students to pose a real question, a question to which they really wanted to know the answer and one that would require them to talk with another person. For some of the women in the class, this exercise proved surprising. To bring genuine inquiry into their relationships with others seemed transformative, changing their experience of relationships even with old and good friends. Others, in reflecting on the exercise, wrote about the effort it took to clear out of their minds "good questions" or "important questions," so as even to know what their real questions were. I thought about why this exercise was particularly revealing for women students and also about the hope that lies in women asking real questions as they enter, via their education, a world whose tradition of storm and shipwreck now threatens civilization.

Some years ago, I sketched out a line of women's development by listening to the ways women speak about morality and about themselves (Gilligan 1977, 1982). The themes that I heard in these narratives had to do with survival, with goodness, and with truth—specifically, truths about relationships and truths about violence. By following shifts over time in the thinking of college students and graduates and also in women who were pregnant and thinking about what to do, I heard a bare-bones concern with survival (conveying a feeling of being all alone) yield to, or sometimes replace, a concern with goodness—with being a good woman as defined by the willingness to take care of, or to take on the cares of, others, a willingness often to sacrifice oneself for others in the hope that if one cared for others one would be loved and cared for by them. The central problem—feeling abandoned by others or feeling one should abandon oneself for others—was a problem of disconnection, and often led to desperate actions, desperate efforts at connection, which was one way in which some women spoke about their pregnancies. With their bodies, women can create connection by having a child who will be with them and love them.

In these struggles over connection, I saw evidence of a central dilemma of inclusion: how to include both oneself and others. To seek connection with others by excluding oneself is a strategy destined to fail. "What connection," girls would ask as these efforts unraveled, "what relationship," women wondered, were they trying to sustain? Yet teenage girls and adult women often seemed to get caught on the horns of a dilemma: was it better to respond to others and abandon themselves or to respond to themselves and abandon others? The hopelessness of this question marked an impasse in female development, a point where the desire for relationship was sacrificed for the sake of goodness, or for survival. Adolescence seemed to pose a crisis of connection for girls coming of age in Western culture. Increasingly, I wondered about the role of education in this crisis.

Listening to different women and following women's thinking and lives over time, I heard concerns about survival labeled "selfish" and replaced by concerns about responsiveness to others as the condition for relationship, which often merged with the conventions of feminine goodness where the good woman is "selfless" in her devotion to meeting others' needs. The strategies of indirection that the need to appear selfless encouraged in women sometimes precipitated a crisis, which then led to concerns about truth: the psychological truth that relationship implies the presence of both self and other, and the social truth that caring for others requires resources but is associated with economic disadvantage in North American society. Facing these truths, women tended either to ask, in effect, why care? or to ask how it was possible for them to live in connection with themselves, with others, and with the world.

From this work, I was left with a lingering question. The developmental sequence I had traced—three levels: survival, goodness, and truth, and two transitions: repairing relationship by correcting an exclusion of others, or of self—did not jibe with my observations of younger girls. In short, the sequence that I had traced by following adolescent girls and adult women through time and through crisis did not seem to be rooted in childhood. Instead, it seemed a response to a crisis, and the crisis seemed to be adolescence. Adolescence poses problems of connection for girls coming of age in Western culture, and girls are tempted or encouraged to solve these problems by excluding themselves or excluding others—that is, by being a good woman, or by being selfish. Many current books advocate one or the other of these solutions. Yet the problem girls face in adolescence is also a problem in the world at this time: the need to find ways of making connection in the face of difference.

Adolescence seems a watershed in female development, a time when girls are in danger of drowning or disappearing. "This is a Photograph of Me," one of Margaret Atwood's poems, captures girls' experience of sinking out of sight or fading from view. Psychologists, noting that in childhood boys tend to react more negatively to stress than girls, find that this pattern reverses during adolescence (Rutter 1986, Werner and Smith, 1982, Elder et al. 1985). In adolescence, girls are more likely to first manifest psychological difficulties (Ebata 1987), and girls respond more negatively to stressful challenges during the early adolescent years (Crockett and Peterson 1987). In addition, episodes of depression increase for girls in adolescence (Rutter 1986); girls are more disparaging than boys in appraising themselves (Gove and Herb 1974) and reveal more disturbances in self-image (Crockett and Peterson 1987).

Evidence that these problems in girls' adolescent development are problems of connection rather than problems of separation (as psychologists traditionally have assumed), comes from recent research—from Rogers, who found that the development of a clear sense of self in girls is related to voicing concerns about care and response in relationships (1987), and from Skoe and Marcia, who found that a strong sense of self in college women is linked with the ability to solve problems of care in relationship while staying connected with both self and others (1988). For girls to remain responsive to themselves, they must resist the conventions of feminine goodness; to remain responsive to others, they must resist the values placed on self-sufficiency and independence in North American culture. Thus for girls to develop a clear sense of self in relationship with others means—at least within the mainstream of North American culture—to take on the problem of resistance and also to take up the question of what relationship means to themselves, to others, and to the world. Josselson reports that women who have tangled with these questions through experiences of crisis in important relationships have a stronger sense of self (1987), and Miller and her colleagues provide clinical evidence of the centrality of connections in women's lives and women's psychological development (1976 and 1984).

Remembering Erikson's retrieval of the old medical meaning of the word "crisis"—a turning point for better or worse, or the Chinese ideograph that combines opportunity with danger, I wondered: are girls, because of their more acute personal encounter with disconnection at adolescence, alerted to problems of connection at a time in history when relationships in general have become corrupted in much the same sense as authority had become corrupted at the time of the Reformation—the time Erikson wrote about in his study of Martin Luther (1958)? Does a girl's sensibility, her fascination with the human social world, and her knowledge about relationships cue her at present to the specter of disconnection on a societal and global scale? In Erikson's analysis of Luther, the corruption of authority within his childhood family sensitized him to problems of authority and thus to the corruption of authority in the late medieval world. Are girls, who are more vulnerable to the corruption of love within the family, also more responsive to disconnection and violation, to the problems of relationship and the problems of violence in the world that they are entering as young women, so that a struggle tends to break out at the edge of adolescence as girls begin to notice and to comment on these problems?

It was in this context that I began to pay more atttention to the eleven- and twelve-year-old girls I was studying and to observe how frequently they appear as stalwart resisters of psychological interviewers, willing to sustain disagreement and reluctant to back down when asked, "Are you sure?" A twelve-year-old, completing a stem on a sentence completion test writes, "A girl feels good when—she has proven her point, the only one who thought it was right too." Another writes, "What gets me into trouble is—chewing gum and not having my shirt tucked in (but it's usually worth it)" (Rogers and Gilligan 1988). A twelve-year-old in a study of youth living in the inner city explains her decision to leave the house (when she was told not to) and respond to a neighbor's need for help by saying simply, "I had to help her . . . it was absolutely necessary" (Bardige et al. 1988).

Girls at this age are sometimes called "bossy." A sixth-grade teacher reports that when she paraphrases a girl's statement incorrectly, the girl is likely to look at her and say, "That is not what I mean." Teachers may find it difficult to deal with the outspokenness of girls at this age. And women teachers may find it especially unsettling to witness some of girls' experiments in inclusion and exclusion—the tortuous clique formations through which girls may discover how it feels to be left out and what it means to be taken in, and which also may provide a kind of dumbshow or dark mirroring of the adult world that girls are seeing.

Mothers sometimes speak of feeling a great loss when their daughters reach adolescence, missing, I think, the outspoken companion whom they found in their daughters prior to that time. And the image of the twelve-year-old girl recurs in poems written by contemporary women. Two poets writing in disparate cultural settings, present strikingly similar descriptions of returning for their twelve-year-old self—imagined as a girl they left sitting alone by the edge of the water. Both poets display the tradition of storm and shipwreck, and their poems contain echoes of Miranda's questions: why all the suffering and where are the women? First, Michelle Cliff, a Jamaican-born poet, in a volume called *The Land of Look Behind* in a section called "Claiming an Identity They Taught Me to Despise," in ·a passage called "Obsolete Geography," writes:

I. Airplane shadows move across the mountains, leaving me to clear rivers, dancing birds, sweet fruits. Sitting on a river rock, my legs dangle in the water. I am twelve—and solitary.

II. On a hillside, I search for mangoes. As I shake the tree the fruit drops: its sweetness splits at my feet. I suck the remaining flesh from the hairy seed. The sap from the stem stains my lips—to fester later. I am warned that I may be scarred.

This twelve-year-old girl, her legs dangling in the water, tastes the pleasures of the natural world, and is warned that she may be scarred.

III. My other life of notebooks, lessons, homework continues. I try not to pay it mind.

IV. Things that live here: star apple, pineapple, custard apple, south sea apple; tamarind, ginep, avocado, guava, cashew, cane; yellow, white, St. Vincent's yam; red, black, pepper ants; bats, scorpions, nightingales, spiders; cassava, sweetsop, soursop, cho-cho, okra, guango, mahoe, mahogany, ackee, plantain, chinese banana; poly lizard, green lizard, croaking lizard, ground lizard.

V. The pig is big, and hangs suspended by her hind legs from a tree in the yard. She is screaming—her agony not self-conscious. I have been told not to watch her slaughter, but my twelve-year-old self longs for the flow of blood. A small knife is inserted in her throat, pulled back and forth until the throat slits, the wound widens and the blood runs over covering the yard. As her cries cease, mine begin. I have seen other slaughters, but this one will stay with me.

In Cliff's dark retelling of the Garden-of-Eden story, the twelve-year-old girl looks at what she has been told not to watch—"her slaughter." Her desire for the flow of blood mixes with the sight of blood flowing, a confusing mixture of blood and blood, blossoming and violence.

Sharon Olds, born in California, in a poem called "Time-Travel," describes a journey to the scene of her childhood. "I have learned to go back," the speaker says, "and walk around and find the windows and doors." The issue, again, is survival, and she, the survivor, has come for her twelve-year-old self. Walking quietly into "the last summer the family was together," she finds herself down by the shore of the lake:

> a girl
> twelve years old, watching the water
> fold and disappear. I walk up behind her,
> I touch her shoulder, she turns her head—
> I see my face. She looks through me
> up at the house. This is the one I have
> come for. I gaze in her eyes, the waves,
> thick as the air in hell, curling in
> over and over. She does not know
> any of this will ever stop.
> She does not know she is the one
> survivor.

These poems, written by adult women, carry the suggestion that Shakespeare's sister—the poet who died young and never wrote a word—died at the age of twelve. And was buried at the crossroads between childhood and adolescence, the meeting place of girls and women. Placing her poem at this intersection, Sharon Olds draws the reader's eye to a startling disjunction: the girl in her poem turns in response to the woman's touch and then looks through the woman. The twelve-year-old girl who feels the presence of a woman whom she is not seeing points to a missing link in the chain of generations—a link that Woolf saw as critical for women and that has to do with education.

Interviewing girls in adolescence, in the time between the twelve-year-old's knowing and the adult woman's remembering, I felt at times that I was entering an underground world, that I was led in by girls to caverns of knowledge, which then suddenly were covered over, as if nothing was known and nothing was happening. What I heard was at once familiar and surprising: girls' knowledge of the human social world, a knowledge gleaned by seeing and listening, by piecing together thoughts and feelings, sounds and glances, responses and reactions until they compose a pattern, compelling in its explanatory power and often intricate in its psychological logic. Such knowledge on the part of girls is not represented in descriptions of psychological development or in clinical case studies, and more disturbingly, it is disclaimed by adolescent girls themselves, who often seem divided from their own knowledge, regularly prefacing their observations by saying, "I don't know."

At a school for girls in a large midwestern city, twelve-year-olds, when asked to describe a powerful learning experience, were as likely to describe an experience that took place inside as outside of school. By fifteen, more than twice as many girls located powerful learning experiences outside of school than inside. With respect to the nature of such experiences, girls at fifteen were more likely than girls at twelve to talk about experiences outside of school in which family or friends or other people they knew were the central catalysts of learning (Braun 1988). Between the ages of twelve and fifteen—the time when dropping out of school becomes common in the inner city—the education of girls seems to be moving out of the public sphere and into a private realm. Is this the time, I wondered, when girls' knowledge becomes buried? Was girls' learning going underground?

This question surfaced in reflecting on my experiences in interviewing adolescent girls at Emma Willard School in Troy, New York. The isolated setting of the residential school and its walled enclosure made it something of a strange island in the stream of contemporary living, an odd mixture of old world and new. In this resonant setting, I heard girls speak about storms in relationships and pleasure in relationships, revealing a knowledge of relationships that often was grounded in detailed descriptions of inner psychic worlds—relational worlds through which girls sometimes moved freely and which at other times seemed blocked or walled. Listening for this knowledge, I felt myself entering, to some extent, the underground city of female adolescence, the place where powerful learning experiences were happening. The gateway to this underworld was marked by the statement, "I don't know"—the sign of repression, and the codeword of membership, or the password, was the phrase, "you know." I wondered about the relationship between this knowledge and girls' other life of notebooks, lessons, and homework.

One afternoon, in the second year of the study, toward the end of an interview with Gail, a girl with whom I had not made much contact, I asked if she was curious about the "it" that she was describing, "the problem" that stood between her and her being "able to achieve anywhere near my potential," the thing that kept her from "getting my act together." Gail said that she did not know whether she would "ever understand what the problem was, but I hope that someday it will be gone and I will be happy." I asked, how it will go away? She said she did not know, but that it would be "sad if it doesn't." I asked if she was curious; she said she did not know. We went on with the interview questions. As she thought about herself in the future, I asked, how did she imagine her life, what expectations did she feel others had for her, what were her hopes for herself? She was waiting, she said, to see if "it happens." She felt she had come up against "this big wall." We went on. At the end Gail said, "Maybe someday I will draw it." It seemed that she knew what it looked like. I asked what color she would make it; "kind of deep ivory," she said. What shape? "A giant block of ice. This tall . . . very thick. A cube standing in front of me." She said that she could melt it, but that she would "have to use very high temperatures."

The water, I thought, that the twelve-year-old girl was sitting next to had frozen. Its surface no longer moved, no longer reflected. It had covered over. What was once liquid had become solid, turning into "this big wall."

The following year, Gail—now a senior—began by talking to me in the language of social science. "I would like to mention," she said, "that having thought about my last two interviews, it occurs to me that it is hard to get the real opinions of teenage girls as young as we are because a lot of girls really don't know what they think." If I had interviewed her on another day, or if I were a different person, I would "get very different things," especially because "a lot of the questions you asked are not questions that I have ever put to myself . . . and afterwards I wondered, you know, did I really mean that. . . . I don't feel you are getting what is important to me; you are getting that and other things in equal weight." I asked, "So there is no way of knowing [what's true and what's important]?" She agreed. I began with the interview questions:

"Looking back over the past year—" I suggested that as we went along she might tell me which questions were ones that she had put to herself and which. . . . Gail suddenly switched modes of discourse. "I actually feel a great deal older this year." One way of speaking about herself ("Teenage girls . . . really don't know what they think") yielded to another ("I actually feel"). The relationship between these two ways of speaking about herself seemed critical. In the terms of her own imagery, one way of speaking shored up the wall between herself and her knowledge and one provided a sense of an opening, a place of entry which led through knowing how she was feeling. "I really feel able," Gail explained, taking the opening,

> to put myself in perspective, about a lot of the things that were confusing me about myself, and I have a tendency to keep things to myself, things that bother me. I keep them in and then I start feeling like this, just harassed and I can't really—everything just warps my perception of everything . . . But I have discovered the reason for my whole block. I mean, I was getting bad grades and I told you about a mysterious block last year that was like a wall. (*I remember that.*) Now, I figured out what was going on. I figured this out last week. It is that all through my childhood, I interpreted what my parents were saying to me in my mind. I never voiced this interpretation.

The unvoiced or unspoken, being out of relationship, had gotten out of perspective, "just warp[ing] my perception of everything." What she interpreted her parents as saying to her was that "it was for me to be independent and self-sufficient from a very early age." Thus, Gail said, "anything that interrupted my sense of what I should be, I would kind of soak up into myself, as though I was a big sponge and had tremendous shock capacity to just bounce back." What Gail was taking in was clearly something that she found shocking, but she felt that she should act as though she was a sponge and could just soak up the shock by herself. So, "I would feel bad about things [but] I wouldn't do anything about them. I wouldn't say anything. That goes with grades and personal problems and relationships"—much of her adolescent life. And then, "last week, last Wednesday, this whole thing came over me and I can really feel that now I can understand what was going on with me, I can put my life in perspective." Thus, Gail explained that she no longer had to not know,

What's happening, what's happening with me? What is going on? Why am I not being able to see? Why is this so hard for me? And then of course when I finally let it out, maybe every six months, it is like a chair casting shadows and making tremendous spokes. Everything becomes monumental. I feel terrible and it is really very disturbing.

With this powerful image of "it" as a chair casting shadows and making tremendous spokes, Gail conveys how the ordinary can become monumental and very disturbing. What is explicit in this passage is that Gail became disconnected from her own thoughts and feelings and found herself asking questions about herself that she then could not answer. The process of knowing in threatening this disconnection had become overwhelming. I asked Gail if she had a sense of what had led her to the understanding she described, and she spoke about a conversation with a friend:

It started when my friend was telling me how angry she was at her math teacher, who when she asked for extra help must have been in a bad mood and was angry with her. I was thinking about the way my stepfather would do the same thing. And then I was thinking about my stepfather and then I decided that I really have been abused as a child, not physically, but even last summer, whenever he has insecurity, he is very jealous of me, he is insecure with my mother, and then he just lashes out at me and criticizes me to no end, very angrily. And for a person who has grown up with that and who doesn't really understand herself, instead of saying, "Wait a minute, what are you doing? I am a person." I would just cuddle up and make like a rock. Tense all my muscles and just sit there and listen to it and be relieved when it is over. And then I was thinking about myself and my reactions to things and I was thinking all year about all the problems I had last year. . . . It is all my holding back. And I really feel I have made a tremendous breakthrough.

Joining her friend in voicing anger in response to anger rather than just soaking it up like a sponge or tensing her muscles and becoming like a rock, Gail felt she had broken through the wall that was holding back her "reactions to things," her feelings and thoughts. "It was amazing," I said, "to see it that way," responding to Gail's precise description of psychological processes—her step-by-step tracing of her own feelings and thoughts in response to her friend's story about anger and the math teacher as well as her analysis of how insecurity and jealousy breed attack. "My mother," Gail said, turning to the missing person in this drama, (and signalling by the phrase "you know" that this was in part an underground story),

> came down the day before yesterday, and I told her about it. She had been worried about me day and night since I was little because of my holding back. She would say, "You are holding your light under a bushel," and then, you know, get very upset once or twice a year, because everything would get [to be] too much, you know. Of course, my mother would have tremendous guilt. . . . "What have I done to this poor child? I don't really know what I have done, but there is something. What is it?"

"You have read *Oedipus Rex*?" Gail asks me. I had. "Well, Oedipus went through his entire life weighing himself by himself, and I have done that and that is what allows me to get out of proportion. I don't talk about anything with anybody, anything that is bothering me."

I thought of the queen in the Oedipus story—Gail's description of her mother had caught the franticness of Jocasta as she tries to keep Oedipus from knowing the truth about family relations. No more truth, she pleads. Was Gail hearing a similar plea from her mother? The problem was that "it"—the unnamed or unspoken truth—"just rolls up like a snowball and it gets bigger and bigger and my perception just warps out of shape," so that like Oedipus, Gail cannot see what in another sense she knows. Her question to herself, "Why am I not being able to see?," resonates with the question she attributes to her mother: "What have I done to this poor child?" But Gail also lays out the logic that suppressed her questions about suffering and about women. Gail reasoned that if her stepfather's attacks had truly been hurtful to her, then her mother would have taken action to stop them. Because her mother did nothing, at least as far as Gail was aware of, Gail concluded that her stepfather's verbal lashings could not really have hurt her. To feel her feelings then posed difficult questions: what does it mean to be a good mother, what does it mean for a mother to love her daughter, and what does it mean for a daughter to love both her mother and herself?

The either/or logic that Gail was learning as an adolescent, the straight-

line categories of Western thinking (self/other, mind/body, thoughts/
feelings, past/present) and the if/then construction of linear reasoning
threatened to undermine Gail's knowledge of human relationships by
washing out the logic of feelings. To understand psychological processes
means to follow the both-and logic of feelings and to trace the currents
of associations, memories, sounds, and images which flow back and forth
connecting self and other, mind and body, past and present, consciousness
and culture. To separate thinking from relationships and thus to make
a division between formal education and powerful learning experiences
is to become like Oedipus, who got things out of proportion by "weighing
himself by himself." Gail ties the return of perspective to the return of
relationship and describes the insight and knowledge that suddenly came
out of the back-and-forth play of her conversation with her friend:

> I talked to my friend, and she talked about her math teacher, and
> I was thinking about my stepfather, and then with all my thinking
> about it beforehand, wondering what makes a difference, I finally
> put it together and bang!. . . . Before when I was getting all tied
> up, everything was a huge wall, that isn't a wall anymore.

The "it" is no longer a wall but a relationship that joins Gail with herself
and with her friend.

The image of a wall recurred in interviews with adolescent girls—a
physical rendering of the blocks preventing connection, the impasses in
relationship which girls acutely described and which were associated with
intense feelings of anger and sadness. Girls' wishes to make connections
with others reflected the pleasure that they found in relationships. Molly,
when asked whether she and her friend depend on each other, says:

> We don't really depend on each other. It's more like we depend . . .
> we are so strong for each other, because we have such a good time
> with each other . . . we are drawn to each other so much that way
> . . . to evoke a certain emotion . . . a happy kind of *joie de vivre*.

And Susan, talking about her relationship with her mother, says that she
and her mother depend on each other,

> but not to the point where if something separated us . . . I wouldn't
> be able to function. . . . I feel better for my dependence on [my

mother] because I know without her I would be missing something in my personality, and I don't think I would be as full or interesting a person as I guess I am. (*What would be missing?*) I don't know. My mother's sense of humor, and just the ability when anybody's upset and you know they are upset, just to sit down and try and talk to them and calm them down and want to have fun. I don't know. I think there is more that I have yet to find.

Pleasure in relationships is thus linked to knowledge gained through relationships, and girls voice their desire to know more about others and also to be known better themselves. "I wish to become better in the relationship with my mother," Ellen says, "to be able more easily to disagree with her,"—disagreement here being a sign of relationship, a manifestation of two people coming together. And it is in close relationships that girls are most willing to argue or disagree, wanting most to be known and seen by those to whom they feel closest and also believing that those who are close will be there, will listen, and will try to understand. "If you love someone," Anna explains,

you are usually comfortable with them. And feeling comfortable, you can easily argue with one another and say, look, I want you to see my side. It's a lot easier to fight with someone you love, because you know they will always forgive you, at least usually they will . . . and you know that they are still going to be there for you after the disagreement.

Perhaps for this reason, girls often speak about conflict in their relationships with their mothers—the person who, one girl said, "will always welcome me." Girls' willingness to fight for genuine connection with their mothers is well-illustrated by Kate, a fifteen-year-old who says, paradoxically:

I called my mother up and said, "Why can't I speak to you anymore? What is going on?" And I ended up crying and hanging up on her because she wouldn't listen to me. She had her own opinion about what was truth and what was reality and she gave me no opening. . . . What she had on her mind was the truth. And you know, I kept saying, "Well, you hurt me," and she said, "No, I did not." And I said, "Well, why am I hurt?" you know, and she is just

denying my feelings as if they did not exist and as if I had no right
to feel them, you know, even though they were.

The counterpart to the image of a wall is the search for an opening,
a way of reaching another person, of finding a place of entry. Yet to
open oneself to another person creates great vulnerability, and thus the
strength of girls' desire for relationship also engenders the need for protection from fraudulent relationships and psychic wounding. "To me,"
Jane says, "love means an attachment to a person," by which she means
a willingness or wish

> to share a lot of things with that person and not feel as though you
> are opening up your soul and it is going to be misrepresented or
> misunderstood. Rather, so that person . . . will know kind of inside
> how far to go and if they go too far, they will understand when
> you say, that's not what I want. . . . Where people accept your
> idiosyncrasies . . . that you can have fun and you can disagree but
> that the argument isn't something that wounds you for months. . . .
> Some people are too quick to say "I love." It takes time to learn
> someone. I don't think you can love on first sight. . . . You can feel
> a connection with someone, but you can't just love them.

These carefully drawn distinctions, the contrast between feeling connected with someone and loving them and between having fun and disagreeing and having an argument that wounds you for months, bespeak
close observation of relationships and psychological processes and also
experiences of being misrepresented, misunderstood, and not listened to,
which have left both knowledge and scars. Jane says she is looking for
someone who will understand when she says, "That's not what I want."
Mira, in contrast, has chosen silence as a way of avoiding being hurt:

> I personally have had a hard time asking questions . . . because I
> was shy and I did not really like to talk to people about what I was
> really thinking. (*Why not?*) I thought it was much safer just to keep
> it to myself and this way nobody would have so much of a vul-
> nerable spot that they could get to me with. And so I thought, just
> the thought of somebody having something on me that could pos-
> sibly hurt me, that scared me and kept me from speaking up a lot
> of the time.

Like the character in Woolf's story, "An Unwritten Novel," Mira keeps her life to herself; her speaking self also is "entombed . . . driven in, in, in to the central catacomb. . . . Flit[ting] with its lanterns restlessly up and down the dark corridor." ([1921] 1972) Belenky and her colleagues have described how women retreat into silence when words become weapons and are used to wound (1986). Adolescent girls invoke images of violence and talk in the language of warfare or about winning and losing when they describe the inner workings of explosive relationships that can "throw us apart forever."

(*What is the worst thing that can happen in a relationship?*)
I guess if people build up resentments and don't talk about them, things can just keep building up until they reach the boiling point, and then there is like a cold war going on. People are just fencing on either side of a wall, but not admitting it to the other person until there is an explosion or something.

If people are thinking on two different planes . . . it is a lack of communication . . . you can't understand. (*Can people on different levels communicate?*) Well, they can try, maybe they can . . . if they are both trying to communicate [but] if one person is trying to block them out totally, the person who is trying to block them out is going to win, and not hear a thing that the other person is saying. If that is what they are trying to do, they will accomplish their objective: to totally disregard the other person.

Other girls describe "building a wall" or undermining closeness:

(*What is the worst thing that can happen in a relationship?*)
Not talking it out. Building a wall. . . . I think that can lead to a lot more because you don't give a chance to the other person to say anything. . . . You are too close-minded to listen to what they have to say. . . . If you don't listen to your friends, they are not your friends, there is no relationship there, because you don't listen. (Emma)

The worst thing is if you . . . stop communicating with that person. Because you don't trust them to know a secret, . . . you lose your trust in them or you aren't even open with them anymore. (*Why is that the worst thing?*) Because after a while you sort of grow

apart . . . or you will feel like you are with them and down underneath you may be angry at the person, but you don't say anything,
so it comes out lots of times in other ways. . . . It undermines the
whole thing, being close to the other person.   (Joan)

Taken together, these observations of the ways in which people move
and affect, touch and are touched by one another, appear and disappear
in relationships with themselves and with others, reveal an understanding
of psychic processes that is closer to a physics than a metaphysics of
relationship—based on tracking voices and images, thoughts and feelings
across the cloud chamber of daily life. Certain observations are breath-
takingly simple in their logic, although profound in their implications,
especially given the pace of contemporary living. Emma says that "If you
don't listen to your friends, they are not friends. There is no relationship
there." Others are more complex, like Joan's exegesis of the indirect
discourse of betrayal: "If you don't trust someone to know a secret . . .
you sort of grow apart . . . or you will feel like you are with them and
down underneath you are angry . . . but you don't say anything, so it
comes out . . . in other ways." Or Maria's explication of the confusing
mixing of anger and hurt:

I am not sure of the difference when I feel angry and hurt. . . . I
don't even know if they are separate emotions. . . . I was angry, I
think of myself in that relationship, that I had let myself be used
. . . that I had let down my guard so much. I was completely vulnerable. And I chose to do that. . . . I kept saying, "I hate him,"
but I realized that he didn't even notice me there because he was
in his own world. So that I think . . . all my anger comes out of
being hurt, and it's a confusion there.

Repeatedly girls emphasize the need for open conflict and voicing
disagreement. Catherine describes the fruitful quality of disagreement in
her relationship with her friend:

We have learned more about ourselves . . . I think . . . she had never
really had a close friend but lots of acquaintances. She didn't get
into fights and things like that. . . . I think she realizes that you
have to have disagreements and things like that for a relationship
to last. (*How come?*) Because if you don't really voice your dis-

agreements, then you don't really have anything going, do you know what I mean? It's just another way, it is another side of you that you are letting someone else see.

Tracy speaks about what happens when disagreements are not voiced, and explains how conflict can become a catalyst for change:

> Some people, when they disagree, do not voice what they feel, and therefore the other person does not know what they are doing wrong to bother the other person. And the other person who is being bothered just assumes that the person could never change. . . . And that bothers them. . . . I think if a person handles conflict badly, it's bad. But conflicts can also be good in a relationship because if a friend voices her opinion, the person can be more aware of that and possibly not change their whole personality but, you know, be more careful.

And Liza describes the raw pain of finding, at the end of a long journey, that you are not able to talk with someone on whom you had depended:

> (*What is the worst thing that can happen in a relationship?*) That you grow up, or sideways, and not be able to talk to each other, especially if you depend on being able to talk to someone and not being able to. That hurts a lot, because you have been dependent on that. It is like walking fifty miles for a glass of water in a hot desert and you have been depending on it for days and getting there and finding it is not there anymore; you made the wrong turn ten miles back.

The knowledge about relationships and the life of relationships that flourish on this remote island of female adolescence are, to shift the metaphor, like notes from the underground. Much of what psychologists know about relationships is also known by adolescent girls. But as girls themselves say clearly, they will speak only when they feel that someone will listen and will not leave in the face of conflict or disagreement. Thus the fate of girls' knowledge and girls' education becomes tied to the fate of their relationships.

When Women's Studies is joined with the study of girls' development it becomes clearer why adolescence is a critical time in girls' lives—a time when girls are in danger of losing their voices and thus losing connection with others, and also a time when girls, gaining voice and knowledge, are in danger of knowing the unseen and speaking the unspoken and thus losing connection with what is commonly taken to be "reality." This crisis of connection in girls' lives at adolescence links the psychology of women with the most basic questions about the nature of relationships and the definition of reality. Girls' questions about relationships and about reality, however, also tug at women's silences.

At the edge of adolescence, eleven- and twelve-year-old girls observe where and when women speak and when they are silent. As resisters, they may be especially prone to notice and question the compliance of women to male authority. One of Woolf's questions in *A Room of One's Own* is why mothers do not provide more rooms for their daughters, why they do not leave more of a legacy for their daughters, and why, more specifically, mothers do not endow their daughters' education with greater comfort. A teacher of twelve-year-olds, after a faculty meeting where women's reluctance to disagree in public became a subject of discussion, told the following story: her eleven-year-old daughter had commented on her reluctance to disagree with her husband (the girl's father). She was angry at her mother, she said, for always giving in. In response, the mother began to explain that although the girl's father sometimes raised his voice, he was loving and well-intentioned—at which point, her daughter interrupted her saying that it was she, her mother, whom she was angry at for always giving in. "I was so humiliated," the teacher said, "so ashamed." Perhaps as a result, when later that year she suppressed her disagreement with a colleague and did not voice her objections to the new rule about lunch that he announced in homeroom one day (because, she said, she did not want to undermine his authority), she thought twice on a day when the rule seemed particularly senseless and excused some girls, in spite of the rule, before others who had arrived late at lunch had finished eating. "Good for you," the girls said, "we're proud of you." It was clear that they had noticed everything.

In his appreciation of the poetry of Sylvia Plath, Seamus Heaney reads a famous passage of Wordsworth as a parable of the three stages in a poet's journey. At first, one goes out into the woods and whistles to hear if the owls will respond. Then, once one discovers that one can speak in a way that calls forth a response from the world of nature, one has to learn to perfect one's craft: to enter the world of sounds—of birdcalls, of traditions, of poetic conventions—until, Heaney says, if one is blessed or fortunate, one becomes the instrument through which the sounds of the world pass. Heaney traces this transformation in Plath's poetry, drawing the reader into his own exhilaration as her language takes off (1989). But Plath's relationship to the tradition of male voices which she was entering and changing by entering, was not the same as Heaney's and her entrance was more deeply disruptive. The same can be said about women students.

A student first must learn how to call forth a response from the world: to ask a question to which people will listen, which they will find interesting and respond to. Then she must learn the craft of inquiry, so that she can tune her questions and develop her ear for language and thus speak more clearly and more freely, can say more and also hear more fully. But if the world of nature, as Heaney implies, is equally responsive to the calls of women and men, the world of civilization is not, or at least has not been up to the present. The wind of tradition blowing through women is a chill wind, because it brings a message of exclusion—stay out; because it brings a message of subordination—stay under; because it brings a message of objectification—become the object of another's worship or desire, see yourself as you have been seen for centuries through a male gaze. And because all of the suffering, the endless litany of storm and shipwreck is presented as necessary or even good for civilization, the message to women is: keep quiet and notice the absence of women and say nothing.

At the present moment, the education of women presents genuine dilemmas and real opportunities. Women's questions—especially questions about relationships and questions about violence—often feel disruptive to women because at present they are disruptive both in private and public life. And relationships between women are often strained. It is not at all clear what it means to be a good mother or teacher to an adolescent girl coming of age in Western culture. The choices that women make in order to survive or to appear good in the eyes of others (and thus sustain their protection) are often at the expense of women's relationships with one another, and girls begin to observe and comment on these choices around the age of eleven or twelve. If women can stay in the gaze of girls so that girls do not have to look and not see, if women can be seen by girls, including the twelve-year-old in themselves, if women can sustain girls' gaze and respond to girls' voices, then perhaps as Woolf envisioned, "the opportunity will come and the dead poet who is Shakespeare's sister will put on the body which she has so often laid down and find it possible to live and write her poetry" (Woolf 1928)—as Plath did for a moment before taking her life. Yet as Woolf reminds us, before Shakespeare's sister can come, we must have the habit of freedom and the courage to write and say exactly what we think.

At present, at Harvard, 7.8 percent of the tenured faculty are women, in contrast to roughly 50 percent of the students and 25 percent of the faculty who are subject to constant review (Harvard University 1989). In Woolf's terms, only a very few women have rooms of their own within the university. As long as this is the case, we need great patience, sustaining friendships, and an interim strategy for girls' education. One strategy followed in this essay is that of the naturalist: to provide detailed drawings of girls' knowledge and resonant settings for girls' voices in the hope that at the moment when some modern day Prospero, donning his magic cloak, says to some twelve-year-old Miranda, "here cease more questions" and " 'Tis a good dullness," she will remember her questions about suffering and about women and heed the voice of the resister inside her.

In my seminar last spring, a black woman was reluctant to turn in the weekly writing that was then read by all of the seminar members. She was new to the university world, she said, and she feared what others would think about her if they were to see her writing. I asked what she imagined they would think, and she said, "That I am out of my mind," conveying in this way her sense of herself as living somewhere outside of her mind and also the dislocation of self, mind, and body, which is rampant among women in the university, and which she, as a black woman and as a newcomer, may have felt more clearly.

For women to be in their minds and in their education raises serious questions for women, for men, and for civilization. Women's entrance into the disciplines brings a recovery of voice and with it the vision that if we do not end a tradition of storm and shipwreck, there may well be an end both to nature and to civilization. But women's questions also stir up conflict and disagreement and thus are more likely to be spoken in relationships where no one will leave and someone will listen.

Sources

Atwood, M. 1976. "This Is a Photograph of Me." In *Selected Poems, 1965–1975*. Boston, Mass.: Houghton Mifflin, p. 8.

Bardige, B., J. V. Ward, C. Gilligan, J. M. Taylor, and G. Cohen. 1988. "Moral Concerns and Considerations of Urban Youth." In *Mapping the Moral Domain*, edited by C. Gilligan, J. V. Ward, and J. M. Taylor. Cambridge, Mass.: Harvard University Graduate School of Education, ch. 8.

Belenky, M., B. Clinchy, N. Goldberger, and J. Tarule. 1986. *Women's Ways of Knowing*. New York, N.Y.: Basic Books.

Braun, A. 1988. Themes of connection: Powerful learning among adolescent girls. Working Papers of the Laurel/Harvard Project, The Study Center. Cambridge. Mass.: Harvard University, p. 3.

Brown, L. M. 1989. Narratives of Relationship: The Development of a Care Voice in Girls Ages 7 to 16. Ed. D. diss., Harvard University.

Cliff, M. 1985. "Claiming an Identity They Taught Me to Despise." In *The Land of Look Behind*. New York, N.Y.: Firebrand Books, p. 19.

Crockett, L., and A. Peterson. 1987. "Pubertal Status and Psychological Development: Findings from Early Adolescence Study." In *Biological-Psychosocial Interactions in Early Adolescence*, edited by R. Lerner and T. Foch. Hillsdale, N.J.: Erlbaum.

Ebata, A. 1987. A longitudinal study of distress in early adolescence. Ph.D. diss., University of Pennsylvania.

Elder, G., T. Nguyen, and A. Caspi. 1985. Linking family hardship to children's lives. *Child Development* 56:361–75.

Eme, R. 1979. Sex differences in childhood psychopathology: A review. *Psychological Bulletin* 86:574–95.

Erikson, E. 1958. *Young Man Luther*. New York, N.Y.: W. W. Norton & Co.

Gilligan, C. 1977. In a different voice: Women's conceptions of the self and morality. *Harvard Educational Review* 47:481-518.

Gilligan, C. 1982. *In a Different Voice*. Cambridge, Mass.: Harvard University Press.

Gove, W., and T. Herb. 1974. Stress and mental illness among the young: A comparison of the sexes. *Social Forces* 53:256–65.

Heaney, S. 1989. *The Government of the Tongue: Selected Prose 1978–1987.* New York, N.Y.: Farrar, Strauss and Giroux.

Josselson, R. 1987. *Finding Herself.* San Francisco, Calif.: Jossey-Bass.

Miller, J. B. 1976. *Toward a New Psychology of Women.* Boston, Mass.: Beacon Press.

———. 1984. Development of women's sense of self. Stone Center Working Paper Series Number 12. Wellesley, Mass.

Olds, S. 1980. "Time-Travel." In *Satan Says.* Pittsburgh, Penn.: University of Pittsburgh Press, p. 61.

Report of the committee to review affirmative action. 1989. Faculty of Arts and Sciences, Harvard University.

Rogers, A. 1987. Questions of gender differences: Ego development and moral voice in adolescence. Unpub. manuscript, Harvard University.

Rogers, A., and C. Gilligan. 1988. Translating the language of adolescent girls. Monograph No. 5, GEHD Study Center, Harvard University.

Rutter, M. 1986. "The Developmental Psychopathology of Depression: Issues and Perspectives." In *Depression in Young People: Developmental and Clinical Perspectives,* edited by M. Rutter, C. Izzard, and P. Read. New York, N.Y.: Guilford Press.

Shakespeare, W. *The Tempest,* edited by L. B. Wright and V. A. LaMar. New York, N.Y.: Pocket Books.

Simmons, R. and D. Blyth. 1988. *Moving into Adolescence: The Impact of Pubertal Change and School Context.* New York, N.Y.: Aldine De Gruyter.

Skoe, E. E., and J. E. Marcia. 1988. Ego identity and care-based moral reasoning in college women. Unpub. manuscript, Acadia University.

Werner, E., and R. Smith. 1982. *Vulnerable But Invincible: A Study of Resilient Children.* New York, N.Y.: McGraw-Hill.

Woolf, V. [1928] 1957. *A Room of One's Own.* New York, N.Y.: Harcourt, Brace & World.

———. [1921, 1944] 1972. "An Unwritten Novel." In *A Haunted House and Other Short Stories.* New York, N.Y.: Harcourt Brace Jovanovich.

Listening to Voices We Have Not Heard
Emma Willard Girls' Ideas about Self, Relationships, and Morality

NONA P. LYONS

Responding to an interview question asking how she might like to see herself in the future, the young woman, a high school junior, acknowledges she would like to "improve or expand on my compassion." She explains:

> With compassion, I'm sometimes not very understanding. I have a habit of putting myself in [another] person's place, which I found is not fair because I would do things differently and I think in a different way. And if they get angry, I would say, All right, how can I understand that? I will put myself in her place. But then I say, I wouldn't get angry at that! That doesn't help very much. [So] I would like to have more compassion toward them, to accept the way they feel really, and respect that.

Having discovered that an old way of understanding others, by putting herself in their place, was not "fair," the young woman holds up for herself a new measure of her development: "To improve or expand on my compassion . . . to accept the way they feel really, and respect that." But in so characterizing her future change, this adolescent girl points to a set of ideas and activities only now being elaborated in the psychological literature on adolescence.

For example, psychologist James Marcia has enunciated a classic formulation of the adolescent transition. Studying identity in adolescence, Marcia construes "identity," following Erikson, as an "internal, self-constructed, dynamic organization of drives, abilities, beliefs and individual history." Marcia sees identity undergoing changes over time, some of which are crucial: "Adolescence seems to be one of these. It is a period of transition in approach to cognitive tasks—from concrete to formal operations; in approach to moral issues—from law-and-order ["duty"] reasoning to transcendent human values; in approach to psychosocial concerns—from others' expectations and directives to one's own unique organization of one's history, skills, shortcomings and goals" (Marcia 1980, 190). But in trying to fit this formulation of the adolescent transition and its cognitive, moral, and psychosocial agenda with an adolescent girl's aspirations for herself in the future, a set of differences and discrepancies emerges.

Taking what traditionally has been defined as the essence of fairness —the capacity to put yourself in another's place—the student labels it "unfair." While it could be questioned if this young woman somehow misunderstands the Golden Rule, it seems rather that she has a different standard for evaluating its usefulness: that is, whether it helps very much. In substituting that pragmatic reality for an abstract principle, "fairness," she holds up not a "transcendent human value" but an empirical one: how to see and respect difference. With a self-chosen goal—to expand compassion and accept the way others feel and respect that—the young woman turns toward a new level of engagement with others, attentive not just to her own but to the unique organization, history, skills, shortcomings and goals of others. Thus, with an ethical standard born of observation, experience, and judgment, this adolescent girl sees and holds for herself a new way of being in relation to others.

The significance of growth in human attachments to an understanding of adolescent development is the subject of this chapter. Through listening to the voices of adolescent girls at Emma Willard School and attending to the way they see themselves and experience their relations to others, there emerges a new way to think about a set of ideas centrally related to development: that is, ideas about self and morality.

For relationships are linked to moral imperatives, to concerns about good and evil, right and wrong. Piaget reminds us that "Apart from our relations with others, there can be no moral necessity" (Piaget [1932] 1965). Questions of value are implied in human relationships. But if morality arises in the relations between people, it most centrally implies a self and involves a question of interpretation: How do individuals see and construct their own understanding of relational problems? What are the moral concerns that emerge in their relationships with others—the questions of right or good?

This chapter describes and explores the connections Emma Willard girls find between their relationships to others and morality. Using data from in-depth interviews during which these high school students were asked to speak about themselves and about moral conflicts they see and try to resolve, this chapter first identifies and shows how a characteristic way of dealing with moral choice is related to a girl's way of considering her relations to others and to a way of describing herself. Two distinct orientations to morality are presented: a morality of justice and a morality of care. Each moral voice implies or articulates a particular conception of relationships—relationships of equality and fairness, or relationships of responsiveness and interdependence. The logic of each is defined. In a clearly speculative way, the second part of this chapter explores how these ideas of self, relationships, and morality may change over time and become significant issues in a girl's development. Finally, in the last part of this chapter, the implications of this work are discussed, especially for considering the education of girls.

Two lines of research converge here to provide a context: research on psychological theory and women's development focusing on self, relationships, and morality; and new work on adolescent psychology. Research in developmental psychology first identified a "different voice" in women's conceptions of self and morality and challenged the field to expand beyond the traditional conception of the self as separate and of morality as justice in order to include both experiences of separation and connection and the values of justice and care (Gilligan 1977, 1982; Gilligan et al. 1982; Lyons 1982, 1983, 1987; see also Chodorow 1978; Miller 1976, 1986; Belenky et al. 1986). New directions in the study of adolescent development call for and urge new research on adolescent girls (Adelson and Doehrman 1980; Adelson 1986; see also Douvan and Adelson 1966). The stark assessment of Adelson in 1980 that "adolescent girls have simply not been much studied" called attention to the "masculine bias" in such accepted psychological categories as "identity" and "morality" and to the fact that girls' experience had not been considered when these categories were created. Adelson suggests that the exclusion of girls from theory-building research may account for the previous lack of serious investigation of such important concepts as relationships, intimacy, and so forth. Recently other researchers have argued that any conception of adolescent development must include not only individuation but connectedness to others as well (Grotevant and Cooper 1983; Youniss 1980; Gilligan 1987). And in 1986 Hartup and Hinde underscored the significance of relationships in psychological development by calling for systematic study of relationships, beginning with simple descriptive data, if a needed science of relationships were to be developed (Hartup 1986; Hinde 1979; Hinde and Stevenson 1986). This chapter focuses on the presentation of a set of ideas and descriptions about how relationships are implicated in identity and moral development of adolescent girls. Using data from the Dodge Study at Emma Willard, this chapter, while not offering a systematic representation of findings, does suggest new hypotheses for future research.

For example, in distinguishing two voices in girls' narratives of moral conflict—the voices of justice and of care—it is important to note that girls who focus on justice and girls who focus on care do not differ in their academic achievement as measured by grades or standardized scores (Hanmer 1987). Yet the different logics of the two moral orientations suggest an interpretation of differences in girls' day-to-day behaviors and their ways of interacting with others. Further, girls' methods of posing and solving moral problems suggest a more general model of problem solving; and how relationships enter into girls' development, as revealed in the two characteristic patterns presented in this work, offer the outline of a new relational model of adolescent development.

This present work, then, makes available needed descriptive data of adolescent girls' perceptions, thoughts, and feelings about relationships and promising hypotheses; it also suggests an interpretation of girls' behaviors, including a way of understanding why a high school junior can say that her development is best measured in terms of expanding her compassion and why she calls that an "ethical" and moral concern.

Two Emma Willard high school students exemplify the contrast between an orientation to justice and one to care as manifest in the thinking of Emma Willard students who took part in this study. The two students reflect as well a larger sample of people, male and female, who have similarly been found to use predominantly justice or care thinking when making moral choices (Gilligan et al. 1982; Lyons 1982, 1983; Johnston 1985; Gilligan and Attanucci 1988). Although it has also been found that there can be a third pattern in the use of justice and care reasoning, that is, a roughly equal use of both justice and care considerations, here the contrast between justice and care predominance is explored.

Two perspectives: on self, relationships, and morality

Responding to the question, what does morality mean to you? two Emma Willard high school students give different definitions, elaborating in their responses how they think about morality and responsibility. Rebecca, a sophomore, says:

Morality? Wow. If I just use the noun 'morals,' I guess . . . I guess just a code of beliefs, you know, a code of honor, that one person would follow that's not necessarily anyone else's beliefs. I think morality maybe is a level . . . of personal integrity someone has. . . . Personal integrity, I think, is also a level of following rules. It is a level of following rules so that you can function, because if I had no personal integrity . . . I would be amoral. . . . So I think also a level of personal integrity also establishes a basis for judging whether something is right or wrong.

The second girl, Beth, a freshman, replies:

I see a moral question as like, say, Is it better to drop a bomb, would that save more lives than it would be to fight? Moral questions are like that, they have drastic effects on life, I think. . . . Should I go out and fight along with my friends, or should I go to Canada and watch my friends die? Or something like that . . . I'm not totally sure that [this situation] is a question of morality. It is a question of responsibility, I think. . . . (*What does responsibility mean to you?*) Something that if I don't do, other people will suffer. . . . My homework is my responsibility because I should, I have to, do it because, if I don't, that will bog other people down and then the class has to go over it again and I wouldn't be helping people and I don't want to hinder people. I don't think that is right.

For Rebecca, morality is a code of beliefs, a measure of personal integrity that is tied to abiding by rules, which can in turn become the basis for judging whether something is right or wrong. Her code is personal, not necessarily anyone else's. For Beth, morality is something that has to do with questions that can have drastic effects on life—like the dropping of a bomb—and yet is tied to ideas about responsibility, which in turn have to do with everyday things like failing to do one's homework because that might bog other people down and wouldn't be helping them. For Rebecca, morality has to do with following one's code; for Beth, it has to do with helping people, being sure to do something so that others will not be hurt or hindered.

While at first glance the contrast between these two responses may not appear especially striking, it does suggest that different kinds of issues can become moral concerns and have implications not just for how a girl constructs the meaning of morality, but for how she might act. Given these different perspectives, it is possible to ask: What are likely moral problems for these young women? In an examination of the conflicts they report, the logic and consistency of two moral orientations—what are called here a morality of justice and a morality of care or response —are revealed. And two ways of being in relation to others are revealed as well.

For Rebecca, who defines morality as a code that gives her a way of judging what to do, an actual moral conflict emerged in trying to determine if she should follow school rules. The situation occurred when she was sitting as an active member of a school disciplinary committee, the Faculty Student Judiciary Committee (FSJ), which determined what to do with students who broke school rules.

> I remember when I was confronted with a situation where I could go out and get drunk with some friends who were on the FSJ. . . . This was at the time when I was saying, Well, if this rule really isn't ethical or moral, then to hell with it and, They don't really expect us to follow these rules, they just don't want us to get caught. But a little voice in me was yelling, It's wrong, it's wrong. And I think of all those people whose cases I sat on, where people were caught drinking . . . [but] I think I turned the girl down more from an extreme fear of getting caught. It wasn't any great moral realization . . . I thought about it and we are not dealing with, Oh, come back to me in an hour. This was minutes, seconds. I said, 'No, thanks. I've got to go.' But through my mind in those few seconds flashed, you know, stuff that I was breaking a rule.
>
> Out of that, I think . . . it forced me, I said . . . it's wrong to break a rule and if you go here, you abide by the rules . . . if you don't like them, leave. So this is another one of my great theories.

In recounting this situation, Rebecca reveals a complex and changing way of thinking about rules and why she will obey them. Forced to respond to the friend who invites her to break a rule, she judges it is wrong and suggests the grounds on which she makes that judgment. Thinking first of all of the cases she herself has witnessed and judged as a member of the FSJ, she goes on to acknowledge as well that it was really no great moral realization, just a fear of getting caught that made her say, No. The implications of not obeying rules have consequences. Seeing that she would be breaking a rule if she went out drinking, she simultaneously reasons that if you go to school here, you abide by school rules. Thus, she judges her own behavior with a standard she uses for others as well. Rules, applied universally across situations, mediate her relationships and her moral decision making, in this instance.

For Beth, who is concerned not to hinder others, moral conflict arises from a situation in her relationship with her mother:

> I was in a situation where my parents are divorced, and I wanted to go to boarding school because I didn't want to live with my parents at that point. And my mother didn't want me to go. I have a younger sister by her second marriage, and she said that I should stay home with my sister and take care of my sister and help the family in that sense. . . .
>
> So I thought about it [and] decided to come back [here]. . . . I guess I took an objective viewpoint . . . and decided that I love my sister and I love my family and I love my mother, but staying there and doing what she wanted me to do wasn't healthy for our relationship. . . . I did have a responsibility toward my family, but that was not to take care of my sister but to make myself a person that wasn't going to be dependent on my family constantly and the only way to do that was to go [here] and . . . make something of myself. And then I could help my family.

In a dilemma caused by the special request of her mother, to come home from school to take care of a younger sister, Beth considers both what is healthy for their relationship and how she can help her family. Asked to comment if she thought her decision was the right thing to do, she goes on to say:

> I felt very guilty. I almost changed my mind . . . but I walked away and tried to think about what I was doing, and I realized that I was right and—for me, I was right—I don't think you could be totally right in that situation because there are different parts, different amounts of being right. And [I] could have done one thing and I could have stayed with my mother and that would have been partially right; or I could have come here and that would have been partially right. But each way I am cheating someone. But I have to work for myself. I have to do things for myself because if I can't do them now, how will I be able to do them when I become an adult and am supposed to?

Concerned then that "each way I am cheating someone," Beth sees no one right way, only different amounts of right. She resolves her conflict by seeing that "making something of myself" is necessary in order to be able sometime "to help my family." From a way of thinking about morality that is constructed as not hindering others, to a definition, resolution, and evaluation of a moral problem, a logic is revealed in this young woman's thinking: Individuals in relation must each be considered in their own contexts and needs.

In contrast, Rebecca, also responding to the question, Do you think it was the right thing to do?, says:

> Definitely. . . . I think it is not fair for this school to ask you to live under some sort of rule, and to break those rules and then sit in on a case where you are judging someone else for doing the very same thing that you did. That is why it seemed like a contradiction to me because you are creating the wrongness the FSJ deals with, and I don't think [it is fair] for someone to sit there and talk about punishing someone else if they had been drinking themselves last night.

Embedded in the two kinds of conflicts these students present are what may be called two kinds of logic, two different ways of thinking about the relationships between people that give rise to different moral considerations. For Rebecca, relationships are construed as if through some kind of contract with an underlying conception of fairness and equality between individuals. All individuals should be, and are, considered in fairness.

Beth looks at the situation from the point of view of each person, including herself, not in strict equality but in each person's terms and contexts. She acts to do what is right for herself and her family—considering their long-term relationship. Here the underlying value is interdependence and responsiveness, responsiveness implying an acknowledgment of the reality of the situation as well as an understanding of each person's particularity and need.

From perspectives of fairness and "reciprocity" or of "response" and interdependence, these young women see and seek to resolve conflicts they term moral conflicts. Other examples from the experiences of Emma Willard students similarly reveal the two orientations to self in relationship or morality (see table 1 on following page).

Table 1

Moral Conflicts Emma Willard Girls Report Framed with Justice and Care Considerations

1. Justice Focus*: Considerations of Self: Respecting and Upholding Rights, Contract or Fairness in Relationships.

I didn't get my math homework done. . . . We had to hand in computer tapes and my friend had an extra computer tape, and I knew that the teacher was absolutely going to freak out and scream at me and I would get into trouble if I didn't hand in a tape. And my friend had an extra one she was offering me, but I couldn't do it. I couldn't take it. . . . Sort of like the principle, damn it, I didn't do the computer tape . . . I couldn't hand it in when I didn't do it. It would have been like cheating.

I don't go to chapel anymore because I find that offensive and I guess that's moral. We have required chapel once a week and I don't like the idea of being required to go, of being forced into religion. I go to church on my own sometimes. I think that's enough for me and I don't feel that I need to go to these required services. It was a big decision.

2. Care Focus: Considerations of Self: Creating and Maintaining Interdependence and Response in Relationships.

I lied to my parents about my grades. I told them that my biology grade was going to be marvelous, and it is not going to be marvelous. . . . Suddenly, my sister who has always been national honor society and all those wonderful things, has gotten horrible grades this past month, and [my parents] called me up and told me this and then wanted to know how mine were. And it was the difference between, knowing my parents, they would go to the ends of the earth if they know both their children were doing horribly in school—my parents are educational fanatics—and so I've told them that my grades are fine, and there was almost a sigh of relief from my father. And I think that outweighed the idea that I was lying to them. . . . I couldn't bring myself on the phone to say, Well, Dad, you are looking at two academic failures for the term. And I think that's a moral dilemma.

My roommate and I were in the same class and I lost my book, and she lost her book. And then I lost my book and she found hers and I borrowed her book one night to do my homework. And I noticed my name in it, and I realized that she had taken my book and erased my name and wrote hers over it. And I had to decide whether I should save embarrassing her by confronting her with the problem and just go out and get another book, or whether I should say, Hey, did you take my book? I know this is my book, and give it back.

I had a problem with a . . . girl whom I [as editor] would tell that I needed her to get something done and I would tell her weeks ahead of time . . . and then when I needed whatever she was supposed to have done, she hadn't done it. And this went on for a long time. . . . And I felt like I needed someone else to be doing the job, and yet whenever I would talk to her, she would say, 'Yah, I really do want to do it and I want to be able to help.' . . . I didn't really want to confront her and I knew I had to. . . . I didn't know if I was being unreasonable in things I was asking her to do—maybe I didn't make it clear to her the things I needed [her] to do.

3. Mixed Considerations of Care and Justice.

Last year some friends and I went out and we were having a little celebration. . . . One girl met a friend of hers and she wanted to stay longer and talk. . . . The next morning we realized that our friend had gotten busted. . . . I didn't know if I should turn myself in or what. In the end, I really had a hard time deciding what to do because I felt it was really unfair . . . she had gotten busted and we hadn't. And the problem was if I turned myself in I would have been responsible for the four other people. . . .

Focus is a term used to indicate a primary or predominant way of framing conflict. For example, if seventy-five percent of all ideas—called considerations—are of one orientation, justice or care, that determines a focus.

Similar issues—different moral conflicts;
Different issues—similar moral concerns

Two perspectives: equality and rights or
interdependence and responsiveness in relationships

In these examples what is first apparent is not just that different issues can become salient moral conflicts for students, but that the same issue can be construed with different meanings. Lying is a case in point. The student who talks about lying to her parents about her grades is seeing a different problem than the student who cannot lie about the computer tapes. For the girl concerned about the tapes, to hand in as hers her friend's homework would have been cheating and, for her, would have involved violating a principle of fairness. She says, "I didn't do the tape. . . . I couldn't hand it in." Applying a general principle to her situation, she declares it not right to hand in her friend's tape. But a different kind of issue concerns the student who lies to her parents about her grades: that is, the direct effect on her parents of the bad news of her failing grades. It is, as she says, knowing her parents in their particularity—the intense value they place on their children's education—that makes her tell them that her grades will be good when they will not. In an instant, as she not only calls up the values of her parents but also enters into their world, she acts to hold off their disappointment for at least a short period of time. In these two constructions, different considerations frame and shape conflict—conflicts that both girls label as "moral."

Similarly, it is possible to examine the underlying perspectives of different conflicts presented and to see a similar logic at work across different situations. For example, the girl who found a moral conflict in deciding not to go to required chapel acts out of her principles and standards in much the same way as Rebecca, who decided it was wrong to break the school rule when she was sitting on the Judiciary Committee. Both act to apply a set of standards they hold about what is the right thing to do in a particular situation. The underlying values are equality and reciprocity, or, fairness. This way of thinking about real-life moral conflict is termed here a morality of justice.

So also, the editor who does not know whether to tell a fellow student that she must get her work in on time acts to respond to the girl in much the same way as the girl who does not tell her parents she will have a failing grade. The logic that shapes their behavior is a logic that acts in response to knowledge of people, considering the pragmatic situation of the individuals involved as well as what constitutes care. This way of thinking about moral conflict is termed here a morality of response, or, care. And this orientation to morality can create a particular set of conflicts for women surrounding care of self and when to respond to self as well as others. For example, the girl who acts to retrieve her textbook from her roommate casts the problem in a particular and familiar form: whether she should embarrass her roommate or sacrifice her own needs and desire to have her book. This issue, which can be central to the development of girls and women (Gilligan 1977, 1982), is discussed later in this chapter.

While it is clear that girls can act out of either of these two moral orientations—and usually the conflicts they report have elements of both—girls also present both modes equally in their thinking. For example, the girl who did not know if she should turn herself in when a friend she had been with was caught outside of school grounds, when she herself had been breaking the school rule as well, presented the conflict as one embodying two terms: What was fair—"it really was unfair"— and what was responsible—"I would have been responsible for the four other people" who would have been implicated as well. Thus her dilemma pits the principle of fairness directly against responsibility for the weal and woe of others.

It seems important to emphasize again that in these examples Emma Willard girls present moral conflicts that include both justice (rights) and care (response) considerations. Here, however, we have been looking at "justice" or "response" to illuminate the characteristic features if one kind of moral consideration predominates in a girl's thinking. For a summary of the central moral issues and logic of the two moral orientations, see table 2.

This construction of morality as involving at least two voices, justice and care, expands the construction of morality described in the dominant model of moral psychology, notably in the work of Kohlberg (1969, 1984). In Kohlberg's model morality is defined as justice, and moral problems are seen to emerge from the conflicting claims of individuals and to be resolved through objectivity and the application of principles of justice as fairness. Fair treatment and broadly contractual rules and individual rights provide a set of related ideas within this orientation to morality. But a second construction offers another definition of morality: that is, morality as responsiveness to another. This ethic is called the ethic of care, or, response (Gilligan 1977, 1982; Lyons 1982, 1983). In this conceptualization of morality as care, moral problems are likely to emerge from the recognition of actual or potential fractures in the relationships between people or from concerns that someone has been excluded or not taken care of. Thus conceived, moral problems are resolved by stepping into—not back from—the situation and by acting to restore relationships or to address needs, including those of oneself.

Table 2

An Overview of the Central Moral Issues and Logic of Care and Justice in the Construction, Resolution, and Evaluation of the Resolution of Moral Dilemmas (Lyons 1982).

A Morality of Care/Response

A. *In What Becomes a Moral Problem*

A morality of "care" rests on an understanding of relationships that entails response to another in that person's terms and contexts. Therefore, what becomes a moral problem has to do with relationships or the activities of care.

The conflicts of relationships are raised as issues surrounding the potential fractures between people, that is, not with the breaking of trusts or obligations but with the severing of ties between people; or conversely, with restoring or maintaining relationships.

The conflicts surrounding the activities of care have to do with response itself, that is, how to respond (or the capacity or ability to respond) to another within the particular situation one encounters and how to promote the welfare or well-being of another or to relieve the individual's burdens, hurt, or suffering—physical or psychological. Included in this construction can be particular concerns about care of self and how to care for self especially in considering care of others.

B. *In the Resolution of Moral Conflict*

In a morality of care resolutions to moral conflict are sought: (1) in restoring relationships or the connections between people and (2) in carrying through the activities of care, ensuring that good will come to others or that hurt/suffering will be stopped for others or oneself.

C. *In the Evaluation of the Resolution*

In a morality of care the evaluation of moral choice is made considering: (1) whether relationships were restored/or maintained and (2) how things worked out or will work out; in some instances there is only the acknowledgment that no way to know or to evaluate resolution is possible. Whether relationships were restored can be measured in several ways: simply if people talk to one another, or if everyone is comfortable with the solution. If people talk and everyone agrees with the solution, one knows relationships are maintained.

How things work out is a measure of resolution in that in seeing what happens to people over time, one then knows if the resolution worked. This marker also carries the notion that *only* over time can one know results, that is, know in the sense of seeing what actually happens.

A Morality of Justice/Rights

A. *In What Becomes a Moral Problem*

A morality of justice or fairness rests on an understanding of relationships as reciprocity between separate individuals. Therefore, what becomes a moral problem has to do either with mediating issues of conflicting claims in the relationships between people; or with how one is to decide conflicts or how one can justify one's decision and actions, considering fairness as a goal between individuals.

The moral dilemmas of conflicting claims have to do with the conflicts of obligation, duty, or commitment stemming from the different role-relationships one may have: between self and others, self and society, or to one's own values/principles. The conflicts with respect to how one is to decide come from the need to have some impartial, objective measure of choice that ensures fairness in arriving at a decision.

B. *In the Resolution of Moral Conflict*

In a morality of justice resolutions to moral conflicts are sought considering (1) meeting one's obligations or commitments or performing one's duties and (2) in holding to or not violating one's standards and principles, especially fairness.

C. *In the Evaluation of the Resolution*

In a morality of justice, the evaluation of moral choice is made considering (1) how the decision was justified, thought about and/or (2) whether values, standards, or principles were maintained, especially fairness.

How the decision was justified or thought about is an important measure to make of living up to one's obligations (duty or commitments) or of fairness. Whether values, standards, or principles were maintained is a measure of the self's ability to live up to one's obligations or principles; it is a measure, too, of the standards used in decision making.

For an expanded logic of the two moral perspectives with a related set of ideas, see table 3. While these summaries were prepared and developed from previous studies of people's use of the justice and care reasoning as well as from the Emma Willard study, it is useful here to identify a set of ideas—of self, relationships, and characteristic features of ways of thinking—that are interconnected to ideas about morality (Lyons 1983, 1987). It is important to restate, too, that most people (including the students presented here) show evidence of both kinds of considerations in their thinking about moral conflict. Yet it is the patterning of these responses so that one mode predominates, shaping the way issues are constructed and resolved, and the logic that this implies that are of interest (see table 3 on page 46).

How these ideas of self, relationships, and morality may change over time and become issues in girls' development is taken up next. Through case materials examining the moral conflicts of two girls—girls introduced in the preceding pages—it is possible to suggest different pathways of girls' development in the adolescent years.

Themes of development: trying to be generous and not selfish

Asked to talk about herself, to describe herself to herself, the young woman, Anne, a high school sophomore, hesitates at first because "It's really hard to do this" but begins a response. As she does, she lays out a set of interconnected ideas.

Describe myself? Um . . . I guess I'm a pretty outgoing person, likes people. Um . . . I'm a pretty intelligent person when I put my mind

to it. It's really hard to do [this] . . . I know what I'm like but it's
. . . Describe myself, like to me? . . . I try to be generous to people.
It is very important to me not to be selfish. Um . . . Have very high
standards for myself and for others, and that's not always good,
but I have them.

Two themes that appear in this response may not at first glance seem
critical. Yet they become central to Anne's growth and the focus of her
conflicts in subsequent years. The themes are "selfishness" ("It is very
important to me not to be selfish"); and "being generous" ("I try to be
generous to people"). As Anne elaborates a context of values, however,
she begins to reveal why "being generous" and "not selfish" will become
issues in her relation to others. Before examining these, it seems useful
to look at the values she identifies as important to her, seeing how they
are revealed in and are part of her everyday life and why.

Answering the interviewer's question, Why is it not good to have high
standards for yourself and others? Anne explains:

Sometimes people are the way they are, and you have to accept
them the way they are. And you can't say that this person is not
good enough for me. . . . Somebody who maybe is an alcoholic or
maybe . . . they are on drugs or something like that, I sometimes
look at and say, That person isn't, you know, blah, something like
that. But I shouldn't do that because that is the way they are and
I think that . . . that is one of the bad things about having such
high standards. And, I like a lot of people around me.

Anne's conflicts about "standards" arise from the concern about accepting people "the way they are." As part of an effort to see others in
their own terms, Anne "tries to be generous."

I like to do things for other people . . . to give somebody something
that they don't have, or help with work or even if they need money. . . .
I like to know, it is a matter . . . I go down and buy a flower for
my mother or something. I like to do things like that. In that way
I take after my mother, but it kind of runs in me now, too, . . . it
is really important for me to see other people happy.

Thus, for Anne, connection to others is a central value, a way of being
toward others that is part of the way she thinks about herself. Its im-

Table 3

The Logic of Two Moral Perspectives*

	Perspective toward others	Conception of self-in-relation to others
The perspective of response in relationships	See others in their own terms; contexts	Interdependent in relation to others
The perspective of rights in relationships	See others as one would like to be seen; in equality and reciprocity	Autonomous/equal/ independent in relation to others

Ideas and images of relationships	Ways of thinking/knowing	Interpersonal ideas and processes
Attachment through response; interdependence of people in relationships; concern with responsiveness, isolation of people; relationships as webs	Particularistic; contextual; question posing; suspended judgment; use of dialogue, discussion; goal is understanding; thinking and feeling held together	Interdependent; emphasis on discussion and listening in order to understand others in own contexts
Attachment through roles, obligation, duty; concern with equality and fairness in relationships; relationships as hierarchies	Objective; generalizing; abstract; ruleseeking; goal is to critique, to analyze, to answer question, to prove; thinking and feeling seen as needing to be separated	Objective; role-related; in order to maintain fairness and equality in dealing with others

*From Lyons, N. *Visions and Competencies: Men and Women as Decision-Makers and Conflict Managers*, Harvard University, 1985.

portance lies not only in "just liking people around me," but also in "the feeling you can give each other." Interdependence is the underlying assumption. Anne describes one way these values emerge in her everyday affairs as she introduces her concern about competition in school.

Academic competition bothers Anne. She muses, "If you get a grade on a test and somebody else gets one lower than you, they are jealous of you, and they have to flaunt it, and that makes you feel bad because you got a high grade. Or like if somebody gets a higher grade than me, I get jealous.... I mean I never try to show it, but I still tend to feel jealous." Declaring that there is "no reason why people should be unhappy because you did well," she continues: "I don't think you should be feeling jealous.... When people do it to me, it wrecks the whole pleasure . . . and I know they feel bad. And that really bothers me a lot."

When asked to say if she is changing, Anne identifies the emerging issues that will challenge some of her values: "New things are becoming important to me. It's like trying to become on an adult level . . . presenting my ideas and trying to make myself be as well as I possibly can, on an adult level, trying to get them up to standard, up to a point where they are not childlike."

Commenting on this difference, between what is adult and what is childlike, she says:

A child doesn't really take the world seriously; he doesn't see all the aspects of the world. And as an adult, you do. You see, you grasp, you grasp what your world is about and what . . . you take things seriously and start to bring them into reality. Whereas as a child it is kind of like a fairy world. I mean you have your family and that's kind of all you ever go outside of, whereas as an adult you are brought into contact every day to the different aspects of the world, be it starvation or poorness or the reality of having to get a job and have responsibility. Whereas as a child you don't have any responsibilities really. Other people take care of those for you so that when you grow to start to become an adult, you start to take on more responsibilities.

To this interviewer's question, Such as? she says:

Such as . . . supporting a family . . . I mean . . . taking care of yourself. When you are a little kid your mother dresses you, and you go to the stage where you dress yourself. And then you get to the stage where maybe you start to pick out your own clothes and just um, yah, you go from the stage where your mother takes care of you, where you start to get some type of individualism, and then you want more independence. And then finally you are independent and you have to support yourself and take care of yourself and see that you are, because otherwise you won't survive.

I look outside my little own world here and when I was little, I never did. I always looked . . . I relied on my mother and my father and my relatives, my friends, just the people that I was in daily contact with, to keep me informed on what was going on, that is important to me, that is going to affect me. And now I've gotten to the point where I look outside myself, my little world. And I look for things, even if it doesn't affect me directly. I look to see what's going on and what's happening and try to get some individualism, too . . .

It could be argued that these concerns for independence and "individualism" are classic statements of concern for autonomy and independence—ideals traditionally identified with the adolescent experience. Yet becoming independent to Anne means not only increasing her autonomy but also her capacity to see others in their reality. It is becoming responsible for "taking care of your world." For Anne becoming independent is joined with being interdependent in a new way.

When Anne describes a conflict, one that seems an everyday happening to adolescents, the values she holds come into conflict with one another: her concern about "selfishness," "being generous," and her emerging "individualism." She identifies the situation as occurring when a friend, a "really good friend," wanted her to go to her house after school, but Anne couldn't reach her mother: "I think she wanted me to stay overnight or something because she had had problems, and I couldn't get ahold of my mother, so I didn't know whether to go or not."

In that situation, her concerns were: "My feeling of what I should do. And what my mother would want me to do. I didn't want to get in trouble." She elaborates what getting in trouble means:

I get yelled at and then I feel bad because . . . I don't know . . . because it hurts, I guess. I mean it always hurts if you get in trouble. Nobody likes, I know I don't like for my mother to get mad at me because I don't think . . . I hate to have my mother upset with me for something. . . . It hurts both of us I think, you know, I don't think she likes to get mad at me either.

"Trouble" is not just an effect to Anne, some punishment, but involves hurt: hurt, both to her mother and herself. "Besides," she adds, "your parents run your life up until a certain point, and when I was at that point I was at that point where I am sure it was a struggle for independence and relying on other people to run my world, so it was kind of, I should let her decide because she runs my world."

Asked what she considered when she was trying to think about what to do, Anne responds, introducing a new concern:

> Well . . . it was something like I want to go for my own selfish reasons because I like to visit with my friend, and I think she needs me there for her, too. I don't think it is just my own selfish reasons, but I think it would be good for my friend to have me there when she needs somebody to talk to or something. And then the other side is I just don't want to do something without Mom's permission. I don't want to get in trouble . . . and that my friend wanted me to come, that also helped affect me and my decision. But the other side was very strong—I mean my mother's feelings on the subject —was very strong. If she didn't like it, then I wouldn't do it, of course . . .

In the end, Anne reveals, "I decided to go to my friend's, which was fine, because my mother wasn't mad anyway. She didn't mind at all." And that, to Anne, was the right thing to do. "Because she would have let me do it, and I wanted to do it, and it was important to my friend that I do it. So three ways in one direction is fine."

In the situation presented here, Anne grapples with the inherent conflict of "trying to be generous" to all the people around her—not wanting to hurt her mother, being there for her friend, as well as doing what she wants for her own "selfish reasons." She struggles to make her own decision, to be independent, and to consider, too, what she would like to do. But unable to grant her own view a place of parity with concern for her mother and concern for her friend, she marks it as "selfish." While Anne does, in fact, go to her friend's—she does do what she wants to do—she does not find a way to deal with or legitimize her own point of view.

Marking her own wishes in a self-evaluating way as "selfish," the task for her—and the difficulty—seems to be in finding a way to hold both self and other together. Individuation while maintaining connections to others is what she grapples with, and her relations to others complicate her task. Thus she juggles her knowledge of her mother with her understanding of her friend's need. But where can her own needs fit? Three years later she describes a different situation.

Anne as a senior

During the interview in her final year of high school Anne comments, "Probably a lot of changes in your life throughout the years caused you to grow, and people you interact with grow around you. So you grow with them." Reflecting on her own change over the three years of school, Anne, a senior now, sums up, "I can look back on myself and . . . think about the decision which I made, or think about the way I felt about myself and when I felt really responsible or really mature. And now it's not a question of, Oh, I feel mature. Because I am. It is there and I know it." Calling herself "hard-working," "personable," "goal-oriented," and "pretty well put together," Anne states, "I enjoy interacting with people, getting to know them, seeing what they think about things." Then in discussing a real-life conflict she faced as a senior, Anne identifies continuities and change, sounding again the theme of "selfishness," but this time, two years later, it emerges in a different way.

Reflecting on the moral conflict she faced recently when she had to choose which colleges to apply to, Anne discloses that she wanted to apply to a certain school but her father could have gotten a tuition break if she attended another college. "Not that he doesn't have the money, but he just doesn't really want to go out and spend fourteen thousand dollars a year to send me to the first school—as opposed to sending me to the just-as-good school." She describes feeling "torn between doing what I felt I needed to do, which was to apply to the school which, for some reason, had really appealed to me, or applying to one that I knew would be best for my father and wouldn't be bad for me either."

In trying to decide what to do, Anne talks about the considerations she pondered: "I considered my father's feelings on the subject [because] it is really important to me to be able to get along, to do what is going to be best for everybody involved." But she goes on, "You know, it was more a question of whether or not I was being selfish in deciding to go where I wanted to apply, or whether I should be realistic almost in a sense, which isn't necessarily realistic, and apply to the place which is going to be best for all of us."

Not abandoning her old concern that "it is really important to me to get along, to do what is best for everybody involved," she now puts that alongside of another: "I considered my own feelings . . . a lot." Still unable to cast aside the issue of "selfishness," it appears now in a new way: that is, whether she is being realistic—in this case, to apply to the school that might be "best for all of us," for everybody. Thus she aligns her interests with the reality factors of her life and the lives of others— whether her father could, in fact, afford the school of her choice. Yet she acknowledges and gives a place to her priorities.

Talking about whether or not that was the right thing to do, Anne summarizes:

> I came to realize that you can't please everybody else all of the time, and if you are working on something that is that important to your life . . . going to school, gaining an education, then you should choose what you really want to do and go after it. If I hadn't, I would have been kind of abating myself, because I would have been saying, Oh yes, you really do want to go too, you really do. But somewhere deep inside me, and it would have come up to consciousness at some point or another, I would really want to do something else. And so I thought that it was best that I do what I really wanted to do. And I think that my father feels that way now, too.

In identifying that "you can't please everybody all of the time" and that if something is important to you, "you should choose what you really want to do" because, as in her case, if she had not she "would have been abating" herself, Anne seems to shift to a new place, reorganizing both her way of being in relation to others and her way of thinking about herself. Her new perspective allows her a way to respond to herself as well as to others.

In this reorganization, what is interesting is that old elements of her thinking are transformed. Issues she identifies in her early years of high school—"being generous to people" and "selfishness" carry new meanings. "Selfishness" is now acknowledged alongside of what is "realistic" given a situation, as well as "what is important to me." Not that acting in a selfish way is suddenly inconceivable; rather, the confusion of labeling what is important to her as "selfish" is being clarified and her wishes given legitimacy. Similarly, being generous to people is mitigated by her concerns and desires; and her desires are tempered by the "reality" of the situation. Thus a new way of thinking about herself cannot be dis-associated from her new way of being and acting in relation with others.

What brings about change

Because the assurance and confidence of this young woman in her own point of view is clear and strong, unlike the faltering voice of her sophomore year, it seems fair to suggest that some change in her thinking has occurred. How this has come about is the question of interest. Turning again to examine the conflicts of her life, we look at the middle year of her schooling and speculate that the conflict she describes there may offer an explanation of change. The situation occurred when her father decided to get remarried, and she had to decide whether to tell her mother. She relates that "it was really a hard decision on my part as to whether and when to tell my mother that, because on the one hand, I knew that it was really going to kill her to find that out, and on the other hand, I thought I had an obligation to tell her." What made the situation a conflict for her was that while her mother and father were divorced, she knew, "my mother still loved my father a great deal."

Asked by the interviewer to say why this was a moral problem, Anne says moral problems usually occur for her when "I am struggling against myself to come to a solution to the problem." In her situation, the values that were conflicting were:

The fact that I had always been brought up to care a tremendous amount about my parents' feelings and the way they feel. On the one hand, that conflicted with itself because my mother's feelings were going to be really upset and my father's feelings were good. So that conflicted with itself, and um, my [long pause] trying to figure out, I guess you would have to weigh the love that I have for my mother, which is in effect my morals, against if I love my mother enough to tell her something [so] that she won't hear [it] from other places and get upset. But then again, that's against mainly the feeling that I've been brought up with that I hate to see any member of my family hurt and that would conflict against that, so the two.

Thus caught in a dilemma of telling her mother what she knew and risking her hurt, or not telling her and risking the pain her mother would inevitably feel when she did learn of the remarriage, Anne decided to tell. But she did so knowing that she and her sister, who joined in the telling, could give their mother "our personal support so she could handle it." If we speculate what this young woman learned from this dilemma, we might say that she confronted the impossible situation—the inability not to hurt another or prevent hurt—and yet saw a way to deal with it.

Two issues emerge in Anne's story. Connection—attachment—is to be maintained as is a growing "independence." But independence comes within attachment to others and transforms both, leading to a new way of being and a new way of interacting with others.

Similarly, Anne says that morality is the "love" she has for her mother and her father. Thus, issues of morality, as she defines them, are not solely issues of fairness or rights as previous formulations suggest (Kohlberg 1969, 1984), nor are they the creation of agreements between people (Haan 1977 and Youniss 1983). Her concerns are for sustaining connections with others, not by a utilitarian calculus of "the greatest good for the greatest number of people," but rather by weighing the love that is her "morals"—responding to others in their own terms and contexts: Do "I love my mother enough to tell her something [so] that she won't hear [it] from other places and get upset?"

While one cannot speak about girls in general without studying girls in other situations, cultures, and social class, it is possible to summarize some issues central to the development of girls we characterize as "connected," or, "interdependent in relation to others." This connected mode of experiencing self and defining morality is more frequently found within the Emma Willard sample of students who revealed a certain set of characteristics:

At adolescence, issues of attachment for girls who were characterized as "interdependent in their relations to others" are the focus of attention in at least two ways: (1) maintaining connections with others, either in renegotiating old attachments or in forming new ones, personal or professional, and (2) how ideas and issues of caring for the self while maintaining connections are dealt with and negotiated within relationships.

The issue of holding together self and other—what has been called here caring for the self as well as caring for others—may be a special issue of development during adolescence for some girls. The special vulnerability may be in finding a way of caring for the self while maintaining connections with others.

Issues and conflicts of what girls label moral as well as issues of "identity" formation take place within relationships.

Before elaborating on some of the implications of this work we turn next to examine another, characteristically different, mode of response found in the answers of Emma Willard students.

Themes of development: choosing between doing
what the rules dictated and maintaining my friendship

In contrast to those adolescent girls whose high school years seem to be a time to work on a new capacity to care for others and oneself, a similar yet different configuration of these issues seems equally salient for other students, students characterized here as "autonomous in relation to others." While issues of attachment, of self, and relationships emerge in their development, there are differences. For these girls relationship concerns seem joined to issues of integrity and one's standards. To see this process at work, we turn now to a young sophomore, Rebecca, whom we have met before and who found as a member of the Faculty Student Judiciary Committee that she had to confront her own desires and standards. Listening first to how she describes herself and then contrasting the conflicts she experienced over her three years of high school, it is possible to examine how her relations to others and her ideas about her integrity and "standards" enter into her thinking.

Responding to the question, How would you describe yourself to yourself? the young woman, Rebecca, begins:

Oh dear. I was thinking about that as I was getting dressed this morning. Um . . . to myself. I don't know, sometimes we have to do creative writing exercises; and Who am I? I think of myself as a person who gets involved. I am doing a lot this year. In fact, I overextended myself this year, but no problem. I like to get involved in things. I think I am well known by a large part of the student body only because I am always sticking my fingers in a lot of business and stuff like that. My personality, I don't know. I have certain aspects of me, like I think I am a very warm person. I think I am very good at articulating how I feel, identifying parts of my life, like I've just done. But that's about it. I can't think of anything right now that I would describe myself as. I'd describe myself as a changed person, definitely.

I think I have changed a lot. I used to think when I was in the 7th and 8th grade that I was a liberated woman . . . but I don't know. I am at the stage now where I don't know if I'm liberated in the purest sense simply because, when in doubt, I always slip back into old traditions and old ways. If I go to a mixer at a boys' school, I don't ask guys to dance simply because I'm afraid of what kind of reaction I'll get. So I don't know if I am liberated, if I'm completely, totally free about, you know, about being liberated in front of men because a lot of people . . . This girl was extremely, extremely liberated or whatever, and she went to [x] boys' school during exchange time and she got nicknames like Amazon, and these guys thought . . .—this school is like the way the world was in 1950, to give you a little background—but they called her the Amazon, Gloria Steinem, . . . and they saw her as some female castrating bitch. They just couldn't handle [it], they didn't understand what she was doing so they tended to reject what she was saying. And I don't want to be rejected like that, and I don't want people talking about me like that. So I don't know how liberated I am. So I think I am a changed person is all I can say right now.

Characterizing herself with some ambiguity, as "good at articulating how I feel, identifying parts of my life" and "I can't think of anything right now that I would describe myself as," Rebecca, in part, characterizes herself in her differences from others. In spite of her tentativeness, she does identify that she is changed. She sees herself as "changed" in relation to a marker—how "liberated" she is. In a discussion of a moral conflict she faced, she picks up the theme of "difference" and identifies as well the issues she will continue to deal with for the next three years: her integrity and the integrity of her standards, her relation to them, and how they mediate her relations to others.

In her sophomore year of school, Rebecca talked about a conflict— one already presented here. "When I was confronted with a situation where I could go out and get drunk with some friends who were on the Faculty Student Judiciary Committee . . . this was at the time when I was saying, Well . . . if this rule really isn't ethical, or moral, then to hell with it. . . ."

Reflecting on that situation, she elaborates how her thinking was changing:

That was one of my extremist theories . . . I just thought, I just went through a stage where I thought that anyone who came here and violated a rule should be kicked out of school because they couldn't handle it. They couldn't come here and totally stay within the rules, you know. And then I went through the thing: Is it possible to go through here four years without breaking a fundamental rule? And I asked someone, who said, I don't think so. So that is something I am going to have to deal with in the future.

In her construction of conflict and choice, Rebecca articulates a complex way of thinking about rules and their meaning in her life and in her relations with others. But as she sees the limits of the new place that she is at—that, indeed, she may not be able to avoid breaking a rule—her thinking is focused not on the situation and the others involved but rather on the values she holds and her integrity in maintaining them in dealing with others. Three years later she describes a different conflict and reveals how some old issues are reconstructed.

Rebecca as a senior

Describing herself as "independent and very outgoing," "involved more in trying to change this environment," three years later Rebecca sees herself as "concerned" with getting things changed. Because she believes "this school has done a lot for me," she wants to help mold the environment so that it is best for "my needs, not only my needs personally, but for the students." Emphasizing why it is important to be concerned and give "because the less control you have over your own environment, the more other people will control it for you and then you end up feeling helpless. And I don't want to feel helpless . . . small and alone," Rebecca sees that for her it is necessary "to try to take control of my life." She tries to do that in school. While these words carry a new meaning, surely signaling a new place for this young woman, old themes reappear.

Focusing on a conflict she faced as a school leader, a proctor on a hall, she describes a situation in which she had to report students who did not follow school rules. Recounting a specific time where a friend of hers asked if she could sleep through morning reports, she says "that was hard" to decide because, "I was caught between choosing between a friend and what was right." Detailing an element of this conflict she says:

It was a difference between choosing doing what the rule said, what the rules dictated, and maintaining my friendship with this girl, at least as I saw it, maintaining my relationship with this girl.

Asked to describe what she considered in trying to decide what to do, Rebecca goes on:

> I considered, okay, I mean, is this going to be, I mean it finally occurred to me that she knew my job, she knew that was my job, and she knew what kind of pressure I was under. And if she was going to sit there and pressure me, what kind of a friend was she? And if I said No to her over morning reports, and she decided this was the end of our friendship, maybe we didn't have that much of a friendship in the first place.

Although seeing her conflict as "choosing doing what the rule said, what the rules dictated, and maintaining my friendship with this girl," Rebecca identifies something new in her thinking as she works out a solution: "I realized that I can do what's right and at the same time not sacrifice relationships. That can work." She elaborates:

> And I realized that you can do what's right. This is something that has become new, too. I realize that I can do what's right and at the same time not sacrifice relationships. And as my friends have gotten older, they have an ability to do that, too. Like, you know, my friend the vice president of [x] and I have all sorts of arguments over what's wrong. It gets to the point where it is more than abstractions, but damn it, I believe this is right and the world is going to die unless this happens. And she believes something else very strongly, and we are able to argue about that. In fact, we are able to fight a lot, and we still get along, and our friendship still works. And that can work. I have discovered that you can do the "right" thing and not sacrifice a relationship. And I don't think that is something I would have learned if I had gone to a co-ed school, because I would have been a lot more desperate about relationships I think.

Rebecca describes her reflections, that her choice was the right thing to do:

> At that point in time, I was at the point that I needed to assert my authority as a leader, and she needed some limits set for her, too, because she was at the period where she was testing me out to see what I would do.

Because it was new in the year, she had known me as somebody who kind of fooled around the year before. I mean by being late to study hall and not regarding the rules as a sacred cow and saying, That is a stupid rule and I am going to violate it because I don't feel it has a lot of merit. And so she was testing me out to see what kind of an authority figure I would be, and I needed to say to her, Hey, you are not going to be able to use our friendship as a tool to push me around with.

While it would be simple to suggest that perhaps this conception of friendship is instrumental, it is more complex. Elaborating on her reasons why this situation presented a moral conflict for her, Rebecca suggests a different way of seeing friendships as she discusses the question of what morality means to her.

What does morality [mean to me]? Oh boy, such big questions, morality? I used to say every year when I did this, oh, it is a system of ethics that you live by. I think it basically comes down to whether you want to do what makes yourself more comfortable or whether you want to try to please other people. And I substitute the phrase what is more comfortable for you, I substitute that in lieu of what's right. Because who's to say what's right. Usually when you do something 'right,' you feel good about it and you know, you know. And it's not that easy. Doing what's right I have discovered is not, you know, it's not some nebulous principle that's impossible to figure out and you feel good about what's right, *and what you do for other people is a sacrifice of what's right* [emphasis added]. Sometimes they don't conflict. But you usually know when you have done something that violates yourself, your concept of what's right, when you feel cruddy about it. And you feel really bad. So to me, that is what morality is.

Thus, identifying morality as a changing conception in her thinking, one more consistent with her own integral sense of "what is more comfortable" for her, Rebecca also seems to identify a point of tension— what you do for other people may be a sacrifice of what's right. Thus the very question of friendship can seem a threat to Rebecca's sense of self.

Change

If we look at the conflicts Rebecca reports at her first and last year of school, we see that "rules" and standards are part of a central set of ideas about herself and her relations to others that change over time. The dramatic shift occurs, however, from year one, when the people involved in breaking a rule were only shadowy figures. In contrast is the problem she constructs as a senior: "choosing between what the rule said and a friendship." Others it seems are now more centrally coming into focus. But what is at stake now is how to maintain what's right with friendship.

Talking about herself in her middle year of school, Rebecca articulates a set of ideas about her relations to others important to her own self-definition. Describing how she thought about herself in the past, she says:

> In the past I really had no notion of myself, of just me and not me in relation to my friends or me in relation to my parents or anything. I see myself. I have a better notion of what I am and who I am and everything. And I didn't before, because I was never, I never felt that I was really separate from my family or my friends so that was a different behavior, a different person.
>
> (*And now?*) Now, well, in friendships before, I felt like I was just part of the group and I would mold myself to a group, and what that group needed I would be. I would change or act a certain way. If they needed an airhead, I would be an airhead. If they needed a jock, I would act like a jock, or whatever. And now I know that this is what I am like and the friendships that I find now, those are going to be people who are going to have to deal with me as I am and like me as I am.

Identifying her separateness as giving her a "better notion of . . . who I am," Rebecca seeks to maintain that identity, to hold on to it even in friendships. People—friends—will have to deal with her as she "is." When asked about change—in particular, things about herself that she would not want to change—Rebecca says:

> Wouldn't want to change? I don't think I would like to change the way I look at life now and the way I see things. I don't really ever want to lose my perspective, from the way I see things now.
>   It's a perspective in that I don't totally divorce myself from the

world, but I am not totally wrapped up in the midst of. If somebody has a problem, usually before I'd get wrapped up in their problem and their problems would become my problem, you know, and I suppose that goes along with like molding into a group, you know.

Now I think the perspective I have now is I can set myself apart from situations, and I can see situations. I can see the humor and I don't get too wrapped up, and I don't take everything too seriously and go overboard, which is what I used to do before.

Now celebrating her perspective that sets her apart from situations and people, that makes it possible that she will not find herself again lost or "molded into a group," Rebecca emphasizes her autonomy and sense of self in relation to others. This theme—consistent across three years of her high school—seems part of a central issue of her development. Manifested not only in her personal relationships, but found too in her schoolwide role as proctor, the themes of separateness, of maintaining her standards or her perspective can be traced across an evolution of a way-of-being in relation to others that has been modified over three years.

In a conflict she faced in her second year of school, a new element emerges in her thinking that perhaps accounts for change. The situation arose for her when her sister was planning to visit her at school at Thanksgiving, anticipating coming herself to Emma Willard. Rebecca wanted to go home for the holiday. Knowing that "the money for her to come here would be my money to go back home," Rebecca tells how she thought about it:

I remember talking to my sister on the phone saying, "you don't really want to come out here now, your grades are so bad." And it was pretty selfish and pretty low of me and so . . . I said to my mom: 'I don't think she should come; her grades are bad.' So she [did not come] but I felt so guilty, I couldn't let myself go home.

Asked what the conflicts were, she says:

The right side was she has been talking, she has been planning on coming out here for a long time and she wants to come. She should come. I promised that to her. My parents have made the arrangements she should come. Then, the other side, was I have never really gone home for Thanksgiving for several years. . . . I'd really like to see my friends.

Reflecting that "I think I hurt her feelings . . . I was willing to walk all over her to get what I wanted. So I guess that's what I mean by hurtful," Rebecca wrestles with a new element in her moral code—not hurting somebody. Framing the conflict in terms of issues of fairness—of what was promised to her sister, what was right—she reflects on it both from the perspective of fairness and that of not hurting someone. Thus over three years, while rules and integrity—the salient themes of Rebecca's development—have undergone change from things outside the self (school rules) to internal self-chosen ideals, the new edge of her growth is seeing the other more clearly. Seeing that another person has a context, goals, aspirations of his or her own, her standards and integrity give way to create a new way to maintain friendships.

Although these issues need more systematic attention with diverse samples of adolescent girls, some features of this way of being in relation to others can be identified:

That issues of a way of being in relation to others characterized as "autonomous in relation to others" seem to center around concern for autonomy, separateness—but only in relation to others.

That one feature of the developmental dynamic of this mode seems to be finding ways to hold on to one's integrity while dealing with one's relations to others. This can be seen in issues of identity and morality.

That seeing others in their own terms and contexts may be the cutting edge of growth and change.

The conflicts that Emma Willard girls reported at grade 10 and then at grade 12 changed (see table 4). In brief this comparison makes it possible to see in relief some elements of the issues discussed.

Themes of change

In examining the conflicts Anne and Rebecca and other Emma Willard girls report, it is possible to see that a transformation in thinking has occurred. From ways of thinking about self in relation to others, nuances can be perceived suggesting the outline of themes of change over time along the following lines.

Response / Interdependent Mode: Themes of Change
Entering oneself in the dialogue. From thinking about simply one's concerns for others, what seems at stake at grade 12 is honoring one's own

Table 4

Nature of Moral Conflicts Girls Report

At 10th grade	At 12th grade
Response mode	
1. Coming to school here: I didn't want to have my parents separated from me; decide between mother and father and school; should I help myself or my aunt (whom I was living with); I wanted to come here but if I went to public school I would be with my friends; will they want me next year [as friends].	1. Whether I should follow my own instinct and go tell the teacher what I think, whether or not to speak to the head of humanities about the teacher, or whether it would be selfish of me not to go?
2. Whether to go with a friend, stay out late when I could not get ahold of my mother.	2. I wanted to apply to a college but my father gets a tuition break at another.
3. What to do with sister who tells me things in confidence.	3. Whether to talk to my friend or not—we are not communicating.
Rights mode	
1. Whether to go out drinking with friends when I sit on the FSJ (Faculty Student Judiciary Committee).	1. Choosing between what the rules said or maintaining my friendship with this girl.
2. Not going to required chapel. I don't like the idea of being required to go.	2. Deciding to begin Stop Nuclear War. How far to stretch myself.

thinking: for example, "Should I follow my own instincts?" or "But I had to decide." Subtly there is a recognition of self, not simply a self-reflective self, but one engaged in the issue of choice.

Naming the psychological realities of self and others that one knows. One now needs to consider in the choices one makes what the realities of others and self are. "My father gets a tuition break at another college." That needs to be considered if I am to honor the particularity of others. But I will also honor my own self. "She was not doing her work—but I had to decide." "We are not communicating."

Speaking out about what one knows. Now the concerns about selfishness that seem to carry over across the years of girls high school experience enter in the name of speaking out. "Whether it would be selfish of me not to go, not to speak out." One must act—speak—if one knows.

Autonomous / Independent Mode: Themes of Change

Bringing others into the dialogue with the self. Here the task is to acknowledge others, their contexts and needs.

Balancing the standards one holds with the needs of friendship, or against other values. For example, "Choosing between what the rules said or maintaining my friendship with this girl."

In each of the two modes—the interdependent or the autonomous—developmental issues involve both tasks of autonomy and tasks of attachment (see table 5 on page 66).

Implications

To gain perspective on the implications of this work, it is useful to consider the responses of some of the teachers of Emma Willard School and the implications they find in this work. Their comments provide one way to consider the validity of this research, that is, its usefulness to the people who work daily with Emma Willard girls.

For example, this research provided the dean of students with a new way to interpret behaviors he found disturbing. Noting that sometimes after "lights out," girls would be found rushing off to another girl's room, and when caught would argue that "I needed to see my friend. She is in a kind of bad way, and I wanted to talk with her." Thinking that this was just an excuse, and not a very compelling one, the dean discovered that the girls really were responding to needs they identified, and that school rules did not come first in the set of values they held about the importance of relationships in their lives. Similarly, a faculty member who had been the adviser to an editor of the school yearbook reported that although he was aware of a conflict the editor reported in trying to get another student to do her yearbook assignments, he had no idea how long it had gone on. He was unaware of how significant it was to the editor and how she had wrestled with the other student's desires to stay on the yearbook staff even though she had not done her assignment.

Similarly, teachers seeing the two moral orientations as embodying two logics now look at discipline issues differently. They recognize that girls may want to be involved in the school judiciary procedures for very different reasons—reasons that will shape their behavior: some to help prevent student troubles; others to have a chance to be in charge of the procedures that will guarantee fairness in deliberations. These views may be compatible. But they are subtly different, suggesting different values that, in turn, lead to different ways of interacting.

Probably the area of most significance to teachers comes in the ways teachers now think about the education of girls. Not only did Emma Willard faculty review and "balance" their curriculum to respond to the inclusion of women within it, that is, to guarantee that women were included (for example, in the novels assigned in reading, in the examination in history of the social features of people's lives as well as the political features), but teachers also became more attentive to their practices in support of student learning: in listening to questions students ask and in reflecting on their own responses; and in trying out diverse approaches, such as cooperative learning, in math classes and on the playing fields (McIntosh 1983). It is possible to show a hypothesized mode of the characteristic features of two approaches to learning implied in the two moral and self orientations: the justice and care modes with their related self-conceptions—the self as autonomous, or separate; and the self as interdependent, or connected (see table 6 on page 68). This model is adapted from recent work of Belenky et al. (1986) and of Bruner (1986). The terminology of "connected" or "separate" knower is the one used by Belenky et al. adopted from my work (Lyons 1982, 1983) and that of Gilligan (1977, 1982, 1987). Here the emphasis is on different features of the learner's goals and interests, which reflect different approaches to learning.

While the two approaches to learning are thought of as clearly complementary although significantly different, understanding and articulating these differences is an important agenda for the future. Most schools tend to foster rule-oriented, abstract thinking, whether in mathematics

Table 5

Developmental Tasks Related to Modes of Self Defined in Relation to Others

Relational modes	Developmental tasks of autonomy	Developmental tasks of attachment/connection
Interdependent in relation to others	Developmental tasks center on issues of caring for self; extricating self from others, but not at expense of connection to others. Inclusion of self—meets self's needs.	Growth continues in understanding others; attachment to others remains as issue of development.
Autonomous in relation to others	Growth continues around issues of separation/ autonomy in relation to others; idea is to maintain integrity of self, not compromise self's standards while in relationships, include others but not at expense of self.	Developmental tasks center around issues of seeing others in their ow terms and contexts.

Mode of change	Vulnerabilities
Enter oneself in dialogue. Name psychological realities one knows. Care for self—meet own needs. Speak out.	Self not cared for because of attention to others; considerations of self are "selfish."
Open self to other people. Attend to others' contexts.	Loss of authentic self ("not me") through compromise of self's standards in relationships; loss of integrity is loss of self.

Table 6

Learners and Learning Contexts: The Relationship of Mode of Self to Learner's Interests, Goals, and Mode of Thinking*

Mode of self / knower	Learner's interests and goals	Learner as thinker and knower
Autonomous (separate in relation to others), "paradigmatic" knower	To question, to prove, to find answers to questions, to solve problems To convince by argument, logic Know how to know truth	Analytical, procedural, truth seeking, rule seeking and using Test for truth: consistency, logic, reasoned hypothesis Transcend time and space and particulars; imagination: to see before proving; thought and feeling held apart
Interdependent (connected in relation to others), "narrative" knower	To question; to find understanding of situations, people, and their contexts; narrative-seeking; to convince by motives, particulars of lives	Tentative and questioning, judgment suspended, fact gathering, synthesizer Test for truth: believability; concern for understanding of human motivation, intention Imagination used to enter into situations, contexts; locate in time and place Thought and feeling held together

*Adapted from Belenky et al. 1986, Bruner 1986, Gilligan 1982, Lyons 1982, 1987.

and science or history and social studies: Less attention is given to features we identify here as associated with a response "connected" learner. Emma Willard teachers, for example, found themselves thinking about student hesitancy and questioning in a different way once they had some familiarity with the two orientations. One recently hired Emma Willard teacher of history, for example, shared an incident with colleagues that he at first found perplexing. He was nearing the end of a class in which he had been emphasizing how the American political system worked in one presidential election during which a deal had been struck between Northern and Southern Democrats and Republicans. One girl raised her hand to ask what grounds the people involved had to trust one another. The teacher, feeling as if the question came from "left field" since it had nothing to do with a systems approach he was emphasizing, was puzzled at his failure to be clear. But in sharing this situation with colleagues he was offered a different interpretation: The girl was more interested as a learner in understanding the motives of those involved. She heard the event as a narrative, a story of an encounter in the relationships between individuals. The logic she sought was not the logic of a system. Rather she sought the logic of understanding, what Bruner calls "believability" (Bruner 1986). Unlike the teacher who sought to transcend time, she was rooted in it—in the particulars of the situation and in the relationship between people. It is this approach to learning, with its different concerns and interests, that educators need to understand better and for which they must listen. They also need to make opportunities for this voice to be expressed and heard. If this is a mode of learning more frequently found in the thinking of girls—although we know it is available to both sexes—we need to be attentive to that. Adolescent girls remind us of the centrality of Piaget's ([1932] 1965) insight that "apart from our relations to other people, there can be no moral necessity." Their thinking about what is morally necessary illuminates and helps us understand how morality, mind, self, and relationships are intricately linked in everyday ways of knowing and learning.

Sources

Adelson, J. 1980. *Handbook of Adolescent Psychology*. New York: John Wiley.

———. 1986. *Inventing Adolescence: The Political Psychology of Everyday Schooling*. New Brunswick, N.J.: Transaction Books.

Adelson, J., and M. J. Doehrman. 1980. "The Psychodynamic Approach to Adolescence." In *Handbook of Adolescent Psychology*, edited by J. Adelson. New York: John Wiley.

Belenky, M. F., B. Clinchy, N. Goldberger, and N. Tarule. 1986. *Women's Ways of Knowing: The Development of Self, Voice, and Mind*. New York: Basic Books.

Bruner, J. 1986. *Actual Minds, Possible Worlds*. Cambridge, Mass.: Harvard University Press.

Chodorow, N. 1978. *The Reproduction of Mothering: Psychoanalysis and the Sociology of Mothering*. Berkeley, Calif.: University of California Press.

Douvan, E., and J. Adelson. 1966. *The Adolescent Experience*. New York: John Wiley.

Erikson, E. 1968. *Identity: Youth and Crisis*. New York: W. W. Norton.

Gilligan, C. 1977. In a different voice: Women's conceptions of the self and morality. *Harvard Educational Review* 47:481–517.

———. 1982. *In a Different Voice*. Cambridge, Mass.: Harvard University Press.

———. 1987. Female development in adolescence: Implications for theory. Unpublished manuscript, Harvard University.

Gilligan, C., S. Langdale, N. Lyons, and M. Murphy. 1982. The contribution of women's thought to developmental theory: an interim report to the National Institute of Education. Unpublished manuscript, Harvard University.

Gilligan, C., and J. Attanucci. 1988. Two moral orientations: Gender differences and similarities. *Merrill-Palmer Quarterly*.

Grotevant, H. D. and C. R. Cooper, eds. 1983. *Adolescent Development in the Family: New Directions for Child Development*. San Francisco: Jossey-Bass.

Haan, N. 1977. *A Manual for Interpersonal Morality.* Berkeley, Calif.: University of California, Institute for Human Development.

Hanmer, T. 1987. Personal correspondence to N. Lyons.

Harre, R., and R. Lamb, eds. 1986. *The Dictionary of Personality and Social Psychology.* Cambridge, Mass.: MIT Press.

Hartup, W. W., and Z. Rubin, eds. 1986. *Relationships and Development.* Hillsdale, N.J.: L. Erlbaum Associates.

Hinde, R. A. 1979. *Towards Understanding Relationships.* London and New York: Academic Press.

Hinde, R. A., and J. Stevenson-Hinde. 1986. "Relating Childhood Relationships to Individual Characteristics." In *Relationships and Development,* edited by W. Hartup and Z. Rubin. Hillsdale, N.J.: L. Erlbaum Associates.

Johnston, D. K. 1985. Two moral orientations—two problem-solving strategies: Adolescents' solutions to dilemmas in fables. Ph.D. diss., Harvard University.

Kohlberg, L. 1969. "Stage and Sequence: The Cognitive Developmental Approach to Socialization." In *The Handbook of Socialization Theory and Research,* edited by D. Goslin. Chicago: Rand McNally.

———. 1984. *The Psychology of Moral Development: Essays on Moral Development.* San Francisco: Harper and Row.

Lyons, N. 1982. Conceptions of self and morality and modes of moral choice. Ph.D. diss. Harvard University.

———. 1983. Two perspectives: On self, relationships and morality. *Harvard Educational Review* 53:125–45.

———. Forthcoming. "Visions and Competencies: Men and Women as Decision-Makers and Conflict Managers." In *Educating Women,* edited by J. Antler and S. Bicklen. Albany, N.Y.: SUNY Press.

———. 1987. Ways of knowing, learning and making moral choices. *Journal of Moral Education* 16, no. 3.

Marcia, J. 1980. "Identity in Adolescence." In *Handbook of Adolescent Psychology,* edited by J. Adelson. New York: John Wiley.

May, R. 1980. *Sex and Fantasy: Patterns of Male and Female Development.* New York: W. W. Norton & Co.

McIntosh, P. 1983. Interactive phases of curricular re-vision: A feminist perspective. Working Paper. Wellesley College, Center for Research on Women.

Miller, J. B. 1976, 1986. *Towards a New Psychology of Women*. Boston: Beacon Press.

Piaget, J. 1965. *The Moral Judgment of the Child*. Glencoe, Ill.: Free Press. (Originally pub. 1932.)

Youniss, J. 1980. *Parents and Peers in Social Development: A Sullivan-Piaget Perspective*. Chicago: University of Chicago Press.

Conceptions of Separation and Connection in Female Adolescents

LORI STERN

Adolescent girls represent the embodiment of a fascinating paradox. While theorists of adolescence describe a time of separation, individuation, and autonomy seeking, theorists of female development have observed that for women, the importance of strong relationships does not abate. In other words, theory tells us that by virtue of being female, adolescent girls especially value their connection; while by virtue of being adolescent, they are attending particularly to their separation. If we accept these theories, how do young women negotiate the contradictory strivings to be separate and yet connected? How do young women formulate these questions that divide theorists? Do they maintain their relationships at the expense of their autonomy, or can a sense of self develop without relinquishing connections? This chapter will address these questions by studying the responses of adolescent girls to a structured research interview dealing with issues of self-concept, morality, relationships, and future aspirations.

Perspectives on separation in adolescence

Anna Freud (1958) in her work on adolescence, defined the central characteristic of this period to be the renunciation of one's childhood relationships. In her view one's adaptation depends on breaking ties. Peter Blos (1967) carried this line of thought further with his classic paper positing the adolescent shedding of familial attachments as requisite for adult involvement in society. While Erik Erikson's conception of identity development includes a social dimension, his related notion of distantiation refers to the response "where intimate, competitive, and combative relations are experienced with and against the selfsame people" (1968).

As described by these theorists, then, the hallmarks of adolescent separation are turmoil and rebellion, traditionally the *sine qua non* of this life stage. Although studies by Offer (1969) and Douvan and Adelson (1966) have called into question the extent to which turmoil and rebellion actually form an integral part of adolescence, individuation and autonomy development are still widely considered the foremost adolescent tasks (Josselson 1980). Indeed, autonomy has been seen not only as the preoccupation of adolescents, but also as the distinguishing feature of the mature individual.

Studies of women and girls, however, seem to contradict any theory considering separation and individuation to be universal adolescent interests. Freud (1905) discussed the fact that women do not undergo the same process of separation that men do. He implies that this deviation signifies pathology:

> At every stage in the course of development through which all human beings ought by rights to pass, a certain number are held back; so there are some who have never got over their parents' authority and have withdrawn their affection from them either very incompletely or not at all. They are mostly girls, who, to the delight of their parents, have persisted in all their childish love far beyond puberty. (P. 93)

Recent theorists have postulated that females' relational ties are strengths and that the role of these relationships in development should be understood in this context. Miller (1984) wrote that a girl "can move on to a larger and more articulated sense of herself only because of her actions and feelings in the relationship." For women, even a task as distinctly self-oriented as identity formation may mean defining oneself "in relation and connection to other people" (Chodorow 1974). Gilligan (1982) refers to "the fusion of identity and intimacy" in women, while Stiver (1984) points out that women's "need to feel related to others is a crucial aspect of her identity and allows us to understand why women are so threatened when there is the danger of alienation."

If some sort of breaking away is a central concern of adolescence while connecting to others is a central concern for females, then we expect that for female adolescents, the conflict between these opposing tendencies will create a major existential dilemma. Based on interviews with female adolescents, this chapter will describe some of the ways they conceptualize and resolve the conflict of breaking away and connecting and how their views relate to some major theories of human development.

Self-descriptions

This study began with an analysis of the responses to the question, How would you describe yourself to yourself?, which was part of the research interview conducted at Emma Willard School. The sample includes the twenty-three young women who were interviewed for each of three years. Hence, the question was asked of the participants each year for three years. While the self-descriptions are not taken at face value as complete portrayals of a person, they do indicate those aspects of the self that are of particular meaning to the participants, and by what categories they measure themselves. A count of the appearance of responses in the most prevalent categories yields the following picture of the relative salience to twenty-three young women of the different themes. Each self-description contains several statements in various categories.

Table 7

Themes of Self-description: Frequency of Occurrence

	Number of statements	Year		
		1st	2nd	3rd
relational style and skills	120	36	43	41
achievement style and skill	53	19	13	21
personal qualities (unspecified)	38	13	11	14
independent, individual	31	7	12	12
likes, dislikes, activities	16	6	6	4
physical appearance	9	2	1	6
ideology	6	3	1	2
role ("a student")	1	1	0	0

The extent to which these young women describe themselves in terms of their interpersonal abilities is striking. Gilligan (1982) has pointed out the apparent paradox that when asked to describe themselves, women include much information about other people, particularly themselves in relationship with others. While this would tend to support the theory that the female sense of self is relational, there is also a consistent tendency by these participants to discuss themselves in terms of their "independence." Although the independence statements only number one-fourth of the relational ones, the theme is pervasive. A count for presence/ absence revealed that nineteen of the twenty-three participants spontaneously described themselves as independent at some point over the three years of interviews. This supports the idea that adolescence is a time in which these girls also have some interest in the ways in which they are distinct from others. Hence, this data indicates that while concerns about relationships are paramount in these women's self-conceptions, concerns about independence are also significant.

In order to further understand the meaning of independence in female adolescence, as described by these young women, I shall discuss four cases that represent four different approaches to the issue. These cases were chosen for their contrasts, in order to give as broad a view as possible of some ways that adolescent girls deal with issues of independence and separation. Because these young women are so different in approach, any common themes may be particularly noteworthy.

Four cases

The following case studies will depict four adolescent girls' approaches to independence. The separation language of psychoanalytic theory is vocalized by Jane, while Judy values her connection to her mother above all else. Anne and Becky represent the more common pattern of incorporating some hybrid version of the two extreme positions.

Much as the psychoanalytic theorists have prescribed, Jane sees a rupture with her parents as a necessary step in her development. She says, "I tried hard to be rebellious, and I went through a long time of that; but it was very successful because I managed to break away from my parents." Unlike the other young women, she sees her mother as dependent on her, rather than vice versa, saying, "My mother is very attached to me. . . . She loves me as herself, and I think my mother has had a lot of difficulty in separating the two of us. It is getting better now that she realizes that I at least have made the distinction."

In contrast, Judy describes herself as someone with difficulties in separating. She says, "My mother was such a big part of my life that I didn't realize I almost didn't feel like a separate person." She would like her relationship with her mother to remain unchanged, saying, "I always want her to be my mother. I don't want her to have her own life." It is difficult for her to become an adult and maintain the relationship without changes, and given a choice, she would like not to grow. She says, "I wouldn't mind staying sixteen my whole life . . . young enough that I could live at home and get the approval I need from my mother." Yet she recognizes the impossibility of this and is left with the unappealing prospect of needing to "grow away from" her mother.

Becky, like Judy, describes a continuing emotional attachment to her mother, saying, "I think she is the only person who it has become impossible or nearly impossible to separate myself from." To Becky, her mother's approval continues to be important to her, and in spite of some severe conflicts, she does not find that this relationship inhibits her growth, and she holds many leadership positions in the school. Her descriptions show that when the relationship would require her to deny her point of view, rather than sacrificing herself to the relationship, she struggles to bring them both into account. "I don't think I am going to see her until Christmas because she is not ready to talk. She is ready to have me say, Oh, you were right, Mom. And as long as she is not willing to communicate with me, I don't want to knock my head against the brick wall."

Anne defines independence as a necessary part of maturity at the same time that she acknowledges the importance of her relationships. Her interpersonal view of development can be characterized by her reflections on her own changes: "People grow, so you grow with them." She describes the struggle she undergoes in seeking to incorporate independent behavior when it is not an automatic response, articulating the importance of being her "own person." Yet she also consistently considers the effects of her actions on others, and on her relationships. "Being independent and also at the same time, being able to make the people around me that mean the most to me, happy. And if I can do that, then I guess I can be successful."

What is independence?

While independence is of importance to these young women, it is unclear exactly what this concept means to them. In common usage, independence and separation are abstract terms that can signify anything from physical self-sufficiency to psychological autonomy. To understand the particular meaning for these young women, it is necessary to examine their conceptions of independence on a rudimentary level: What are independence and separation? How do these young women use these terms, and what meanings are attached?

In Anne's earliest interview, while independence is looked on as desirable, it is also a somewhat mysterious entity. In describing her own development, she says, "You go from the stage where your mother takes care of you, where you start to get some type of individualism and then you want more independence and then finally you are independent."

Independence, then, is alien to her. It is something one "gets." Her struggle to assimilate independent behavior before she is actually comfortable with it is apparent in the moral dilemma she describes. She describes making a decision to go to a friend's house without asking her mother's permission.

> I was at the point where I am sure it was a struggle for independence and relying on other people to run my world. So it was kind of, I should let her decide because she runs my world. But then there was the other side, too. Independence, and I need to get out, and I have to make my own decisions. It's got to come sometime and it is my decision, and I should make it.

It is interesting that she defines this struggle for independence as a moral issue. Yet this is not a struggle for independence where she sees herself pitted against others. Rather, it is an internal struggle about incorporating apparently external standards. Independent action, at this point, is perceived as what she *should* do. The motives for it seem quite alien. This sense is reiterated in her evaluation of her action, which hinges on her mother's approval. She responds to the interviewer's query, Did you think you made the right decision? Why? as follows:

> Uh-huh . . . because she would have let me do it and I wanted to do it and it was important to my friend that I do it, so three ways in one direction is fine. *(How did you know it was the right decision?)* I didn't. I didn't know that at all. *(How did you know afterward?)* I found out from my mother that it was fine with her, so that was fine. *(Can you summarize for me what made it the right decision?)* My independence and my mother's approval and my friend's feelings and that made it the right decision.

It is apparent that although Anne discusses independent action as if it were a goal in itself, acting on her interests alone does not justify behavior. In fact, she juxtaposes it with apparently contradictory desires to please her friend and gain her mother's approval. Is this an example of underdeveloped autonomy, or does it indicate a complexity in Anne's reasoning that merits understanding? For these answers, let us look to her other responses.

When Anne is asked to describe the ways that she has changed, she describes the process of becoming more involved in the world around her and connects this change with her developing "individualism." While individualism might imply a heightened self-interest, for Anne it is contrasted to a self-centered approach to the world.

> Now I've gotten to the point where I look outside myself, my little world, and look for things, even if it doesn't affect me directly. I look to see what's going on and what's happening and try to get some individualism too. *(Individualism?)* Just not relying on everybody else to take care of your world.

Anne says that for her, independence is linked to an enhanced ability to look outside herself, precisely the opposite of what the word implies. A similarly paradoxical definition of independence is given by Becky, who says, "Being independent means that I can handle crises that I go through without totally falling apart—to have enough personal strength, you know, to go through crises and to be able to depend on other people." The notion that independence means being able to depend is quite striking. Is this another example of somebody who doesn't understand the meaning of independence? Or are these young women conveying a sense that to them independence means acknowledging interdependence, rather than behaving counter-dependently.

Becky discusses this further: "I don't think anybody is really self-sufficient, no woman is an island. And I think that whenever you go through a crisis, of course you have to handle it yourself, but there is always support, you know." Jane articulates a similar belief: "Everyone is dependent on other people because everything that gives anyone pleasure comes from other people. You read a good book, well, someone wrote it. You see a good movie, someone acted in it." Judy echoes this with the assertion that independence does not mean breaking ties: "I think I have realized that I can always stay close to my mother, even if, you know, it's different depending on her and staying close to her . . . you can be independent and still stay close to somebody like that."

Is such contradictory language a thin disguise for unresolved dependency needs, caused by women's difficulties in separating, such as Freud described? Yet these young women are also quick to discuss the distaste they feel at being too much like (or too close to) someone else. This is illustrated in Anne's description of her relationship to her sister:

Feelings that we both have about things that are alike is also important ... the ability to feel the same way is also important, to be able to have the same ideas, and the same ideas also helps us to stay close because we don't immediately have to explain the way we feel. But we just know it, intuition or something.

Yet Anne follows this with:

I hate it when someone says, you're just like her. I take it as a compliment, but I don't want to be just like her. I want to be just like me. I don't want to be just like anybody. Because it is important to be my own person.

Is Anne contradicting herself by stating that she wants her sister to be able to think and feel like her without their being alike? It seems there is a fine line between being similar enough to someone for mutual understanding, but not so similar that one's sense of uniqueness is lost. Anne says, "I feel everybody's got to have their individualism to some extent, even though I think it's good that we feel alike in a lot of ways. It's also really important that we aren't totally alike." Rather than demonstrating lack of differentiation, Anne seems to describe a coexistence of identity and intimacy, where experiences can be shared while a sense of self is maintained.

In a similar vein, Jane describes the process of recognizing that she is not a duplicate or an extension of her mother.

I feel that by giving me the kind of life that she wanted, she kind of transferred herself to me; and because I am her daughter, she assumed that I am her. I mean not literally, you know, not as an insane kind of me, that is me over there in the room. But kind of a sameness between us that really isn't there. We are similar in many ways, being mother and daughter, but we aren't the same, the same person. She, in a certain circumstance expects me to react the way she does, and I think this is another part of the guilt I felt as a child, I didn't react the way she did, therefore I assumed I was wrong, so. (How does that make you feel now in terms of the way she sees you?) Well, it used to really anger me, and now I understand it. So it doesn't anger me; it is a kind of inconvenience sometimes. You know I love her anyway, and it doesn't inhibit our relationship except that a lot of the times she has trouble understanding me.

Becky discusses coming to terms with the fact that she is biologically a separate organism.

I remember, this is really strange, but at moments being kind of stricken with fright. I would look in the mirror and say, This is me, these are my hands, and I am all alone, and I'm not glued to any other person. So I feel a lot less intimidated by myself and being alone and not being with others.

Hence, these young women acknowledge and even value their abilities to differentiate themselves from family members or friends. At the same time, however, they feel that their experiences are more meaningful when they can be shared. Becky discusses both sides of this issue: "Now I know that this is what I am like and the friendships that I find now, those are going to be people who are going to have to deal with me as I am and like me as I am." But she later says, "If it was my mother, of course I would always put her before myself because in a weird way, it wouldn't be worth it if I did anything for me, because who would I show off what I had done?"

While this may appear as a bind, these young women do not seem to experience it as such. In fact, this is the most striking feature of their notions of independence. Self-determination is allowed to coexist with actions that take others into account. Although our language implies that independence is the polar opposite of dependence, these women tell us that these are not mutually exclusive experiences. In fact, we have seen that their discussions of independence involve unusual juxtapositions where separation and connection are linked. Becky says that being independent means being able to depend on others, while Jane says that in order to really love her parents she had to break away from them. For Judy, being independent of her mother can involve remaining close, while Anne says that individualism involves looking beyond herself. While each young woman expressed positive views of independence, they all included qualifiers that the concept itself is somewhat fallacious. Apparently, the independence that is discussed by these women does not require renouncing interpersonal attachments.

In the face of these contradictory statements, one question that remains is, Why do these women value independence? What purpose does it serve, and what motivates its pursuit? For these answers, let us look again to the responses of these four women.

Why become independent?

One theme that emerges from these discussions of independence and separation is that it is an unavoidable fact of life. "You have to support yourself and take care of yourself and see that you are, because otherwise you won't survive," says Anne. "Whereas when you are a child, you always know that you will survive because there is always going to be someone there." This attention to taking care of her physical needs occurs in her first interview, while in her third year, she discusses a similarly pragmatic reason for eschewing "dependency":

> It can be harmful if you are only dependent, say, on one person, because if that one person does something and just completely betrays that dependence or that trust you have in them, then you are done. You don't have anywhere else to turn.

Judy echoes this with the opinion that it is important to be able to generate her own self-confidence.

> I am becoming my own person, which I have to anyway, because when my mother is not around anymore and I am fifty years old, I hope I am stable enough to become confident with myself, because I always try to get reassurance from my mother. I always say, 'Mom, is this okay?'

This view that independence and separation are imposed externally, rather than by one's own desires is noteworthy, particularly in light of the psychological descriptions of women's problems in separating; however, these women also consistently describe motives that are internally experienced. Again, these discussions have a paradoxical quality, for here the young women describe independence that is for the sake of their relationships. Jane, the strongest advocate of separation in this group, provides a clear illustration.

> I managed to break away from my parents, the feelings that I had. I couldn't really love them until I had broken away from them and staked out my own identity. And now I can really love them much more than I could then.

This is quite different from Blos's prescription for "the loosening of infantile object ties, in order to become a member of the society at large, or simply, of the adult world." While psychoanalytic theory defines the purpose of separation as serving to induct the individual into "society," Jane's separation was for the purpose of returning to her parental relationship with an enhanced capacity to love. It is unclear how Jane feels her relationship is improved by her independence, but this question is dealt with by the other young women.

Anne says that by being able to meet more of her own needs, she will develop the ability to recognize her mother as a person in her own right and thereby improve the relationship.

For Becky, "there is a time for every kid when they stop seeing their parents as perfect and start seeing them as human beings." Like Anne, she describes a new ability to see her mother realistically, rather than as an omnipotent provider. This ability to see the other in her own terms has been linked with "honest and mutual relationships" (Attanucci 1984). Anne calls the new experience of taking the other into account a "total relationship." To these young women, this capacity is predicated by their increased independence.

Hence, that independence, for these young women, involves an increased capacity to care for themselves. By decreasing the extent to which others must meet their needs, these women are able to perceive others in a new way that enables them to attend to the other as a person. Seeing their parents as people rather than caregivers opens new possibilities for their relationships. As Gilligan (1982) points out, interpersonal connection requires the inclusion of both self and other. Consequently, the ability to perceive the other more accurately leads to a capacity for including the other more wholly in the relationship, which enhances the connection.

While independence for these young women fosters their relationships, Anne describes a process whereby her relationships also foster her personal growth.

I'm going to become more independent, and I'm going to be able to continue to see it as more of a relationship. . . . As I realize that my mother's not just there for me and as I become more independent, that's going to cause me to stop seeing it as just taking my mother for granted if she is always there to do everything for me. If she didn't do anything for me and I did it all for myself, she's just going to be a person, rather than somebody who's God and going around doing everything for me.

If there are a lot of people in your life that you are happy with, and who make you feel good, they make you feel good about yourself in one way or another, indirectly or directly. And that means that you can go out and do a lot for, you know, just do a lot more than you could, because you feel good.

Hence, while the prevalent motive for developing independence is to improve relationships, relationships are bound to the experience of independence in two ways. Independence is most valuable to these young women to the extent that it serves their relationships, and their relationships enable them to venture further into the world of independence. This is not dissimilar to Winnicott's (1958) thesis that the capacity to be alone requires a sense of the other's presence.

Likewise, Bowlby has written (1980):

Paradoxically, the truly self-reliant person when viewed in this light proves to be by no means as independent as cultural stereotypes suppose. An essential ingredient is a capacity to rely trustingly on others when occasion demands and to know on whom it is appropriate to rely.

Discussion

Theorists of adolescence have emphasized the need to develop independence during adolescence while female-developmental theorists have described the unwavering importance of relationships in the female life cycle. These two contradictory lines of thought place adolescent females at a peculiar crossroad. The implication has been that they must choose to follow the route either of separation or of connection, where separation leads to maturity and connection leads to femininity. In this paper, I have used interview data in seeking to understand how adolescent girls conceptualize these problems and in describing their ways of addressing them.

The data have shown that issues of separation and of connection are both foremost concerns for these young women, but they seldom place these two approaches to relationship in opposition by constructing conflicts where they must choose either separation or connection. Rather, separation and connection are seen as two compatible aspects of a person. These aspects not only coexist, but each can also function in the service of the other. Developing independence is seen as improving the capacity to meet one's own needs, so that others can be appreciated as people rather than as instrumental providers. In reducing the preoccupation with receiving care, these women report a heightened capacity to look outside themselves and attend to others. At the same time, relationships provide the support one needs to push one's own development further.

The fact that these young women do not dichotomize separation and connection is difficult to understand in psychological terms. The apparently conflicting desires to see oneself as part of a larger whole, and yet to feel like an individual have often been reconciled by psychologists' "cutting and pasting" the two concepts together. For example, Erikson's stages two through five focus on increasing individualism while the later three focus on developing interpersonal connections. A similar solution is offered by Kegan (1982), who describes development as a vacillation back and forth between psychologies of independence and of inclusion.

From such a perspective, these young women seem persistently to contradict themselves. The apparent paradoxes that they present, however, reveal not confusion but a conception of the self that is, by its nature, in relation to others. Thus, even separation and independence occur within a context of relationship.

This context of relationship is, for these young women, an underlying assumption that must be understood in order to appreciate the meaning of their terms. A complex understanding of relationship is revealed as they describe how their increased individual capabilities (resembling "independence") are used not to foster breaking away but to be funneled back into the relationship. These young women's discussions of separation and independence uncover a basic premise that assumes the presence and importance of relationships. Thus, separation is not pitted against connection but involves a redefined ability to respond to (and consequently to connect with) the other.

With the persisting importance of attachment in their lives, these young women assimilate their new abilities to relate to others in various ways. Relationships without independence become just as problematic as independence without relationships, for neither is prior to the other. Independence, then, involves the renegotiation and reframing of relationships in light of their new ability to consider the other person. Chodorow (1980) wrote that "differentiation is not distinctness and separateness, but a particular way of being connected to others." These adolescent girls have shown how the meanings of separation and independence shift when considered in the context of ongoing relationships.

Sources

Attanucci, J. 1984. Mothers in their own terms. Ed.D. diss., Harvard Graduate School of Education.

Blos, P. 1967. "The Second Individuation Process of Adolescence." In Vol. 22 *The Psychoanalytic Study of the Child*, 162–86. New York: International Universities Press.

Bowlby, J. 1969, 1973, 1980. *Attachment and Loss*. New York: Basic Books.

Chodorow, N. 1974. "Family Structure and Feminine Personality." In *Women, Culture, and Society*, edited by M. Rosaldo and L. Lamphere. Stanford, Calif.: Stanford University Press.

————. 1980. "Gender Relation and Difference in Psychoanalytic Perspective." In *The Future of Difference*, edited by H. Eisenstein and J. Jardine. Boston: G. K. Hall.

Douvan, E., and J. Adelson. 1966. *The Adolescent Experience*. New York: Wiley.

Erikson, E. 1968. *Identity, Youth and Crisis*. New York: W. W. Norton.

Freud, A. 1958. "Adolescence." In Vol. 13 *The Psychoanalytic Study of the Child*, 255–78. New York: International Universities Press.

Freud, S. 1962 (orig. 1905). "The Transformations of Puberty." In *Three Essays on the Theory of Sexuality*. New York: Basic Books.

Gilligan, C. 1982. *In a Different Voice*. Cambridge, Mass.: Harvard University Press.

Josselson, R. 1980. "Ego Development in Adolescence." In *The Handbook of Adolescent Psychology*, edited by J. Adelson. New York: John Wiley.

Kegan, R. 1982. *The Evolving Self*. Cambridge, Mass.: Harvard University Press.

Miller, J. 1984. The Development of Women's Sense of Self. Wellesley, Mass.: Stone Center Works in Progress.

Offer, D. 1969. *The Psychological World of the Teenager*. New York: Basic Books.

Stiver, I. 1982. "The Meanings of Dependency in Male and Female Relationships." Wellesley, Mass.: Stone Center Works in Progress.

Winnicott, D. W. 1958. "The Capacity to Be Alone." In *The Maturational Processes and the Facilitating Environment* (1965). New York: International Universities Press.

LYN MIKEL BROWN

Feminist thinkers must self-consciously and critically confront various traditions of political discourse, feminist and nonfeminist. There are among us, for example, those who seek solutions to our public and private dilemmas by depriving us of a grammar of moral discourse and forcing all of life under a set of terms denuded of a critical edge. In so doing, they would deprive the human object, female and male, of the capacity to think, to judge, to question, and to act, for all these activities are importantly constituted by an everyday, ordinary language infused with moral terms. —*J. B. Elshtain, "Feminist Discourse and Its Discontents"*

Jean, seventeen years old, in her third year of the Dodge Study at Emma Willard describes the following real-life conflict in response to the question, Could you describe to me a situation where you had to make a decision and you weren't sure what was the right thing to do?

A girl who just recently left this school—she is, was, a freshman here, and she was thirteen years old, and she had a lot of problems at home. And she was having a lot of problems here . . . trying to cover it all up by being really loud and obnoxious. . . . She said once to me that [when] she came here, the thing that she wanted more than anything was to be accepted. But she was doing everything in her power to not be accepted. . . . And so she was getting really unhappy here . . . and everybody ragged on her. Plus the fact that she was doing poorly in school and there was a lot of threats at home about if you don't get A's and B's . . . and she was really unhappy. And last Tuesday she was sitting in front rocking back and forth hugging herself and saying I can't stand it here. She was talking about how she just wanted to kill herself and she just couldn't handle it anymore. And all I could think about was what if this little thirteen-year-old-girl really tries to jump out a window, how will I feel after that? And my immediate answer was I'd just feel like garbage. So the next day I said, Well, even if [she] gets mad at me and never wants to speak to me again, I'd rather she be alive and never want to speak to me than be dead and not have the chance. So I went and told the counselor. . . . And so I said, 'I have a friend, a real friend, who is not very happy and who is really seriously considering suicide.' And as soon as I said 'suicide,' she just said, 'what!?' And I said, 'Yes.'

(When you were trying to decide what to do, what was the conflict in this situation?) It was between, well, doing what I knew positively was the best thing for [her] and what I was thinking, the whole thing. Well, she told me something as a friend, and in private and . . . she could have just been pulling my leg and being very upset and didn't really mean it. And should I really go, and maybe I'll be wasting [the counselor's] time. And then I thought . . . I considered just trying to talk to [her] myself and just listen and be a friend.

(Without bringing in the counselor?) Without bringing in the counselor and just listening to her and trying as hard as I could to be [the counselor], be like [the counselor], without [her] presence.

Jean struggles between the imperative she felt to help her friend, the possibility that she may not have the full or accurate story, and the realization that revealing her friend's situation may sever their relationship. Acknowledging her doubts, she acts. She cannot risk her friend's life. Surprisingly, when Jean was asked if she considered the situation she described a "moral" problem, she responds:

No, it was just a question of what was best for [my friend], and I realized getting her out of school was the best for her because she would have had a breakdown or something. Thirteen is really kind of young to have a breakdown at a boarding school.

For Jean morality is:

Kind of the rules, rules you grow up with and what you internalize from what your parents tell you and what you get from your environment, which is something you decide you want to live by— your rules you live by, that you will stick to and change with the situation, not change, like if the weather is bad I will change my morals, but something where it is a difficult situation and you realize that your morals don't really fit the situation.

(What makes something a moral problem for you?) If it really doesn't fit in. Right now a moral problem is something that although it might agree with what I think—what fits with my ideal, kind of my formed idea of morals—but violently contrasts with my mother's ideas of morals and the morals that I have to live with at Emma Willard, because all three have to work themselves out inside of me before I can decide to do what's right. And so it's difficult combining the three because although they have some common points, they have very, very different points also. So I have to decide whose morals I should use and it depends.

Jean's response poses an intriguing question: How does one make sense of the discrepancy between Jean's struggle, her use of prescriptive moral language, her felt imperative to respond to her friend, and the value she places on their friendship, on the one hand; and her contention, on the other, that for her, this situation did not create a moral problem? The apparent discrepancy in Jean's case is not an isolated example but typifies a pattern that appears in nearly 30 percent of the interviews in the third year of the study at Emma Willard.

It has been suggested repeatedly that female development may not fit neatly into the traditional developmental models in psychology exemplified by such theorists as Freud and Erikson, or Piaget and Kohlberg (Chodorow 1978; Douvan and Adelson 1966; Erikson 1968; Gilligan 1982; Lyons 1983; Miller 1976). The value placed on separation and individuation as developmental endpoints have resulted in a lack of attention to the centrality of attachment and relationship for healthy psychological development. Those who have begun to attend to the voices of girls and women find that female identity development may challenge such established definitions of the nature of self and relationship (Belenky et al. 1986; Gilligan 1982, 1987; Josselson 1987).

By examining the moral conflicts generated by four adolescent girls and their subsequent responses to questions about morality and responsibility, this chapter considers these observations while addressing two central questions: (1) What does it mean that the responses of conflict and responsibility these young women express are not labeled "moral" responses, either by themselves or by the existing theoretical paradigms charting the development of "moral reasoning"? and (2) What does a description and analysis of these cases suggest about the relationship between female identity development in adolescence and the nature of morality?

Four stories of conflict

An analysis of cases similar to Jean's reveals a number of patterns or themes. First, in these narratives the conflict, though described in various contexts and situations, takes a similar form. The manifest content of the narratives has to do with personal relationships; they are stories centrally concerned with attachment and with dialogue. The struggle or conflict focuses on an imperative to act or respond in a manner they describe as good, right, or best. This imperative results from knowledge of the other's particular situation or knowledge of the interdependence of relationship. In other words, the imperative to act arises from the experience of relationship and the belief that to turn away from a person in need, particularly a friend, is wrong (Gilligan 1982; Gilligan and Attanucci 1988).

Jean's case clearly illustrates this pattern. Her need to act in a way that is "best" for her friend arises from an understanding of the particularities of her friend's situation. The story she tells clearly indicates she knew the pressures impinging upon her young friend and that she knew them through shared experiences and communication with her. This knowledge of her friend's feelings creates an imperative to respond, and Jean does so in the face of doubt and ambiguity. She is uncertain both of her assessment of the situation and of the consequences should she act—that is, would her action ultimately threaten the friendship.

Kate, also seventeen, describes a similar imperative, although the context of her conflict (and its immediacy) is much different from that of Jean's. Kate struggles to decide whether or not she and a friend ought to speak to the school administration to express dissatisfaction with a teacher, when she was not personally having trouble with the teacher's style. She says:

It was a hard decision for me whether or not I should go. I don't know, for me everything was fine, because when I was interested I could go and talk to the teacher. I certainly had no problem going and doing my own research, making my own assignments. I work best that way. *But I had to think from this perspective* [emphasis added]. I can see how this is a problem for the other people, and it is not fair for all of them to be having this. They aren't getting what they should be out of this course and they need someone. Everyone talked about it. Someone had to go and talk, and it was, you know, it was a question of *would it be selfish of me* not to do it, because things were fine for me, but I knew there was a problem [emphasis added]. So I went and talked, with this other girl, to the [administration].

For Kate the difficulty centers on whether and how to act given her knowledge of the members of the class who were experiencing difficulty and, as she discusses later in the interview, her understanding of the potential repercussions of her action for the teacher and the class. She explains to the interviewer, "But I had to think from this perspective." By knowing that she knows—knowing by stepping out of her perspective and seeing that, for the others, from their point of view, there was a problem—not speaking on their behalf would be seen by her as a "selfish" choice. For Kate, then, "selfish" refers to deliberate inattention. It means being self-centered, looking out for herself alone when she could be responsive to others, turning away when it is clear to her that "they need someone" and that from *their* perspective they "were really, really upset." Kate understands that it is precisely because she and her friend are *not* having a difficult time with the teacher that they *should* be the ones to speak up. She explains why:

Everyone was really frustrated with it and because this friend of mine and I weren't having real problems with the material, we didn't have the same kind of frustration. We didn't have the same resentment. We just felt that something maybe should just be said so that the situation should be corrected ... the hardest thing was that we didn't want it to be malicious or something ... because we didn't feel that way at all. It was both of us, I guess for the obvious reasons. We like her [the teacher] very much and we didn't want to hurt her feelings, and we weren't saying the way she was teaching the class was wrong. It was just that ... students weren't advanced enough to handle the kind of classroom situation.

It is important to Kate that the teacher understand the spirit in which she and her friend act—that she understand their intent and the complexity with which they view the situation. She and her friend worry about the consequences of misunderstanding—tension in the classroom, hurting the teacher's feelings, and the potential for tension between the teacher and the administration. Though Kate acknowledges issues of fairness—"it is not fair . . . they aren't getting what they should be out of this course"—she also recognizes her act as a response to need—"they need someone."

Kate, like Jean, makes a choice to speak in spite of her uncertainty. Within the boundaries of a particular story, each story highlights responsiveness; each emphasizes knowledge of the other(s), of their particular situations, of their particular needs.

Faye also illustrates this pattern. As editor-in-chief of the yearbook, she must decide whether or not to confront a girl who is not doing her job. She says:

> It's like I kept feeling torn between should I get someone new and say you are fired, or should I just keep waiting. . . . I guess my conflict was I didn't really want to confront her, but I knew I had to. . . . I wasn't really sure if I was being reasonable in the things I was asking her to do. Part of me wanted to go yell at her, and when I would see her upset *about the things that were going on in her life* or just other things that she was busy with, I couldn't just go and say, you know, Why aren't you doing this? *I felt I couldn't just look at my situation*, that this is the most important thing, because I realized there were other things going on . . . but . . . it was getting to be too much work for other people [emphasis added].

Faye finds that she cannot simply act on what first appears to be a clear-cut violation of expectations—that her classmate is not doing her job. The classmate's perspective, when taken into account, makes the issue more complicated. Faye acknowledges that in order to attend to the needs of all involved in the situation, she must recognize that not only is her own work and the work of others increasing because this person is not doing her job—which justifies firing her—but she must include the possibility that she may have been asking too much, or that perhaps there were other things happening in the classmate's life that may be affecting her work. She recognizes clearly that "I couldn't just look at my situation."

As mentioned earlier, these girls do not describe their real-life dilemmas as "moral" dilemmas or problems. Although their rationale takes various forms, there are similarities that appear to be key to understanding "morality" from their perspective. For some of these young women, morality is defined much like developmental psychologists concerned with morality would expect it to be defined, that is, as rules, standards, principles that guide the self, protect relationships, or order the social world (Colby and Kohlberg 1987; Kohlberg 1984; Piaget 1932). Moreover, "morality" framed in this way is described as something taught in school, by parents, or, more generally, by "society." Frequently it has a quality of being outside themselves, as prior to themselves. Defined in this way it is, in Piagetian (1932) terms, "heteronomous" morality, or in Kohlbergian (1984) terms, "conventional" morality. As such, since it is defined by others or by the external situation, it can be, and frequently is, manipulated or changed depending on the situation.

As Jean stated earlier, morality is "the kind of rules you grow up with and what you internalize from what your parents tell you and what you get from your environment, which is something you decide you want to live by—your rules you live by, that you will stick to and change with the situation." Rules, then, are chosen and "stuck to," yet they are also flexible and contingent on her environment. For Jean a moral problem is something that contrasts her morals with her mother's or those of Emma Willard School. She knows three moral points of view, each equally viable, similar in quality. The difficulty for her is in "combining the three" or deciding *whose* morals to use. Yet Jean's struggle to solve the conflict she experiences with her friend does not reflect a morality defined as "the rules you live by." Her conflict reflects a struggle to sort out what her friend "really" needs and who she is or ought to be in relation to her friend. Rather than an externalized or "internalized rule," Jean's conflict highlights responsiveness to relationship. She is concerned about the welfare of a friend she has observed closely. She is concerned about the veracity of her observations. And she is concerned about the consequences of her action—for her friend, for their relationship, and, as importantly, for a definition of herself as a moral person. Rather than a choice among various a priori moral points of view, Jean's choice will have implications for her own moral identity.

Kate's discussion of "morality" has a similar quality to Jean's. Like Jean she does not consider her situation to be a "moral" problem. The interviewer asks, Would you describe the situation that you just described as a moral problem? and Kate answers:

It's really hard to say what's moral and what's not. I have—at any given point in time—I have certain sets of maybe principles that I have never really sat and defined. They aren't—morals frequently have religious connotations and things like that . . . I don't have morals that are just for the sake of morals: Someone says this is how it is. I have principles of my own *that shift as I get older.* But I am always, you know, I live according to . . . *But they are flexible.* I would weigh any given situation and . . . it is never a black-and-white, right-and-wrong situation [emphasis added].

(*Would this situation you described, be within the realm of a moral problem?*) In the sense that I just mentioned, if you call that a moral decision, yes. But it wasn't. In a way it wasn't really, because I never questioned what I was doing, as really right or wrong. I felt I was doing the right thing, but I felt badly about it.

(*Why?*) Afraid that it would be misinterpreted or harmful or. . . . (*To whom?*) The faculty member, the head of the [administration]. It might make a tension there. It might make the class worse. It might, there were all kinds of things, you know.

(*You started describing morality and what morals were. Do you want to elaborate on what you said?*) I think that is really all. It is never something I think of as moral. Because in my mind I think of morals as being very structured, binding kind of—*and the principles I have for myself aren't that way, so I never really call them morals* [emphasis added].

(*What do you base those principles on?*) Oh, I really don't know. All kinds of things. What I have learned, you know, social influences and things like that. (*Can you give me an example of one that is presently important?*) I don't know, I don't ever really think about them. They just happen. I can't deny the fact that there are guiding things in my life like that, because, you know, society just has them. But I never really sit down and think about them. So it's hard to know where and what they are just because they are such an integral part of my actions and my everything.

Kate makes a distinction in her description of morality that Jean does not. When discussing what morality means to her, she distinguishes between morality that is given a priori in the social world, such as religious beliefs, and those she considers to be her own moral principles. She describes those in the external world as "morals for the sake of morals, someone says this is how it is"; a morality in which things are "black and white, right and wrong." Her own moral principles, much like Jean's, are "flexible," not like the "structured, binding" kinds of principles in the world. She does not, in fact, refer to them as moral principles; she doesn't really think about them. "They just happen." Yet, they are the guiding things in her life; things that are integral to her action and, as she says, "to my everything." In the same way, Kate's real-life dilemma does not fit the definitions of morality she describes as structured and binding principles. Her experience of conflict does not raise questions framed in dichotomous terms—right or wrong, black or white. Her moral conflict emerges when, as she says, "I felt I was doing the right thing, but I felt badly about it." For Kate, the conflict is neither dichotomous nor defined a priori. It is an experience more closely aligned with her feelings and knowledge. Moral issues in a given situation are "weighed," but the personal struggle arises from acknowledging her responsibility for the web of feeling and relationship that could potentially fracture as a consequence of any action she might take. Whatever she chooses to do, someone is potentially hurt or "misinterpreted," and as a result she feels "badly," although she believes she was "right" to have acted the way she did.

Ann, also in her third year of the study, responding to a painful and complex dilemma about whether to speak with her best friend who was not being communicative, also illustrates this pattern. She describes her conflict:

> My friend sort of went through this period when we were not communicating with each other, and I saw myself as having to make a choice. Was I going to continue to be her friend, or was I going to totally wipe her out? Not really wipe her out, but erase her as one of my social friends, until she came around to me and said, 'What's the matter?'

While struggling to decide whether or not to speak, Ann considers how much she needs her friend, especially at that time of "transition" in her life. She explains, "If she got angry with me she would divorce herself from our friendship. At that point I knew I wouldn't be able to handle such an emotional thing. Such a break in a relationship that had been strong for so long." Ann also realizes that her initial decision not to speak up may have been self-serving:

I mean my action not to talk with her was basically very selfish.

(What do you mean by selfish?) I was thinking of myself. I wasn't thinking of her. I wasn't thinking that she needed to prove something to herself, that she had to show herself that she could survive.

In contrast to this experience with her friend, Ann defines a "moral problem" as "whether to go out and get drunk or not." When asked what morality means to her she states:

> When I think of moral I think of a defined right and a defined wrong, and there is no way of falling in between . . . morality tells me my values. *This had nothing to do with my values. It just had to do with life, my friendship with somebody* [emphasis added].
>
> *(What does morality mean to you?)* Morality means what's right and what's wrong. You have a set of moral things: you know, don't smoke, don't have sex before you get married, don't drink, don't drive fast. Those are values that I think society in general and your upbringing gives you and your parents reinforce. Morality in my mind is I have a certain set of beliefs—honesty, trust—and morality is whether I am going to stay with them. . . . It [this situation] was sort of like my feelings . . . and your feelings are connected with your morality. Your feelings sort of control what you think is right or wrong, depending on the situation. But in this way I don't think it was a moral decision. It was my feelings.

Ann struggles with how to integrate feelings—so central to her conflict with her friend—and morality. She distinguishes between inside—her feelings—and outside—a set of beliefs she has taken from society or her upbringing, and this distinction causes her confusion. "Morality," itself, is something distanced from herself and her feelings; it is something that tells her what to value, yet has nothing to do with "life, my friendship with somebody." She and the conflict she experiences with her friend are detached from the realm of morality as defined by the world around her, except perhaps for some vague notion she has that her feelings somehow impact what she values. Ann reiterates a list of "don'ts" that she acknowledges are both societal and parental but not apparently examined or personally owned. Morals are things that she takes on or discards. In contrast, Ann locates the problem with her friend around the issue of perspective. She realizes that both she and her friend had reason to act the way they did, and as a result it was selfish of her not to allow her friend room "to prove something to herself." Knowing what she, herself, needed and attending to what her friend knows and feels, she experiences a conflict that threatens their relationship. She feels a personal responsibility for the way she thinks about, feels, and acts with regard to her friend.

Kate's narrative exemplifies a third prevalent theme heard in these cases: There is a clear and readily available language with which to talk about an "impartial" morality (Blum 1987)—that is, a rights or justice-based morality (Gilligan 1982; Kohlberg 1984; Lyons 1983)—since it is a morality defined and transmitted by the culture. But these girls struggle and appear confused when they attempt to apply the terms of this morality to their situations of moral conflict. An impartial morality does not capture the complexity of their conflicts, yet they have no other language in which to speak if they wish their thoughts to be understood and legitimatized. A corollary to this theme is the tendency for these young women to de-emphasize, in some cases to devalue, their "particularized" (Blum 1987) knowledge of relationship—a knowledge derived from their observations, feelings, and personal experience. Early in her interview-narrative, as Kate struggles to clarify how she perceives the conflict, she says:

> It's difficult to know when you are being fair in any kind of judgment on a teacher. (*What do you mean by fair?*) It's hard to know from . . . the teacher in a class has a very good perspective on things and could be, you know, the teacher's method could be leaning toward certain things that I don't know. I hadn't talked to the teacher, that kind of thing. (*So fairness would be?*) I don't really mean fair or unfair. It was a situation where I didn't know if I was—I felt that someone should represent the other students by talking to the [administration]—but I felt personally, I felt badly that I would, that I was doing this, because I myself didn't really have any complaints, except that I felt that other students weren't satisfied and that there literally was a problem.

Kate discards fairness as the construct she would use to explain the situation as she perceives it. It is not a situation that can appeal to justice for the right resolution, but one that appeals to understanding and knowing as a way to avoid harm. Later in the interview she struggles with definitions of the words "responsibility," "respect," and "honor." She says, finally:

> These are issues that are very hard to talk about without using the words that are, that mean things other than I really intend them to mean. . . . I am trying hard not to use respect or right or wrong. But it is hard to describe something like this without it. *(The words that come up are honor and respect?)* Just because I can't think of anything else, but I don't even really use those. It is more of an instinctive feeling.

Again, these words—fairness, honesty, respect—do not explain what she means, do not feel true to her experience. Kate clearly struggles with a way to understand and talk about her experiences. The words that she might use are inadequate. As a result she appears frustrated and moves from attempts at explication to a sort of vacuous generalization—her experiences become "instinctive feelings." To hear only this attempt and not the rich description of her real-life conflict that precedes it would make Kate's reflection on her experiences seem vague or confused. Yet, listening to the care and thoughtful attention with which she reflects on her decision and the complexity of feeling she attributes to herself and others, it becomes more difficult to dismiss her as someone confused. On the contrary, it becomes more obvious why she cannot reduce an emotionally and intellectually complex problem to one general concept—that is, to simply an issue of fairness or honesty. To do so would not be accurate or represent the reality of the situation as she perceives it. It would, in a sense, remove her from a stance of observer and knower.

Kate's struggle to find a way to talk about her experiences reflects the complexity of her dilemma. It is a struggle that recurs in the other interviews. As a result, these adolescents may either express what their experiences *were not* in an attempt to clarify what they *were* or they may subtly de-emphasize or devalue them. Thus, Jean replies that it wasn't a question of morality: "It was *just* a question of what was best for her . . . doing what I positively knew was the best for [my friend]. . . ." And Kate relegates her perspective to "instinctive feelings." In a similar vein, recall Ann's statement of her real-life dilemma: "It had nothing to do with my values. It *just* had to do with life, my friendship with somebody . . . my feelings . . . I don't think it was a moral decision. It was my feelings." In addition, Faye, whose role as editor-in-chief of the yearbook put her in a position to consider the complicated practical and emotional difficulties of firing a classmate, said, "it was *just* me being able to say 'no'." In fact, saying "no" entailed a time-consuming and painful struggle to include the classmate's perspective and feelings, the feelings of co-workers who were affected, and her own perspective.

Jean, Kate, Faye, and Ann exemplify a relational complexity in their interview-narratives of conflict. Each acknowledges and attends to a variety of people and issues in their process of decision making; each explains a way of knowing that involves moving from their perspective to understanding another's, a process that displays not only an awareness and appreciation of the other's point of view, but also an ability to reflect critically on the self's thoughts, feelings, and actions. This complexity and capacity to take a critical perspective in the stories they tell seems absent from their definitions of morality as a priori standards or rules for behavior externally defined by parents or society. Also absent is a sense of a participating, autonomous, freely choosing self—they talk about morality as something imposed on them, as something they must learn, a code they should obey. In their real-life dilemmas, however, they struggle with the complexity of the situations, with what they know of those involved; they take on the risks of action, acknowledging what they do not or can not know.

When is a moral problem not a moral problem?

The discrepancy between the way in which these young women have discussed their real-life conflicts and their definitions of "morality" remains to be explored. Three possible interpretations emerge, depending on how the question—"Do you consider the situation you described to be a moral problem?"—may have been heard and understood in the dialogue between interviewer and interviewee. First, it may have been the case that the young women selected out and responded to the word "problem," that is, their response may indicate that they perceived the dilemmas they described to be "moral," but perhaps not moral "problems." Second, it is possible that they focused on the word "moral," that is, their response might indicate that their dilemmas were indeed problems, but they would not consider them to be "moral" problems. Third, they may have heard the following question: "Do you consider the situation you described to be a 'moral problem'?"—emphasizing "moral problem" as a single term. In this case, the response, No, it was not a 'moral problem,' may be interpreted as, Yes, the situation was moral; yes, the situation was a problem; but, the difficulty or the conflict I experienced was not with the 'moral problem,' but with some other aspect of the experience. The interpretive task, therefore, is to determine which of the three possible alternatives best explains the intended meaning of the responses given by each of these young women. This is an important task because understanding the responses of these female adolescents to this particular question tells much about how they understand and define morality—and how they perceive and experience the interface between their definitions and those of the wider culture.

In order to determine which of the three questions these young women heard, it is important to return to the interview texts—to the conversation between the interviewer and the interviewee. In other words, the response to this question cannot be isolated from the overall conversation or dialogue in which the question is embedded. A close examination of the text of the interviews reveals that the first possible interpretation, that the young women in this sample felt their real-life dilemmas were not "problems" for them, seems unlikely. Consider the struggle and psychological ambivalence they described while making or coming to terms with their decisions: Jean is uncertain even though she knows she must protect her friend. Kate's statement, "It was a hard decision for me whether or not to go," and Faye's, "I kept feeling torn between should I get someone new and say you're fired, or should I keep waiting," illustrate the problematic, or, conflictual nature of the real-life dilemmas they discuss. Consequently, it is relatively easy to refute this first possible interpretation.

The second and third interpretations, however, are not so easily dismissed. The second, that these young women perceived their real-life dilemmas as problems but not problems within the category of "moral" problems, seems more viable. Each girl distinguishes between, on the one hand, a morality of "right and wrong," "black and white," or, on the other, a morality in which she must sort out standards held by herself from those held by authority figures or institutions, such as school or church, and the conflicts in the real-life moral dilemmas she experienced and described. They use moral language to describe their real-life dilemmas—that is, prescriptive statements about what they ought to do in such a situation—yet, they do not rely on general rules of behavior or impartial standards of right and wrong. *If* morality is defined as standards for behavior or role obligations, then these young women seem accurate in their observations that the dilemmas they describe are not "moral" problems.

The stories these young women tell indicate that what matters most to them, what they care for and show concern for—in essence, then, what they value—has little to do with such definitions of morality. Recall Ann's assertion that "It had nothing to do with my values. It just had to do with my life, my friendship with somebody . . . my feelings. . . . I don't think it was a moral decision. It was my feelings." Ann distinguishes "values" from the feelings of conflict she experienced in her dilemma. For Ann, decisions about life, feelings, friendship do not fall under the same rubric as those "values that I think society in general and your upbringing give you and your parents reinforce." Yet, clearly, she cares for her friendships, her life, and attends to her feelings in her story of conflict. What sense can be made of this?

At least one answer to this discrepancy is to consider growing theoretical and empirical evidence for the idea that there are two different conceptions of morality or two ways in which one might come to know the moral world: one that relies on impartial rules or role obligations, another that focuses on particular attachments, relies on attention to the specific context of a dilemma and the special needs of all involved, often including the self (Blum 1987; Gilligan 1982, 1986, 1987; Lyons 1983). Gilligan and Attanucci (1988) describe dimensions of human relationships that provide different ways of organizing social and moral reality:

> The distinction between justice and care orientations pertains to the ways in which moral problems are conceived and reflects different dimensions of human relationships that give rise to moral concern. The justice perspective draws attention to problems of inequality and oppression and holds up an ideal of reciprocity and equal respect. The care perspective draws attention to problems of detachment and abandonment and holds up an ideal of attention and response to need. Two moral injunctions—not to treat others unfairly and not to turn away from someone in need—capture these different concerns.

The idea that a morality of rights and a morality of response represent different dimensions of relationship that move along different developmental paths suggests the possibility that the young women represented in this paper tell their stories of moral conflict in a care voice. Their dilemmas draw attention to detachment and abandonment, rather than to inequality and oppression. Jean cannot turn away from her thirteen-year-old friend who is contemplating suicide. Kate cannot abandon her classmates in their confusion. She says, "Someone had to go and talk and it was, you know, it was a question would it be selfish of me not to do it, because things were fine for me, but I knew there was a problem." In this case, the split between "morality" and feelings, or standards of behavior and care and concern for others, has to do with the simple fact that "morality" has a specific and rather narrow meaning in this culture. It is a word of power, carefully and specifically defined and legitimized by Western culture as having to do with concerns for justice and excluding the concerns for care and attention to others that pervade the stories told by these adolescent girls. In other words, the values and concerns expressed by these girls in their dilemmas are not moral problems as morality has been defined for them by those in authority in this society.

If, in fact, there are two moral voices, two frameworks within which two ways of speaking about the moral world can be discerned, the girls in this small sample choose to speak in a care voice. This choice may clarify why their stories of relationship reveal reflective, complex thinking, while their references to societal rules and roles remain either simplistic or opaque. Their capacity for reflection and perspective—and for autonomous action—is less obvious in their discussion of an impartial morality of rights, because their experience does not easily translate to this language. Only by acknowledging and attending to a morality of response is it possible to appreciate the capacity of these young women for autonomous choice and critical perspective. These girls struggle to find a solution that would integrate the needs of all involved in their complex real-life dilemmas. They are aware of the painful consequences someone might have to experience as a result of their choice. The failure to find one "right" solution sustains the experience of real moral dilemma that cannot be easily solved by reliance on a hierarchy of principles or standards (Gilligan 1982; see also Nussbaum 1986 for an elaboration of this point). What is remarkable is the ability of each of these young women to act while acknowledging the inevitable consequences: that is, that someone will experience some hurt regardless of what she chooses to do.

While the notion of two conceptions of morality, or two moral voices, sheds light on the above cases and provides a powerful theoretical rationale for the distinction between the descriptions of real-life dilemmas provided by these girls and a more traditional definition of morality, there is still a third possible interpretation—one that may, in fact, go hand-in-hand with the second. As stated above, perhaps these girls perceive their dilemmas both as problems and as moral; but the concern or the real difficulty they feel or experience is with neither. There is some evidence that for these young women there is yet another dimension to the difficulty they experience; one that has more to do with their feelings about others and themselves as moral actors than with the rubric under which they would place their actions. Consider, for example, Kate's assertion that "I felt I was doing the right thing, but I felt badly about it." What seems to make Kate feel bad is the realization that whatever she chooses to do, ultimately someone—either the teacher or the students—could be hurt. Recall that she is unsure about a number of things: "Maybe the students weren't advanced enough to handle the kind of classroom situation," she wonders. But also, maybe she doesn't know enough about the teacher's motives: "It's hard to know . . . the teacher in a class has a very good perspective on things and could be, the teacher's method could be leaning toward certain things that I don't know. . . ." Kate is troubled by the nature of her involvement and the feelings that emerge for her as she acts. She realizes there are things she may not know, or cannot know fully, and that to act under such circumstances feels bad. Her perception of her responsibility for knowing arises by virtue of the relationship she has with her classmates and with the teacher. She cares that they learn and understand but also that her teacher not be hurt unnecessarily. To act as she does is right. But the real problem for her has to do with what it means to make such a choice and to face a loss knowingly, to claim her perspective and to act on her best assessment of the situation, given what she knows she cannot know and the risk that entails. This interpretation of the implications of action and her felt responsibility to the others in her dilemma hinges on Kate's question, Would it be selfish of me not to do it?

Consider, in addition, Jean's case: For Jean, doing what she considers to be the right thing in the situation involves her in an action in which she feels uncomfortable because it causes her to betray her relationship with her friend; that is, to tell the counselor about her friend's plans, when she told her friend she would not. The "moral" choice is clear (". . . even if [she] gets mad at me and never wants to speak to me again, I'd rather she be alive and speak to me than dead and never have the chance . . ."), but the tension or pull she experiences ("between . . . doing what I knew positively was the best thing for [her]") surfaces as a result of her involvement and relationship with her friend. Paradoxically, by virtue of this interdependence, she perceives herself as a responsible knower and chooser and yet as someone who cannot fully know but who must act because she cares. Jean's way of knowing focuses her attention on potential consequences for those involved—to her friend, to the counselor, to herself—and puts her in a position of responsibility for the consequences; therefore, she must be accurate in her perceptions of the situation. Yet given what she knows of her friend and her situation, Jean is not sure what is the way best to care for her. She is uncertain, not of the moral thing to do, but of her perceptions, her construction of the situation. The problem is in failing the relationship and therefore in failing herself, her personal responsibility. Her choice is right, but she feels badly about the potential for loss, the result of betrayal or misunderstanding.

Faye also illustrates the difficulty of choosing, claiming her perspective in spite of what she does not know and who she may hurt. She struggles as she considers what she doesn't know about her classmate's situation: "And it was also a conflict that I wasn't really sure if I was being unreasonable in the things I was asking her to do. . . . And I was conflicted about it because I thought maybe I didn't make it clear to her the things that I need to do. . . . I couldn't just look at my situation, that this is the most important thing because I realized that there were other things going on. . . ." Faye knows she cannot fully know. Her task is to claim the power of her perspective, to trust that she has enough information to choose. Her difficulty has, in part, to do with her realization that to act raises questions about herself as a knower and accurate perceiver. To act in ways that one feels are good or right is to bring one's perspective into the world; it is to claim a public space, a "moral identity" (Blasi 1983). This is a task these young women find extremely difficult. Their response—No, the situation was not a 'moral problem'—may indicate the struggle they experience has more to do with claiming a moral stance, with acting in the face of potential loss or in the face of the risks of not knowing.

Blasi's (1984) notion that "a morality that actually works, not only in this or that action but also in one's life in general, must be rooted in some form of identity" (p. 136) is central to this way of understanding and interpreting these cases:

From this perspective, the central moral issue, also for psychologists, concerns one's responsibility for knowing and in using knowledge. The core of immorality is not wanting to know, blinding oneself, acting against one's knowledge. The ultimate sin, if one can use in this context an old-fashioned and unscientific term, is the sin against the light and the spirit. It should be said, incidentally, that the very idea of responsibility for knowledge is alien, not only to noncognitive theories but also to Piagetian cognitivism. From a different angle, responsibility to what one knows—about right and wrong, about others and oneself—is integrity. Integrity acquires, then, a more precise meaning: It is not logical consistency, nor consistency among personality traits, not the resolution of dissonance between cognition and action, when it is the need to reduce one's anxiety; it is, instead, a responsible actualization of what one knows to be right and true. (Blasi 1983, 206)

This responsibility "for knowing" and "using knowledge," a function of claiming a "moral identity," is what seems most problematic for these young women. Jean, for example, knows a great deal—about her suicidal friend, about their relationship—yet, she acknowledges there are things about her friend she does not know. Does she know enough to make the best choice? Will her choice be "a responsible actualization of what [she] knows to be right and true;" will it have integrity?

Blasi's (1984) notion of responsibility for knowledge and for the self as moral actor acknowledges the centrality of perspective as key to understanding the interview-narratives of these girls. Referring to Erikson's (1968) notion of fidelity as "the human virtue that is intimately associated with the development of identity" (P. 130), Blasi ties moral identity to moral action. Thus moral action becomes a question of self-consistency, of personal integrity. Blasi states:

From my perspective, moral identity is directly related to moral action, providing one of its truly moral motives. As already mentioned, one aspect of fidelity, the basic virtue that Erikson considers as inherently tied to the development of identity, consists of a concern with being authentic and true to one's self in action. In my self mode [Blasi 1980, 1983], the connection between moral identity and action is expressed through the concepts of responsibility (in the strict obligation to act according to one's judgment) and integrity. These two concepts are closely related and derive their meaning from a view of moral action as an extension of the essential self into the domain of the possible, of what is not but needs to be, if the agent has to remain true to himself or herself. Responsibility, in this sense, stresses the self as the source of "moral compulsion." Integrity, instead, emphasizes the idea of moral self-consistency, of intactness and wholeness—all essential connotations of the self as a psychological organization. (1984, 132)

Jean knows what she knows through communication, through dialogue in relationship, and struggles to use that knowledge responsibly. Her uncertainty, although it does not immobilize her, creates a problem. Given that theories of female development highlight the importance of sustaining relationship for the development of the self, Blasi's concept of responsibility provides a lens through which the struggle of these female adolescents can be seen to have integrity. The moral reasoning, moral feelings, and moral action in which these young women engage are given coherence by a moral identity achieved through and defined by relationship. In Blasi's sense, their acts have integrity—in their "moral-consistency," their "intactness and wholeness."

The fact that the young women chosen for analysis in this paper did *not* consider their real-life dilemmas to be moral problems has placed the definition of "morality" in tension throughout this paper. The analysis of these cases restates the question of discrepancy as a question of perspective—not which perspective is the better or more correct in its description of morality, but how one is to understand each in its own terms.

These cases illustrate that the struggle to engage actively in a decision that affects another, to care and to attend to another, is a worthy one for these girls. Standards and role obligations are terms that do not accurately describe their experiences, yet they *are* often terms that describe parental, religious, and societal notions of morality. These cases, therefore, illustrate how a culture and a psychology that recognize and value a narrow vision of morality may exclude the moral significance of the experiences of these young women.

Their narratives, however, also illustrate a more complicated point. If, as Blasi contends, the connection between moral identity and action is expressed through responsibility to one's judgment and the self's integrity, for these young women the discrepancy between their relational understanding of morality and the view of morality legitimized in this culture suggests the integrity of the self may be at risk. In other words, if what is morally imperative for them, or what defines and sustains their "moral identity," is not valued or considered truly "moral" by the culture at large, one would expect a loss of trust in the self's perspective and judgment and the self's moral integrity; a loss revealed in these interview as the difficulty these young women have in calling a moral problem a "moral problem."

Thus evidence of insecurity and self-doubt in describing their relational dilemmas as well as difficulty framing their real-life conflicts in a traditional moral language—one that appears not to fit their experience—can, in fact, be heard in these cases. The loss may be of a sense of self as a moral, caring self and of trust in a logic of interdependence and responsiveness derived from personal experience. These cases suggest that evidence of this loss may be found in females during adolescence, a time when, as Gilligan (1987) argues, young women come face to face with cultural traditions and social conventions that may not legitimize their understanding of themselves or their perspectives on the world.

Sources

Belenky, M., B. Clinchy, N. Goldberger, and J. Tarule. 1986. *Women's Ways of Knowing: The Development of Self, Voice, and Mind.* New York: Basic Books.

Blasi, A. 1980. Bridging moral cognition and moral action: A critical review of the literature. *Psychological Bulletin* 88:1–45.

———. 1983. Moral cognition and moral action: A theoretical perspective. *Developmental Review* 3:178–210.

———. 1984. Moral identity: Its role in moral functioning. In *Morality, Moral Behavior, and Moral Development*, edited by W. Kurtines and J. Gewirtz. New York: John Wiley.

Blum, L. 1987. Particularity and responsiveness. In *The Emergence of Morality in Young Children*, edited by J. Kagan and S. Lamb. Chicago: University of Chicago Press.

Chodorow, N. 1978. *The Reproduction of Mothering: Psychoanalysis and the Sociology of Mothering.* Berkeley: University of California Press.

Colby, A., and L. Kohlberg 1987. *The Measurement of Moral Judgment.* New York: Cambridge University Press.

Douvan, E., and J. Adelson. 1966. *The Adolescent Experience.* New York: John Wiley.

Erikson, E. 1968. *Identity: Youth and Crisis.* New York: W. W. Norton.

Gilligan, C. 1982. *In a Different Voice.* Cambridge: Harvard University Press.

—. 1986. "Exit-Voice Dilemmas in Adolescent Development." In *Development, Democracy, and the Art of Trespassing: Essays in Honor of Albert O. Hirschman*, edited by A. Foxley, M. McPherson, and G. O'Donnell. Notre Dame, Ind.: University of Notre Dame Press.

—. 1987. "Adolescent development reconsidered." In *New Directions for Child Development, No. 37: Adolescent Social Behavior and Health*, edited by C. Irwin. San Francisco: Jossey-Bass.

—. 1987. "Remapping the Moral Domain: New Images of the Self in Relationship." In *Reconstructing Individualism: Autonomy, Individuality, and the Self in Western Thought*, edited by T. C. Heller, M. Sosna, and D. Wellber. Stanford, Calif.: Stanford University Press.

Gilligan, C., and J. Attanucci. July 1988. Two moral orientations: Implications for developmental theory and assessment. *Merrill-Palmer Quarterly* 34:223–44.

Johnston, K. 1985. Two moral orientations—Two problem-solving strategies: Adolescents' Solutions to Dilemmas in Fables. Ph.D. diss., Harvard University.

Josselson, R. 1987. *Finding Herself: Pathways to Identity Development in Women.* San Francisco: Jossey-Bass.

Kohlberg, L. 1984. *Essays in Moral Development.* Vol. 2 of *The Psychology of Moral Development.* San Francisco: Harper and Row.

Lyons, N. 1983. Two perspectives: On self, relationship, and morality. *Harvard Educational Review* 49(1).

Miller, J. 1976. *Toward a New Psychology of Women.* Boston: Beacon Press.

Nussbaum, M. 1986. *The Fragility of Goodness.* Cambridge: Cambridge University Press.

Piaget, J. 1965 (Orig. 1932). *The Moral Judgment of the Child.* New York: The Free Press.

Save the World, Save Myself
Responses to Problematic Attachment

JUDITH P. SALZMAN

Mothers are supposed to love you no matter what you do.
—Emma Willard Student

I would like to discontinue the tradition of mothers down through the ages hating their daughters.   *—Emma Willard Student*

Character is formed by mothers.   *—Emma Hart Willard, 1814*

A new context for understanding problematic attachment in adolescence

Woven through Emma Willard girls' observations on relationships are statements that verify an important but long-lost truism of folk wisdom: Mothers' power to assist or impede children's development does not end with the onset of puberty. In their narratives of family experience, young women explain how the transformation of attachment[1] and the new awareness of self that emerges from this process are an essential part of their psychological experience, and one not easily provided outside the family context. In this chapter, one learns from students who face a special challenge in maintaining maternal attachment why they make this effort, on their own behalf as well as for the sake of preserving relationships. Because they have compelling reasons to think about the meaning and quality of attachment to mothers, they hold these relationships up to strong light and examine them perhaps more carefully than most adolescents would be inclined to do. For this reason, the comments of the nine girls discussed here provide particularly rich, detailed examples of a phenomenon only recently acknowledged in the research literature: The persistence of family attachments throughout adolescence.

In contrast to the majority of Emma Willard students, there emerged over the course of the investigation a small group of nine girls, whose testimony revealed patterns of ongoing problematic attachment, of the sort that led one of them to comment ruefully on the tradition of daughter hating, which she hoped to abolish in her own generation. For Laura, Rebecca, Megan, Kate, Alison, Jenny, Nell, Susan, and Claire (real names have been changed for this presentation), the customary provisions of caregiving (that is, maternal nurturance, dependability, protection, understanding) have not been sustained. In this group of nine, primary attachments were consistently seen as sources of pain and uncertainty— thus, "problematic"—rather than as the "secure base" and haven of refuge described by their classmates. A close reading of their interviews suggests that these girls, who have ample reason to give up on attachment, are instead as passionately concerned with it as the rest of the sample and often determined to preserve or improve it—without parental help, if necessary.

While established theoretical perspectives on adolescence have minimized the contribution of attachment to adolescent development, the nine stories of problematic attachment considered here suggest the alternative possibility that connection to parents may remain critical to the adolescent's emergent sense of self. Indeed, as illustrated by these narratives, even in difficult circumstances, young women may struggle to maintain connection in order to know themselves and to be known by their parents.

John Bowlby, a developmental theorist who has argued persuasively on behalf of primary (familial) attachment as an ongoing developmental requirement, has articulated a position that seems to fit the evidence provided by Emma Willard students. Bowlby's stated view is that "intimate attachments to other human beings are the hub around which a person's life revolves, not only when he is an infant or toddler, but throughout his adolescence and his years of maturity as well, and on into old age" (Bowlby 1969, 442). His theoretical work seeks to clarify the importance of primary attachment, which so perplexed Sigmund Freud, who admitted in an essay he wrote in 1931 that "everything in this sphere of this first attachment to the mother seemed to me so difficult to grasp in analysis" (Freud 1931, 226). In theory, as in clinical practice, Freud found it hard to explain how attachment as a primary, social event (as opposed to a convenient means to reduce drives, such as hunger or sexual desire) operates in human development. Not surprisingly, then, orthodox assumptions regarding adolescent development have not fully recognized the continuing importance of family attachments; they highlight instead the adolescent's urgent needs to cope with sexual and aggressive feelings, which are seen to threaten family connections.

Bowlby's view opposes Freud in its assumption that attachment is a basic instinct even more urgent than the needs for nourishment or sexual expression.[2] With respect to adolescence in particular, he criticizes the psychoanalytic view of "adolescent development as requiring a radical withdrawal of attachment to parents," which derives from theories of dependency and libido. He claims that this analytical position "unwittingly tends to encourage the idea that an adolescent developing compulsive self-reliance is developing satisfactorily. For example, tears are identified as regressive; and it is believed that during normal development an adolescent 'is forced to give up a major love object' and that 'developmental exigencies require a radical decathexis of the parents' "[3] (Bowlby 1980, 374).

In Bowlby's volume entitled *Loss* (1980), the author makes some helpful distinctions between secure and disturbed, or, "anxious" attachments and describes the various ways in which an "anxiously attached" child may be forced to edit out of awareness certain feelings or perceptions about the attachment in order to preserve the relationship and his own safety within it. Psychopathology in this view (particularly childhood depression) is seen to result from stresses within attachment that lead to the child's defensive exclusion of certain aspects of self (especially angry or needy feelings) from the attachment bond.[4]

Bowlby notes that the manifestations of anxious attachment become especially visible when an anxiously attached child suffers a major separation or loss. In such cases, the fault lines of prior anxious attachment are exposed and may reveal one of the following: *(a)* anxious, ambivalent dependence, characterized by a combination of longing, fear, and anger. Such children may be clingy, fearful, but they are also full of rage at caregivers who try to comfort them and appear inconsolable; *(b)* compulsive caregiving characterized by the child's insistence on taking care of a fragile, bereaved parent and denying his or her own wishes for care; *(c)* false self-sufficiency, characterized by avoidance of caregivers and insistence on an exaggerated independent stance.

Bowlby is careful to point out in these descriptions (from clinical case material) that the children's distress is not simply the result of loss, not an expression of normal mourning, but a pathological variant of mourning determined by the quality of prior and/or ongoing attachments. In making this distinction, he suggests, by extension, a view of "secure versus anxious" adolescent attachment, in which the inevitable "loss" of old perceptions of parents may be successfully mourned by adolescents with secure prior attachments and followed by the establishment of attachment on new terms. Anxiously attached adolescents, by contrast, would reveal the fault lines of disordered attachment in this transition and be unable to move easily from the older terms of attachment to newer, more adequate ones.

Problematic attachment: the study and its purpose

Bowlby has given us a theoretical framework and some predictions concerning the activity of attachment in adolescence. The Emma Willard students cited here contribute rich and detailed examples of this activity, specifically as it demonstrates the ways in which girls respond to the stress of problematic or "anxious" attachment, without resorting to disengagement. In their accounts of family experience, these nine students shared the assumption that connection to mothers would survive the challenge of adolescence, and their interviews yielded numerous examples of the ongoing function of primary attachment.

In particular, these girls noted that while they no longer needed their parents to help with the practical end of caregiving, they did count on them to "be there" in the spiritual sense, to offer solace and support and to remain as a "secure base," from which girls could venture out into the world or return in difficult times. In addition, they cited two critical functions of attachment that appear to assume special importance at adolescence: the recognition of the adolescent as a "new voice" within the family; and the subsequent recalibration of family decision-making processes based on this recognition. These changes, in line with those documented by Gilligan and others, seem to mark the difference between attachments in which the developing self may thrive and those in which it may be constrained.

The observations of girls in this subsample yield numerous insights into cases of brittle or "stuck" attachment at adolescence, where the possibilities for recognition of a newly differentiated adolescent self within attachment have been blocked. Girls who face such a dilemma may generate a variety of coping styles, of which three are prominent here: (1) *role reversal*, which corresponds in some respects to Bowlby's description of "compulsive caregiving" in order to preserve an anxious, ambivalent attachment; (2) *hostile avoidance*, which has points in common with Ainsworth's "avoidant" classification for infants and with Bowlby's notion of false self-sufficiency at adolescence; and (3) *transformation*, a category for which there is no equivalent in the literature on infants, probably because it only becomes a true developmental option at adolescence.

This third coping style, evolved by one of the nine girls (Rebecca) out of equal parts desperation and courage, is particularly informative, because it suggests a way for adolescents to find a means of staying attached without resorting to the compromises of self demanded by the other two approaches. In doing so, it offers an alternative to Anna Freud's rather pessimistic view of the likely outcome in cases of problematic attachment: that "where a parent is unable to support or welcome developmental progress, the child's dilemma is most easily solved through accommodation to the parents' needs" (A. Freud quoted in Levinson 1984, 388). Rebecca's narrative challenges Freud's prediction with its account of finding an extrafamilial "secure base" in order to return to attachment on improved terms. By first renouncing and then returning to a relationship with her mother, Rebecca is able to address an impasse in family attachments without negating herself or permanently disengaging herself from her mother.

Despite the observed differences in coping styles and their relative merits for ensuring developmental progress, one common truth unites all nine girls in this subsample: none of their experiences may be assimilated to a developmental theory of "detachment" from family. Rather, their testimony supports the following claims of an attachment perspective:

• Attachment remains operative in adolescence, even when it is flawed or painful. Where attachment is a source of anxiety and pain, girls' responses do not reveal a pattern of nonattachment (as suggested by Weiss, 1982, for instance), but rather two types of *anxious* attachment predicted by Bowlby, and a third variant not envisioned by the theoretical model. The persistence of attachment may be seen even in three cases where girls' mothers have literally abandoned them.

• Attachment persists as the powerful "organizing construct" in developmental experience cited by researchers on early development. Its effects can be seen in the adolescent's constructions of self and morality and in interpersonal experience outside the family as well.

• Where attachment has proven unsatisfying as a source of nurturance, girls may resort to precocious sexual involvements in a bid for attachment rather than for actual sexual gratification. This reliance on sexual behaviors to satisfy longings for attachment conforms to Bowlby's stated view that one must discriminate between the goals of the sexual and attachment systems. Or, as proposed earlier in this paper, where the attachment system falters, the sexual system may come into play in substitute fashion. In such cases, the goal is not so much sexual gratification as it is the establishment of attachment.[5]

Common experiences within problematic attachment

After selecting these nine girls for the problematic attachment subsample, it became apparent that these students shared more than the mere fact of a stressful connection to their mothers. Three additional family experiences formed a cluster around the problematic attachment itself and contributed to an overall common perspective on attachment. This common perspective, as will be seen later in the chapter, may be correlated in a complex and interesting way with aspects of the girls' lives *outside* the family environment as well as within it.[6]

High-conflict divorce

When the subsample of problematic attachment students was drawn from the Emma Willard interviews, it appeared that a large majority (seven out of nine) of these girls had witnessed a high-conflict separation and divorce between their parents. (In an eighth case, the girl's mother was widowed.) A number of the seven reported that their mothers would "come crying" to them with details of marital difficulties. Daughters would then be sworn to secrecy, so that any shared information could not be communicated to their fathers. The net effect was often to deprive the girl of any real relationship to her father. In only one of the nine cases, in fact, did a girl cite a countervailing close attachment to her father that might offset the stress of a problematic relationship to their mothers. More commonly, girls reported experiences similar to that described by Kate, a junior at Emma Willard:

> And with my parents breaking up, that didn't really have a large impact on me. . . . Really, the only way it affected me was it affected my mother so much, and therefore, she brought her problems onto me and really worked on making me unhappy. And that was a reason, I guess, why I left home, and I just talked to her yesterday, and I said, 'Please don't tell me these awful things that my father does, you don't want me to hate him, and I don't want to hate him.' And she said, 'Well, I don't really care.' She is at a point where she hates him, and she wants me to hate him, too.

A second girl, Laura, said she worried about having to be in the presence of both her parents at graduation, because she feared the tug of war that might ensue:

> If they start nagging, they will start nagging through me. My mother will say something, and my father will have a rebuttal, but at *me*. They won't be fighting at each other. It will be yelling through me.

Girls in this group have learned to avoid situations in which they might become a lightning rod for parental conflicts that have little or nothing to do with them. Staying out of the way seemed a means to survival for Laura, who described family life as a war zone from which she often wanted to flee:

> With my parents' battle, they are not killing each other, but they are killing me, because they are making me go through this little thing of theirs. Spats in the middle of the dining room where she dumps a glass of water in his lap and he throws the butter, and I don't want to be there.

These tensions left girls in a precarious situation: facing a difficult relationship to their mothers, yet with scarcely any relationship at all to their fathers. It wasn't simply the fact of divorce that they shared; it was a particular kind of divorce experience, which left daughters in a highly vulnerable position vis-à-vis their parents.

Connection as pain

Not surprisingly, then, all nine girls in the subsample held in common the conviction that intimate connection to other people is often a source of pain. They had observed that one courts disillusionment in wishing for permanence or safety in relationships. Laura, whose mother left when she was very young, expresses her wariness in this way: "I couldn't deal with having another person taken away from me."

Another student, Alison, whose mother has also left the family, admitted that she was frightened by other people's gestures of care:

> As soon as I saw people caring for me, I found myself screaming at them, because it hurt. If I gave my love, I got hurt in every case I can remember.

In the course of dealing with her family, this student discovered that it sometimes felt safer to be isolated by her own sadness than to let herself be lured into involvement with others: "When I started being happy, it was like I missed being sad, like the sadness was a good thing sometimes." Sadness surrounded her, like "a wall that I could take in when I wanted it."

Commenting on the fragmented quality of her family experience, Alison says, "It always started separating and got dispersed and complicated . . . and so I just sort of dealt with it because I had never really learned to love these people [her family] and not to feel hurt."

Inability to resolve conflicts

Clearly, one of the most dangerous feelings to permit oneself in fragile relationships such as these is anger. Without exception, all girls in the subsample experience the open expression of anger as either risky or futile, with the result that they have not learned any satisfactory means of resolving conflict within attachments. Instead, they have become experts at one or both of two alternative strategies: either denying the existence of conflict or walking away from it. Many of the girls report "leaving the room," "walking away," "forgetting about it" as customary responses to family arguments. Others have disciplined themselves to replace anger with feelings of love, as if to relieve themselves of the unsettling effects of disagreement.

Overall, their prevailing attitude is one of resignation. Susan, who entered the study as a sophomore, observes that "We don't ever get the point across" in arguments, so the effort involved seems useless. Alison echoes this belief: "There is always conflict, and I don't know how to deal with it," while Jenny concludes that "we have to leave in order to stop . . . change the subject . . . push it aside." "I generally ignore them," is the response of Nell, yet another student, to her own family battles. The consensus in the group is that one has little to learn within the family regarding the resolution of conflicts, and that they only serve to disrupt attachments.

Girls' inability to use family attachments as a context for learning about conflict resolution emerges as one of the most striking characteristics shared by the group. Its effect, essentially, is to deny girls an opportunity to explore various means to ease the tension between self-expression and honoring others, which constitutes an important developmental task at adolescence. Instead, these girls face an endless series of either/or situations, in which they may attempt to assert their own wishes at the risk of being made to feel, in their own words, "bad" or "guilty"; or, alternatively, to convince themselves that mothers' refusal to acknowledge their daughters' perspective in the conflict is appropriate ("I have to realize my place, that I'm a child," as Kate put it); or further, to assume that because they love their mothers, anger *itself* is not appropriate and must be denied.

Variations in problematic attachment: three subgroups

Up to this point, the discussion has focused on experiences shared by a majority or by all nine students in this subsample. To recapitulate, the basis of this shared experience may be summarized as follows: involvement in high-conflict divorce; a view of intimate connection to others as painful; inability to learn about conflict resolution within attachment experience.

One might expect, given these similarities, that all nine girls would describe their experiences of problematic attachment in a single common language, or that their responses to the experience could be uniformly categorized. If one examines patterns of response suggested by the girls' interviews, however, the larger group of nine separates into three distinctive subgroups. Each of the three has its own way of characterizing a problematic attachment to Mother, and each has its own ways of coping with that experience. A subgroup of five girls was characterized by the tendency toward mother-daughter *role reversal*. A smaller subgroup of three were girls who appeared more openly *hostile* and somewhat intimidated by mothers perceived as powerful, ambitious, and competent. Girls in this subgroup usually preferred to steer clear of their mothers and certainly felt no obligation to function as their caregivers.

A third "subgroup," designated as *transformation*, consisted of a single student, Rebecca, whose relationship to her mother bore all the earmarks of a problematic attachment but who mentioned very few of the additional developmental themes associated with problematic attachment in her interviews. Because Rebecca's narrative yields important clues about how one may survive the challenge of problematic attachment, it must be considered separately from the rest.

Role-reversal subgroup

Looking first at the largest subgroup, those girls who described a particular sort of psychological reversal in relation to their mothers, one finds that the girls invariably perceive their mothers as unstable or needy:

Susan—"she's so nervous about everything"; Megan—"a little off her rocker"; Laura—"a mess"; Alison—"didn't know what she was doing [as a mother]"; Kate—"so confused that she really doesn't know what she thinks and what she feels . . . very unstable, irresponsible . . . in so many things she does I feel she does the wrong things." Three of the five mothers in this subgroup (as opposed to none in the other two) actually left their families and their caregiving responsibilities altogether. It is no wonder, then, that in this subgroup daughters sometimes had trouble distinguishing between the person needing care and the one offering it.

In some cases, this led to a real confusion of roles. Laura, for example, comments that she doesn't think of her mother and herself as mother and daughter. They share a life of socializing together, and the only stated difference between them is that "she's forty-five and I'm seventeen." Kate, another girl in this subgroup, sees herself as her mother's intellectual and spiritual mentor, ready to dispense advice, love, or help in time of trouble. According to Kate, "I feel it's more I'm the mother and she's the daughter, in a way." She believes her mother has "definite potential to grow" and asserts that she "could learn a hell of a lot from me." Susan observes that she is expected to be there for her mother, especially to offer sympathy over marital conflict, but finds her mother too wrapped up in her own troubles to reciprocate much of the time. Alison recalls that her mother looked up to her daughter from early on and trusted her daughter's judgment more than her own. In two of these families, in fact, mothers' reliance on their daughters was so great that they urged their daughters not to apply to boarding school in order to keep them near at hand.

In this subgroup, the mothers' inability to maintain a consistent caregiving position in relation to their daughters created serious kinds of confusion. It was these girls who often identified with their mothers' vulnerabilities, leaving them in some doubt about their own emerging identities. To the extent that they saw themselves as *like* their mothers (needy, struggling, dependent), they experienced difficulty in liking or accepting themselves. More than the girls in the other two subgroups, they were predisposed to express rather harsh judgments about themselves or to admit a lack of confidence in themselves.

In their own eyes, these girls rarely felt "good enough" to meet their own standards. "I don't like myself, the person I stand for," says Laura. Kate regrets that "I always feel like I haven't made enough progress and I am never really growing. . . . I still need to work on my personal growth."

Similarly, Alison believes that "I have not established enough strength within me," and she says that her apparent competence is merely a veneer. The girls seem to feel a distracting tension between the self they think they ought to be and a shadowy inner "me" known only to themselves. The outer self may have been required to appear sophisticated, wise, gracious, or brave, but the inner self has not caught up with these exalted expectations, nor has it been given time to.

Associated with this attitude of harsh self-judgment is extreme *reluctance* on the part of girls in this subgroup to feel justifiably angry at their mothers. (Megan illustrates this pattern.) While all nine girls described in this chapter experience undeniable difficulty in following anger through to the point of conflict resolution, in the *role-reversal* subgroup girls struggle even to admit that they feel angry, or that their longing for care may not have been fulfilled. Rather than confront conflict with their mothers, they turn quickly to a position of love, sympathy, or forgiveness. Laura trivializes conflict with her mother, for instance, by stating that their only problem is the difference in their ages and in the fact that they can't always go to bars together. Kate, Alison, and Megan assume a stance of sympathetic acceptance, claiming that anger would be inappropriate, given their mothers' circumstances. They talk of attachment in terms of "hurt" rather than anger, as if willing to absorb pain instead of inflicting it on mothers already in sufficient distress. Nevertheless, in the many statements of ambivalence about mothers made by this subgroup, one hears signs of a struggle to maintain the sympathetic perspective in the face of opposing emotional currents.

Hostile avoidance subgroup

For the three girls identified as members of the second subgroup within problematic attachments, the pattern of "stuck places" and concomitant coping responses looks rather different from that associated with the first subgroup. In the first place, the mothers of students in this subgroup are described in terms almost diametrically opposed to those offered by the first subgroup. These mothers emerge as "workaholic," powerful, ambitious, occasionally domineering, and invariably wrapped up in their professional lives. Girls perceive them as intimidating, sometimes intrusive, but admirable. The developmental risk posed by these attachments, then, is not a sacrifice of self for others, but the possibility that these girls will feel the "wind taken out of their sails" by mothers with whom they fear they cannot compete.

All attest to their mothers' strengths and their devotion to work:

JENNY: When I was little, she was always working. . . . She would spend the whole day till seven or eight at night, and so we had an aide who would take care of me and my brother so she could work all the time. . . . I didn't understand what was going on, why she had to stay locked up in a room with some stranger.

NELL: I would say that I don't know the real essence of her, because she does so many things. . . . There was something important she was doing. . . . It was sort of like she wasn't just someone who was my mother, she was a person who was doing things in life as well. . . . I would be friends with her if she weren't my mother.

CLAIRE: She is a manager for [a store] and since we were never around each other when I was younger . . . she went to work a week after I was born, and then I went through babysitters after that. And she would leave at 5:30 A.M. and come home at 7:00 P.M. and so we never saw much of each other. . . . I feel as though I know the *outside* of her, as in outside she is competent and she's independent and she's strong and she's stubborn and she stands up for what she believes in, but I feel as if I don't know her [inside] at all.

Through these girls' descriptions runs a thread of mixed admiration, resentment, and apprehension about how one may contend with such a strong, determined parent. Indeed, they have come to see themselves as unable to engage in effective communication with their mothers, because any dialogue quickly degenerates into a battle of wills. The quality of these exchanges implies a "power struggle":

NELL: If she does something I don't like and I do tell her, she will say, 'Don't yell at me, young lady!,' and she will really scream at me about that. 'Well, look, you told me . . . ,' and she says, like, 'Well, I don't like your tone of voice!'—Like, excuse ME! And then there is a whole fight about that, and it ends up that whatever it was isn't resolved.

Like Nell, Jenny reports a series of endless, unresolved conflicts with her mother: "We don't get along at all. We fight all the time."

And Claire makes a comparable observation:

We constantly fight about things, except they get to be real nasty wars, because she will refer to it a year later. She will refer to something I did, and at the present time I will be sarcastic and I will be vicious about it and I will be cynical and then mean, and then it will end [without resolution].

All three girls believe that their mothers "fight dirty," that they don't listen to their daughters; that they pull rank, change positions, or attempt to impose their own viewpoints unfairly. Nell protests that neither of her parents recognize who she really is:

If they knew that they didn't know everything about me and would admit that I am a separate person and they don't know everything about me, then that would be different. But they just sort of assume that they know all about me, even though they don't, and since they assume that they already know everything about me, they wouldn't try to understand any more.

In this subgroup, the girls respond to their frustration over being unheard, unrecognized, unfairly attacked by attempting to conceal parts of themselves from mothers or by avoiding painful confrontations. Because they fear that conflict will end in capitulation, they try to preserve their integrity by avoiding engagement whenever possible. If, however, conflict proves inevitable, girls report that they often fall victim to a particular sort of power play on their mothers' part, which results in an impossible situation for the girl. First, the mother will take a certain position and the daughter will comply. Then the mother will change her mind or criticize the girl for doing exactly what was initially requested. Here is Jenny's version of this maneuver:

My brother graduated from school. . . . My mother kept telling me I probably wouldn't want to go because it would be boring . . . I made plans to be with a friend of mine. . . . My mother said to me, 'Are you coming to R's graduation?' And I said I really wanted to stay with my friend. And my parents came back, and they said, 'Your brother was disappointed that you didn't come and your brother's girlfriend's parents were there and they were really disappointed.' . . . And that was like two years ago, and I still feel guilty about the decision I made.

Jenny has since decided that the best way to deal with her mother is *not* to deal with her; that is, to leave home and conflict behind her:

> I came here because I can't stand my parents and I couldn't deal with that. . . . We had gotten outside help and that didn't work, and nothing worked out and I just kind of gave up and came here.

Nell's strategy is to protect herself by not revealing too much to her mother: "When I was little I used to sort of tell her things, but now I sort of feel that I don't want her to know too much about me."

In personal crises, she says she would prefer to turn to friends for help: "I don't think I would turn to my mother, because of the power struggle. I just wouldn't put her in control about something."

Claire has practiced the art of avoidance (and concealment) with parents for as long as she can remember. She recalls how, as a small child, she would have a tantrum at the dinner table and hold her breath in order to be allowed to go off and eat dinner by herself. Now, she says, she makes contact with her mother only when they go shopping together, and that most topics of discussion other than clothes are too inflammatory to explore. Most of the time she prefers to keep things from her mother and to "just deal with things on my own."

Nell and Jenny are not always as successful as Claire in their efforts to keep their distance from their mothers. On the contrary, they both admit to longings to have their mothers take charge, make decisions, bail them out of difficulties, or take responsibilities for their daughters' own failures. As Jenny frankly states: "She likes me to make my own decisions, and I don't like to. If it messes up, I want someone else to blame." Nell makes a comparable observation regarding her ambivalent wish to have her mother take care of college application details for her. In these admissions, the girls reveal how hard it is for them to feel empowered, to face difficulties on their own. Indeed, they are so accustomed to yielding to their mothers that opportunities for independent action may have been few and far between.

Transformation subgroup

Rebecca's attachment narrative, as stated earlier, has to be considered in a class by itself. Reflecting on her relationship to her mother, this girl cites all the criteria for problematic attachment as defined in this discussion, including (for a limited time) her mother's literal absence from the home. She describes her mother as hurtful, unreliable, uncaring:

> She's not nice to me, and she doesn't like me. . . . I don't think she would really care if I was happy or not. . . . She has lied to me, she has accused me falsely of things, and she's hurt me a lot generally. And because she's so close to me, the fact that she *is* my mother, that's one of the most important relationships I have had in my life.

In her first interview, during her sophomore year, Rebecca articulates three of the major reasons for feeling in a "stuck place" in relation to her mother:

> From the earliest days you get your first impression of yourself from your parents. And I . . . never got a lot of positive reinforcement from them. And it's just been something that I had to struggle with through my life.
>   I didn't know my mother from myself. In a way, I didn't know who was who. . . . I think she's the only person who it has become impossible or nearly impossible to separate myself from.
>   She [mother] had her own opinion about what was the truth and what was reality and she gave me no opening, . . . and she is just denying my feelings as if they didn't exist and as if I had no right to feel them, you know, even though they were there.

What strikes the listener about Rebecca, however, is not simply the candor and clarity with which she identifies the characteristics of her "stuck" attachment, but the fact that she refuses to remain in this admittedly frustrating position vis-à-vis her mother. Even though her profile appears to meet all the criteria for problematic attachment, including maternal abandonment in a situation of great need, nevertheless in her three years as a participant in the Dodge Study at Emma Willard, this girl succeeds in finding her own voice, learns how to express anger to her own satisfaction, and avoids entering into emotionally compromising romantic involvements. Instead, over the course of this period, she utilizes all the extrafamilial opportunities at her disposal to move out of her painful position, without actually renouncing attachment in the end.

She links the beginning of this welcome shift within attachment to conversations with a school adviser, who appears to encourage Rebecca to heed her own voice and who plays the role of respectful adult listener. In this context, she begins to consider the possibility that "hey, this is her [my mother's] truth and she just doesn't want to listen to me. So that was very important and I just made that realization" (that her mother's "truth" need not obliterate her own).

Following this liberating moment, which seems to have been encouraged and supported by the counselor, Rebecca proceeds through a series of revelatory experiences through which she is able to differentiate her own from her mother's perspective and to attain some real comfort in her new awareness. As a junior, she makes the following observation:

> I've grown. I have kind of grown apart from my parents. Or, I don't think we have become less close. It's just now I am beginning to see more, you know, me *myself*, and not me and Mom and Dad.

And in a similar vein:

> In the past I really had no notion of myself, or just me and not me in relation to my friends or me in relation to my parents or anything. I see myself—I have a better notion of what I am and who I am and everything and I didn't before, because I was never . . . I never felt that I was really separate from my family or my friends. . . . I feel a lot less scared about myself, because when you associate yourself so much with others that you can't kind of separate yourself from a group, you feel there are times, you are all alone, and you have to think, Wow! I remember, this is really strange, but at moments kind of being stricken with fright. I would look in the mirror and say, This is me, X. These are my hands and I am all alone, and I'm not glued to any other person. So I feel a lot less intimidated by myself and being alone and not being with others.

Rebecca obviously enjoys having, at last, her own "perspective," but she also acknowledges the limits of independence (in the sense of needing no one else):

> I don't think anybody is really self-sufficient, no woman is an island. . . . I can't imagine going through a rough time, like if somebody I was close to died, without somebody there to talk to or somebody to be with me or hold my hand through it. But the inner

strength, the desire to overcome and go on would really have to come from me.

Rebecca believes that the critical turning point in her relationship to her mother (and to herself as well) came when she began to accept inevitable limitations in the mother-daughter bond. Of all the girls discussed in this chapter, only she is ultimately able to make what sounds like a balanced appraisal of this relationship. In answer to the question, You maintain a relationship? she responds, "Yeah, we maintain a relationship. Whether that relationship is primarily good or bad I don't know. I mean, I don't have any bad feelings about it any more." By senior year, she is able to reflect much more coolly on her mother than in the past:

> I see her as a middle-aged woman with her own life and her own problems, very separate from mine, and it is very fascinating for me to see her as a person, a real whole complete person who makes bad judgments and who yells when she is upset and who really doesn't function rationally all the time. So she is important to me. She doesn't really influence me any more, but she *is* important to me.

Rebecca observes that her mother (and not she, herself) still has a problem directing anger, but she has learned that her mother's anger is not meant to cancel out her love for her daughter; and further, that:

> Even when somebody lets you down, or even when you are really mad at them, you can still feel affection for them and you can say to yourself, I am real mad! But you can separate your feelings of anger and also know that you love that person at the same time.

With this statement, Rebecca expresses her understanding that she may feel angry at her mother without destroying their relationship or being destroyed by it. Along with this insight comes permission to recognize the whole range of similarities *and* differences between her mother and herself. She says:

> My mother and I are basically caring people and outgoing people and I see a lot of her in me. But it doesn't scare me. It used to terrify me, because I used to think, Oh God, I am going to end up like her!

Rebecca has devoted considerable energy and attention, with the help of at least one concerned adult, to ending up like *herself*, neither a carbon copy nor a reverse image of her mother. In the process, she has acknowledged her disappointment with the limits of attachment to her mother and has begun to mourn the loss of caregiving gestures that are simply not in her mother's repertoire. This profound recognition enables her, then, to reclaim those aspects of connection to her mother that are clearly worth preserving: a pleasurable identification with her mother's many admirable qualities and recognition of the fact that her mother, in her own fashion, really does love her.

Correlations between problematic attachment
and three domains of adolescent experience:
moral reasoning, leadership, and heterosexual relationships

The quality of familial attachment in this group of girls reveals both a set of common assumptions stemming from the fact of stressed attachment and three rather distinctive variations in the style of attachment. The same dual pattern holds true for aspects of the girls' thinking and experience outside the family context. In each of three domains—moral reasoning, leadership, and relationships with men—the students in this subsample stand apart, as a unit, from their classmates in rather striking ways. But it is also possible to observe differences in the meaning of these domains of experience that partly parallel the differences among role-reversal, hostile-avoidant, and transformation subgroups. For each girl, the particular organization of these experiences is unique. Yet there are sufficient themes in common to warrant a guess that the girls have learned certain lessons within attachment that influence the way they look at extrafamilial experience.

Tension in moral perspective

Girls with problematic family attachments differ from most of their classmates in this study in that they rather consistently reveal significant discontinuities between the place of self and the place of others in their moral perspectives. For this group, it was difficult to envision a morality that was inclusive of both self and others at the same time. The manifestations of this tension differed according to the particular style of problematic attachment. In the hostile-avoidant subgroup, one hears girls arguing from a strongly self-protective stance that tends to ignore the claims of others. Conversely, in the role-reversal subgroup, girls judge themselves harshly by certain rigid, idealistic moral standards but extend extreme compassion toward others. This latter position, and its inherent tensions, are often illustrated most powerfully in girls' expectations of goodness in themselves, as contrasted with an attitude of nonjudgmental acceptance or compassion toward their mothers. Megan, now in her senior year, describes this sort of dilemma as she has known it:

> At this point, [my mother] is sort of sick herself, I suppose . . . my mother's a little off her rocker, I suppose, and emotionally she's not very stable. She's a wonderful . . . I mean, I am not biased at all . . . She's wonderful, she's smart, she's creative, very much all these things. But I think she has trouble dealing with reality, and I think, I don't want to judge her. . . . Because I have felt hurt by her and she has hurt me doesn't mean that I hate my mother or she's so this or so that, because I know she has hurt me, and the way she has hurt me has been beyond her control. I believe because of her sickness and her problems dealing with reality and dealing with a lot of other things, she's hurt me because of that. But I don't hate her. I hate the fact that she hurts me, but I cannot say I hate her for it. That's always been one of my problems, being able to say these things about her, because I feel guilty because I do. I love her so much and I know that won't change. I don't want to, you know, it's just hard to say bad things about people you love, and . . . that statement—'I hate her'—that's really strong and it scares me. Every time I think something bad I feel guilty, because then I say, Oh God, but I love her so much!

In this subgroup, it appears that reluctance to express anger at mothers contributes to a general position of extreme moral relativism vis-à-vis others, an inability to include *oneself* in a morality of care, yet a significant moral investment in "taking care of the world." Taken together, these factors constitute a distinctive moral orientation, split between a set of abstract principles for oneself and gestures of care for others. More than any other developmental theme, it is this moral orientation that distinguishes the "role-reversal" subgroup from the other girls discussed in this chapter.

Here is how three of the girls explain their moral relativism regarding other persons and their contrasting code of moral expectations for themselves:

KATE: With the word 'unfair' you get into problems like, unfair to whom? And who is being unfair, and why is this happening? . . . You really have to know everything about the situation. It was unfair to drop the bomb on Hiroshima. But then, something good did come out of it, because we know what awful things [a nuclear bomb] can do . . .

In response to the question, What does morality mean to you? Kate replies:

What's good and bad and then your idea of what's right and wrong, and it is going to differ for each person, and my morals aren't necessarily *the* right morals and *the* universal morals. So that's why I can't really say what morals are [for other people].

For herself, however, Kate has drawn up a long list of stringent requirements for moral behavior, including abstinence from alcohol or sex and "always being careful not to hurt others." She describes herself as committed

to strive every day to better myself from the day before and every night to look upon that day—how I did, assess it—and then go on the next day and strive to attain those attributes and qualities which I would like to attain.

Alison appears equally at odds about whether or not one set of moral directives can apply equally to herself and to others. Of herself, she demands a great deal: to help the hungry, not to take from the earth what she cannot give back, to "stay on the path" of selflessness and service. Yet she worries that to apply such standards to others "would mean that everyone has to change their standard of living," which leaves her wondering if "I am being like the nasty missionary who goes to the [native] and saves him from Hell. How do I know that I am right, or how do I know that I am wrong? How do I know?"

Megan expresses a similar conflict between what she would expect of herself as a moral person and the way she judges others. Regarding a classmate's life-threatening dilemma and her own inability to respond definitively, Megan says:

I am controlling her life, . . . and I am making a judgment for her. And if she is incapable of making that judgment, that is yet another judgment—to say that she isn't capable. So what am I supposed to do? . . . I couldn't decide what was right [for her classmate].

To judge another person by one's own moral code is, according to Megan, "violating somebody's right to be their own person." Megan continues:

> You can't . . . I mean, to say and judge means that whatever you are saying is right and *you* know what's right. You know it's right for them and you know it's right in every situation. And you can't know if you are right. Maybe you are right. But then again, right in what way?

In another manifestation of tension between the girls' expectations for themselves and for others in a global sense—a "take care of the world" attitude—while at the same time neglecting to include *themselves* in the universe of those needing care, Laura reports that she has given gifts to her friends until she herself is penniless. She asserts that she would "never hurt anybody," yet acknowledges that she is very careless of her own health and safety. She feels that she has a "responsibility in this world to love everyone," but about herself she is not clear. Indeed, she perceives herself as "not having any caring about myself *whatsoever*, you know what I mean?"

Alison and Kate reveal the same contradiction in their deep concern for the world at large, as contrasted with a certain indifference to their own personal needs. Kate states her attitude about caring in the following way:

> I care about things, about nature, about people, about the development of things. About what happens, on any scale, to the country, to the world, to people, to a person, to their feelings. . . . And at one point, I was so sensitive to that, that I would just . . . because people were dying of hunger, I wouldn't [eat] for a week. I wouldn't eat because I would feel so guilty about that.

She goes on to acknowledge that her extreme altruism has, in the past, left her feeling depleted, robbed of her "self": "Before, if a friend of mine left who I loved very much, I would let her take half of me with her, so I was no longer a whole person." Similarly, she acknowledges feeling "responsible for the future of our planet . . . for my mother, for my father, for doing anything I can for him . . . for my older sister, to be a mother to her."

Yet in trying to be the glue that holds her family together, in expending constant effort on others' behalf, Kate feels burdened and weary:

> There are times I would not like to be responsible for . . . that I would just like to be responsible for myself. I think that's a big enough burden of its own, and sometimes I don't have enough energy to be responsible for all these people. . . . Times when I am down, when I have so many problems myself that I can't deal with, I don't *want* to be responsible for helping friends or loving my family. I just want to be drawn into myself.

Alison outlines a similar difficulty in her own experience. Like Kate, she expresses her conflict about self-nurture, even to the point of feeling guilty about feeding herself while others go hungry. Yet about the necessity for serving others, she is adamant. Her goal is to

> affect a large portion, as many people as possible, to help . . . I see myself in a big way saying big things. I see myself going to school for a long time and learning a lot. I want to write a book that is very, very solid and hard to say, No, you are wrong. So that I can give it to the president and say, Look, Mr. President, you are wrong and you are going to hurt all these people and you are going to hurt yourself. . . . I want to say something big. I want to change the world.

Within the hostile-avoidant subgroup, one sees a different profile of engagement with moral questions. As one might expect, given the emphasis placed on self-protection and resistance to capitulation in this group's attachment experience, their perspectives on morality differ from those in the role-reversal subgroup. Reviewing the interviews with these girls, one finds many frank references to looking out for oneself in moral conflicts. "I usually just think of myself . . . paying attention to your own opinions rather than worrying about what everyone else thinks and what everyone is telling you to do." Further, it is seen as positively *immoral* to engage in something that "makes your self-worth decline." The cluster of items identified as hallmarks of the role-reversal subgroup is conspicuously absent for this subgroup. Nowhere does one find the extreme *relativism* characteristic of the self/other tensions delineated by the first subgroup. Instead, the tension is reversed: honoring the *other's* needs becomes the challenge, when the other is perceived as in conflict with oneself.

Girls in both the role-reversal and the hostile-avoidant subgroups represent tensions between self and other in the resolution of moral conflict. This tension may account, in part, for another common finding: the dramatic predominance of "justice reasoning" in moral dilemmas presented by these nine girls. While care reasoning relies on a felt *connection* between the welfare of self and other, justice reasoning more commonly recognizes the mediation of the *separate* claims of self and other through principles of fairness. It may be, then, that girls living in a state of frequent tension between self and other (within the family) learn to consider moral issues rather differently from girls who rest assured that the family is responsive to everyone's needs, at least most of the time.

As with her description of attachment itself, Rebecca cannot easily be classified with either of the other two subgroups in her discussion of moral conflicts. Like the other girls in this sample, Rebecca shows an inclination toward "justice reasoning" in her discussion of moral conflict (in her case, a clear predominance across three years of interviews), but what intrigues the reader is the individual mixture of views that contributes to the overall orientation—a mixture as distinct from the other two subgroups as they are from one another. At first, Rebecca's moral reasoning has the self-protective ring of the second subgroup. Her reasoning signals some conflict about whether or not one may safely expect others to demonstrate care in relationships. Over the course of three years, however, she travels from a stance based on the assumption that involvement with others' battles can invariably "do nothing but get yourself into trouble," to one in which she feels capable of fully considering the other person's needs in a conflict. As a sophomore, she cheerfully asserted that her moral perspective rested on "the world according to me." By senior year, she has shifted sufficiently to claim that "my purpose is people," and that moral action can mean both "doing the right thing *and* not sacrificing relationships." This shift exactly parallels her transition from an inability to feel safe or whole in conflict with her mother to a position in which she can hear herself much better in the relationship, although not without reservations.

Assumption of leadership positions within the school community

Outside the family context, problematic attachment appears to have generated two distinctive coping responses in members of this subsample: a tendency to seek experience in leadership positions, and involvement in important relationships to older males. The connection between these two phenomena is not readily apparent, but as one listens to their narratives, one begins to understand how, in both categories of experience, the girls may seek a second chance to feel satisfactorily "attached" to another person or group of people.

Leadership opportunity, cited as a focus of Emma Willard life for five of the nine girls in the problematic-attachment subsample, proves distinctly more successful in gratifying the girls' wish to connect than does their experience with older males. While it does not promise the nurturance or protection of a true attachment, it does offer other critical developmental opportunities to girls in problematic family situations. In accepting leadership positions, girls have the chance to address a piece of development cited earlier as a critical omission in all cases of problematic attachment: *that of learning to confront and resolve conflicts.*

While none of the nine girls felt they were able to practice this skill at home, they clearly could engage in such negotiations as student leaders. They speak about learning to be responsible, to listen and to mediate, to balance the demands of various factions, with obvious pride and satisfaction. For example, Alison, who seems tentative and vulnerable in intimate relationships, nevertheless exercises admirable power and skill in organizing the entire student body in a campaign against poverty and in stating her own political position both forcefully and diplomatically. On behalf of others, she need not lose herself or back down from conflict, as she sometimes does when purely personal needs are at issue.

Similarly, Claire reflects that through her experience in a student leadership position, she is gaining insight into her habit of forgetting to represent herself in interpersonal conflicts, and she is learning that it is all right to speak up on her own behalf, to use her own "voice" in negotiation. She admits that "I am so used to being publicly responsible to other people, that I forget that when I am by myself and not with other people, I don't have to do that any more," and she returns again to the same issue:

I think I need to resolve a lot of conflicts with responsibility— feeling responsible for myself and paying a lot more attention to my relationships because I feel that if emotionally my relationships are really bothering me, that I can't really be productive in my work, and just secure in my relationships making sure that there aren't any lines of miscommunication.

Claire's role as a leader has, in a sense, provided a mirror in which she can examine for herself what happens to her in relationships, but free of the distortion or tension present in her attachments at home. While her difficulty in facing conflict is, by her own admission, far from resolved, nevertheless her work at school gives her the opportunity to recognize some profound connections between her public and private selves and to practice a transfer of learning from one context to the other.

Alison and Claire, as members of the role-reversal and hostile-avoidant subgroups, respectively, engage in their leadership roles with great satisfaction, but each does so in a way characteristic of her attachment subgroup. In the first subgroup, three out of five girls hold leadership positions, but for them, the leadership experience is focused on a certain set of characteristics as opposed to others. Kate, a member of the role-reversal subgroup, sums up this focus by distinguishing between two types of leadership roles girls seek:

I guess there would be two kinds of leaders. One who people *follow* [an authority figure], and that would be a leader. But I think a leader [can also be] someone who takes responsibility for other people and other things. . . . I am not the conventional leader. I think other people are better at that kind of administrative work, technical stuff. . . . But [I am] a leader in another sense.

Like Alison, Kate emphasizes responsibility to others and certain spiritual qualities, rather than administrative competence or power, as criteria for leadership. In this respect, her conception of leadership fits with both her personal history and her moral perspective.

In contrast, Claire, as a member of the hostile-avoidant subgroup, emphasizes self-worth and executive qualities in her perspective on leadership. Commenting on her experience as a student leader, she emphasizes the enhancement of her own self-esteem, as well as the quality of her work, in a leadership position:

Because I know I am competent and I know I can get a job done if I am just given the chance. And I am glad other people are willing to give me a chance to get something done and to voice my opinion and to be active in the community—as myself and also as someone representing a group of people.

She goes on to describe how her own consciousness is being raised and changed by her work and how she finds the experience of leadership self-affirming. In this respect, she resembles the first kind of leader described by Kate—the type who stresses competence—rather than the second type who, like Kate herself, sees leadership primarily as an opportunity to answer the needs of others.

As in her moral perspective, Rebecca is also distinctive in her leadership experience, which by her own admission, has given her a real "voice" at Emma Willard. Over the course of three years she has assumed the role of "homemaker figure" to other girls in her hall and has learned concurrently that one can maintain relationships in a leadership role without sacrificing one's personal integrity. She has learned how not to feel helpless, how to express concern for others without compromising her personal integrity. In her own words:

I don't want to feel small and alone, and the only way I found I can stop being depressed at this school is to try to go out and change the things that are depressing me, because usually they arise from the fact that somebody is trying to take control of my life.

In a sense, Rebecca has "saved herself" and found her own voice at Emma Willard by learning to be connected to others, without *capitulating* to others. She claims that "I have discovered that you can do the right thing and not sacrifice a relationship" in practicing conflict resolution as a school leader. Less elegantly, she says she has learned not to opt "for what made other people happy and what made me feel like a real schmuck!" Transferring this valuable lesson to the realm of intimate relationships, Rebecca observes that you can feel really mad at someone you love but "separate your feelings of anger and also know that you love that person at the same time." In other words, she understands that conflict can be expressed without annihilating love, and that a durable relationship can permit differences of perspective. One doubts whether Rebecca could have gained this hard-won understanding without benefit of her intensive leadership experience at Emma Willard, and with only the lessons of turbulent family attachments as her point of reference.

Turning to an older male

A third way in which primary attachment experience seems to have affected most of these girls is their tendency to seek nurturance from an older boy or man—sometimes as much as fifteen or twenty years their senior. Unlike leadership experience, however, such involvements seem destined to repeat rather than to correct some of the difficulties of problematic attachment to parents. Almost all the girls (eight out of nine in the subsample) cited this type of relationship as having great meaning for them. In these relationships, girls appear to seek the comfort and protection missing in the attachment bond to their mothers and sometimes trade sex in return for the promise of attachment. (It should be noted that this type of relationship was not characteristic of a majority of girls who participated in the Dodge Study at Emma Willard, who more often reported on friendships or romances with boys closer to their own age.)

Unfortunately, girls discover that such a promise is rarely fulfilled. Instead, they find that the man wants the relationship "only on his own terms," that they are made to feel "inferior" vis-à-vis the other person, and that they are likely to wind up experiencing a loss of self in some respects similar to what they may have suffered with their mothers. Girls repeatedly observed that they did not feel truly known or recognized in these relationships. "He didn't know who I was. . . . He really hurt me" was the way one of the girls summed up her experiences. Yet again, as in relationship to mothers, the girls were invariably willing to absorb the pain or cost of these attachments into themselves and to rationalize their actions, sometimes to an astonishing degree. The narratives of two girls (Alison and Claire) illustrate this willingness in dramatic fashion.

Alison, whose mother left her, was essentially "adopted" by her boyfriend at age fifteen. She admits that he has been mean, obnoxious, and hurtful to her, but she cannot end the relationship because her longing for nurturance is so great that she is willing to accept the terms of "love" set by J., her boyfriend. Alison is aware of her vulnerability in relation to J.:

> I don't know. I guess he is strong and I need to hold onto something strong because there was nothing else. And I used to hold on and I don't know, I just overwhelmingly love him for no reason at all, I guess. I think about it all the time and I think it is really ridiculous, but I can't . . . I don't know what to do about it.

That Alison's hunger for attachment goes unappeased in this relationship is vividly illustrated by a dream she reports:

> I had gone to see him . . . I was sitting there and he came and I saw him and he came closer to me, and then he said, 'Hello, how are you? I miss you.' And then, 'But I have to go.' And he walked away. And so I followed him, and I kept running after him, and he kept looking back and then he would turn the corner and hide . . . and then he disappeared because he didn't want to get too close. A friend of his came up and we started playing war and we were fighting in the dark, and all the people around were killing each other . . . and J. wouldn't come, and I kept screaming for him to come back and help me and *he was in the wrong world* and he couldn't do anything else.

At least in her dream, Alison knows what her waking self cannot admit: that her relationship to J. provides none of the criteria of secure attachment—neither accessibility, communication, dependence, nor nurturance—in sufficient amounts. But as she herself has pointed out to the interviewer, "There was nothing else."

Claire's narrative, though happier and more hopeful than Alison's, has many points in common with hers. She, too, has turned to an older man at a particularly vulnerable time in her life. Her father is gone, and her mother is emotionally, if not physically, inaccessible to her. Over an extended period, Claire responds to the man's invitation to seek him out, should she ever need someone. But, as she observes, she has ended up doing the lion's share of giving and caring in the relationship and has asked for virtually nothing for herself in return. The interpersonal balance in this relationship is epitomized by Claire's explanation of her recent decision to have sex with her friend:

> I am giving something to the relationship. I am making him feel secure about the fact that I will be there, even if he doesn't need me. . . . It just didn't bother me, the fact that maybe he didn't care.

When asked whether or not she had considered her own pleasure or interest in deciding to have sex, Claire responded that she had never given any thought to her own desire for sex in considering what to do.

The central theme emerging in Claire's description, as in Alison's, is acceptance of a relationship on the other person's terms. Nevertheless, as Alison's dream signaled to her that, at least unconsciously, she admitted inconsistencies between what she longed for and what she actually received in her attachment to J., so Claire's narrative reveals powerful tension between what she wants to believe about her liaison and what the facts belie. She gets tangled in contradictions about trust versus suspicion, giving versus taking, dependence versus independence. After declaring that she has entrusted her "emotional being" to her friend, she then wonders whether or not he might, in fact, be taking advantage of her. At one point, she asserts that he cares for her, and at another acknowledges that "maybe he didn't care." Like Alison, she appears to rationalize many inconsistencies in the relationship out of her need to preserve it. She forgives the fact of her recognized inequality on the ground that "I'm a lot younger," "more like a child." In response to the interviewer's questions, So that makes you feel obliged to *give* more? Is it to make up for the fact that you are not equal? Claire replies, "Yah, I think that's what I feel."

Unlike moral perspective and leadership experience, girls' reports on their romance connections yield no striking differences between the two major subgroups. One might expect the hostile-avoidant girls to be more self-protective in relation to men than the girls in the role-reversal group, but the data do not support this view. Only Rebecca again stands out as different from the other eight. Initially hostile to boys and wary of their power to damage a girl's self-esteem ("It terrified me that males, little adolescent males, had the power to make me feel so disgusting, so worthless as a person"), she, as a senior, admits enjoying their company. She still guards against the possibility of what she terms an "abusive relationship" and sometimes worries that one particular friendship with a boy may not be properly balanced in certain respects. Nevertheless, she manages to maintain a clear sense of what she wants in that relationship and not to fall into the trap of simply accepting the boy's terms unquestioningly. She knows she depends on her friend, and that he in turn respects her and will not violate her trust in him. In this experience, she differs from all the other girls in the problematic-attachment sample. She has successfully moved from a position in which she says she "had a very negative view of myself because I had been rejected by boys" to one in which a heterosexual friendship actually feels "therapeutic" to her.

It is hard to account for the fact that Rebecca at no time sought solace or "attachment" in the kind of relationship described by Alison, Claire, and others. She may have chosen wisely in seeking nurturance first through a counseling relationship, at a time when she felt particularly vulnerable to exploitation in heterosexual encounters.

Summary

Taken as a whole, the elements of girls' development experience in each of the three subgroups bears the unmistakable imprint of lessons learned within a particular type of family attachment. For those in the role-reversal subgroup, the connection is to mothers whose apparent need for care exceeds their ability to give care. Because the psychological demands on daughters in this group lead them at times to ignore, forget, even deliberately sacrifice their own personal needs for the sake of others, they must struggle harder than the other girls in this chapter for psychological survival. Nevertheless, as can be seen in their narratives, at least two of them (Kate and Alison) have evolved coping strategies—in their intense commitment to others—which ultimately force their confrontation with the unresolved issue of self-care. Through opportunities provided within the academic environment, they have come to the point of addressing an important "stuck place" in their own development.

As with the first subgroup, the patterns of developmental stress and coping associated with the second subgroup appear closely related to the quality of the girls' attachment experience. One is tempted to say that theirs is the developmental advantage, because some maternal qualities of strength and stubbornness seem to have influenced these girls' coping styles. Unlike the other subgroup, they seem more consistently able to hear their own voices, their own anger, even though (like the others) they doubt that their mothers hear *them*. Nevertheless, they, too, face developmental tasks that were bypassed in family attachments but are certain to reappear for them in other contexts. Specifically, these girls have learned to fear revealing themselves to people whom they care about, people with the power to hurt them. As a result, they have cultivated the habit of censoring certain truths about themselves within relationships, of holding a lot inside, of hiding their inner vulnerability. Claire describes her habit of self-concealment this way:

> I am not honest even to those closest to me, because I don't want to get that involved in a relationship. I don't want to trust that much in a relationship, so I don't really allow them to see the real

me, and I am constantly lying about the person that I am and how
I feel.

Nell explains that "I hold a lot inside me," that she has in the past
lived not as the real "me," but as a series of self-protective personae: the
actress, the poet, the intellectual. All three girls struggle with the dilemma
of how to be taken seriously in a relationship with a man, when one
cannot risk being truly known by the other person. While girls in the
first subgroup appeared sometimes heedless of pain or unwilling to protect themselves from it, these girls have grown "suspicious" even of the
most intimate attachments (as Claire confesses about her male friend).
Reclaiming a sense of trust in others poses a thorny problem for this
subgroup, just as listening to the claims of the self does for girls in the
first subgroup.

As for Rebecca, an analysis of her apparent success in navigating
certain obstacles posed by a problematic attachment yields the following
set of ingredients: the gifts of intelligence and talent, leadership opportunities within the school, and wisdom in seeking professional counseling
at a critical moment in the adolescent passage.

From Rebecca, one learns the power of attachments during adolescence
made *outside* the family to create a developmental "bridge" of sorts.
This bridge allows the adolescent to move out of a stuck position in two
directions: both toward the larger world, and back into the family as
well. Events at Emma Willard appear to have enabled Rebecca to reclaim
attachment to her mother on improved terms. While their relationship
remains difficult for both participants, it no longer threatens the process
of development as it may have in the past.

Conclusions

The narratives of adolescent girls presented in this paper represent a
small part of the spectrum of changes in emotional bonds to parents that
may occur at adolescence. In fact, for eight of the nine girls in this group,
attachment bonds often proved either too brittle or too vulnerable to
permit certain essential transformations at adolescence. As a result, these
girls face the prospect of entering adult attachments without having practiced certain skills within family attachments. In particular, they lack
experience with expressing their own wishes within attachment and having these wishes honored, if not granted. Moreover, they have missed
out on opportunities to develop strategies for conflict resolution other

than the habit of silencing oneself or turning away from conflict altogether.

Persistence of attachment

While this small group must be considered atypical in the degree of stress they have endured within attachment, the perspective of attachment theory suggests that these students are representative of most adolescents in one important respect: that is, in the degree to which primary attachment continues to be important to them. Virtually all the girls discussed here (with the possible exception of Claire) remain emotionally involved with their mothers. No other relationships reported on by girls in this study compare to the primary attachment bond in strength or influence.

While these girls may be aware of missing elements in relationships with their mothers, on the whole they prefer to maintain a problematic attachment, even at some cost to themselves, rather than suffer a state of true nonattachment. This preference is consistent with Bowlby's (1973) view that adolescence is not a time for "radical decathexis" of family ties, and that behaviors resembling decathexis may be understood as a posture of "false self-sufficiency" in most adolescents. In the group of girls described here, Nell and Jenny conform to this position in many ways, but even they, when pressed, confess that they long to lean on their mothers. Only Claire steadfastly denies any need for attachment to her mother, but in her case the desire for attachment seems to have been transferred almost entirely onto another relationship.

Transformation within attachment

The girls in this group illuminate some aspects of the relationship between attachment at adolescence and ongoing ego development. It appears that for their own sake, adolescents must confront rather than ignore constraining elements in their primary attachments. When these elements remain, certain developmental tasks cannot be addressed. To the extent that one of the girls in particular (Rebecca) has succeeded in this confrontation, she offers clues to a possible general pattern of changes within adolescent attachment that may parallel her own experience. One critical component of this pattern seems to be a reclamation of self, which was formerly "lost" or invisible within attachment.

Rebecca says she can now look at herself and happily recognize her own image, whereas in the past awareness of herself as a distinct individual often frightened her. She experienced herself as desperately "glued" to her mother: that is, in a literally "stuck" relationship. Through a variety of extrafamilial opportunities, including therapy, school leadership positions, friendship, and work experiences, Rebecca has developed a sense of herself that no longer gets lost or obliterated, although she acknowledges that she still needs her mother. She knows that this relationship continues to have special importance for her, but it no longer has the power to render her sense of herself invisible.

The second component of Rebecca's developmental experience, which may also be characteristic of necessary changes in attachment for adolescents, is the capacity to accept a new set of perceptions about parents as well as oneself. Rebecca has moved from a position in which she both idealizes and reviles her mother to one that seems more neutral and more realistic. Her mother has become for her a "real whole complete person" instead of a magically powerful figure with the capacity to negate her daughter's truth.

It is obvious that the data considered here raise many more questions than can be answered by a handful of narratives. It could be argued, for instance, that attachment remains important for this group of girls precisely because their family ties have been troubled, and that in a comparable group of "securely attached" adolescents the issue of attachment has long been resolved and dropped. Two sources of evidence mitigate against such a view, however. One is the growing body of developmental data (Grotevant and Cooper) that documents the persistence of attachment in normal adolescent development. The other comes from perusal of interviews from the sixty-three participants in the Dodge Study at Emma Willard who were not classified in the problematic-attachment group. Many of these girls describe transformations of attachment similar to those reported by Rebecca. The attainment of change was much less arduous for them than for girls in the problematic-attachment group and usually required less in the way of extrafamilial assistance. Nevertheless, the goal in all cases was similar: to maintain attachment, through a series of new recognitions of self and other demanded by adolescent maturation.

Notes

1. In this chapter, the term "attachment" will be used in a manner consistent with its meaning for attachment theory—that is, as an enduring

affectional relationship between child and caregiver, the aim of which is protection, comfort, and nurturance for the child. In adulthood, such relationships may exist on more mutual terms between partners in a long-term pair bond, such as marriage. The hallmarks of attachment include its enduring quality, its promise of protection in times of stress or danger, and the experience of grief and mourning following loss of the loved person.

2. Among the essential points of Bowlby's perspective are the following characteristics of attachment: attachment is a primary instinct, not secondary to the fulfillment of physiological needs; the goal of attachment behavior is proximity to a primary caregiver and is seen to be intensely activated under stress (for example, danger, pain, separation from caregiver); a child may be attached to more than one caregiver but will show a preference for one in particular, especially under stress; attachment is a separate behavioral system from that of feeding or sex and serves distinctly different needs—specifically, those of contact, emotional comfort, and protection in time of stress. Bowlby explains that "each system develops through its own maturational stages and differs in the underlying variables which produce and control its particular response patterns" (Bowlby 1969, 232). Thus, attachment charts a separate (though sometimes overlapping) course from that of sexuality in early development and does not fully intersect with sexual behaviors until the establishment of an enduring adult pair bond. (Note that attachment is seen as active and adaptive throughout the life cycle.)

3. In his discussion of terminology, Bowlby also compares the meanings of "cathexis" and "affiliation" to that of attachment. Cathexis has two drawbacks: It suggests a closed energy system, and it does not permit a "discussion of differences between a person to whom attachment behavior is directed and one towards which sexual behavior is directed" (Bowlby 1969, 229). Affiliation, as conceived originally by Murray in 1938, is a much broader concept involving all manifestations of friendliness and goodwill, a general desire for companionship, and is not specifically directed toward a particular other person or persons. Thus, Bowlby clarifies three phenomena often lumped together under the general heading of "love": attachment, sexual passion, and friendship. While all three of these may coalesce in a single adult relationship, what is commonly termed "love" may consist of one or more of these in various combinations, especially at other points in development.

4. This formulation is similar to the genesis of the "false self" in Win-

nicott, (1965) and to Sullivan's "self-system" (1953), both of which envision the child's response to destructive parental impingements by accommodating to the parent, in order to preserve the attachment. One extreme example of this accommodation would be a child's preservation of attachment by submitting to physical or sexual abuse.

5. Methodological Considerations: The interviews of the nine students included in this subsample from the Dodge Study at Emma Willard were selected according to four criteria suggested by Ainsworth's empirical studies of attachment, and parallel those used by Greenberg in the development of his Inventory of Adolescent Attachments (Greenberg 1983). These criteria (proximity/accessibility; communication/understanding; dependence/trust; nurturance/protection) have been established in past investigations as valid indices of the quality of attachment to parents and are currently operationalized in several recent studies of adolescents and young adults (Kobak and Sceery 1986; Main et al. 1985; Kenny 1986). Among participants in the study, nine emerged who perceived their attachment, to mothers in particular, as markedly deficient in at least three of the four categories of attachment cited above. A second selection of cases by an independent reader yielded 90 percent interrater agreement, with 100 percent agreement on the nine cases discussed here. Thus, the judgment of problematic attachment for the nine girls in this subsample is assumed to be valid, given that the girls' own perceptions are accurate.

On close reading, the interviews of the nine girls in the problematic-attachment subsample revealed twenty recurrent developmental themes pertaining to self, relationships, and oral orientation. The interviews were then coded according to these thematic categories to note patterns consistent over all nine cases and differences that would help to discriminate among possible subgroups. It was hoped that detailed examination would shed light on the relationship between perceived attachment status and other developmental domains, such as self-esteem, moral reasoning, and interpersonal experience outside the family. Actual patterns of correlation found in this manner between attachment status and other aspects of development did, in fact, help to delineate the three attachment styles mentioned above (role reversal, hostile-avoidant, and transformation). Moreover, they provide a running commentary on how profoundly adolescent girls' experience may be organized around issues of primary attachment.

6. Please note that all of these factors, both intra- and extrafamilial, emerged as more strongly associated with the fact of problematic at-

tachment than one would expect by chance. This does not mean, however, that the presence of one or more of these factors in an adolescent's experience signals the presence of a necessarily problematic attachment. In other words, one may not read backward from the fact that a girl has lived through a high-conflict divorce and assume that she must, therefore, be involved in a problematic attachment with her mother. This point is essential to keep in mind while reviewing the observations made here.

Sources

Ainsworth, M. 1969. Object relations, dependency and attachment: A theoretical view of the mother-infant relationship. *Child Development* 40:969, 1–25.

Ainsworth, M., and M. C. Blehar. 1978. *Patterns of Attachment*. Hillsdale, N.Y.: Erlbaum.

Bowlby, J. 1969. *Attachment and Loss*. New York: Basic Books.

———. 1973. *Separation, Anxiety and Anger*. New York: Basic Books.

———. 1980. *Loss, Sadness and Depression*. New York: Basic Books.

Chodorow, N. 1978. *The Reproduction of Mothering*. Berkeley: University of California Press.

Freud, S. 1931. "Female Sexuality." In *The Complete Psychological Works of Sigmund Freud* vol. 21, edited by J. Strachey. New York: Macmillan.

Greenberg, M., et al. 1983. The nature and importance of attachment relations to parents and peers during adolescence. *Journal of Youth and Adolescence* 12:5.

Grotevant, H., and C. Cooper. 1983. *Adolescent Development in the Family*. San Francisco: Jossey Bass.

Kenny, M. 1986. Extent and function of parental affection among first-year college students. Unpublished manuscript, University of Pennsylvania.

Kobak, R., and A. Sceery. 1985. The transition to college: working models of attachment, affect regulation, perceptions of self and others. Unpublished manuscript, University of Denver.

Levinson, L. 1984. Witches—bad and good: Maternal psychopathology as a developmental interference. *Psychological Study of the Child* 39.

Main, M., and N. Kaplan. 1985. Security in infancy, childhood, and adulthood: A move to the level of representation. *Child Development* 209:3–4, 67–104.

Sullivan, H. S. 1953. *The Interpersonal Theory of Psychiatry.* New York: Norton.

Winnicott, D. W. 1965. *The Maturational Processes and the Facilitating Environment.* New York: International Universities Press.

———. 1971. *Playing and Reality.* Harmondsworth: Penguin.

Unfairness and Not Listening
Converging Themes in Emma Willard Girls' Development

ELIZABETH BERNSTEIN AND CAROL GILLIGAN

Editors' Note: In 1979 when Robert C. Parker became principal of Emma Willard, he was intrigued by his sense that girls personalized criticism to a far greater extent than the boys he had taught at previous schools. In the second year of the study, questions about unfairness and listening were added to the interview. This chapter discusses girls' responses to these questions.

That's unfair to me because you are not listening to what I am saying, and you are not treating me like someone who is allowed to have their own views and values. —Rachel, 11th grade

Fairness and listening are not concepts that are typically associated with each other. Fairness seems to belong more to the public realm of laws and rules; listening, more to the private realm of interpersonal relationships. Fairness evokes strident feelings, such as indignation and anger; listening, softer feelings of sensitivity and concern. Finally, fairness is typically viewed as a quintessentially moral concept, while listening generally is not. To be treated fairly is commonly viewed as a right; to be listened to, a wish or a need.

The Emma Willard girls unsettle these conventional modes of thinking. Remarkably, for these girls fairness and listening appear to be intimately related concepts. They speak of listening as a profoundly moral phenomenon, and fairness, a profoundly interpersonal one. Most significantly, the connection between the two concepts appears to be an outgrowth of development. That is, over time Emma Willard girls seem to experience a convergence of public and private concerns, so that listening becomes increasingly an issue in the public realm of school and world affairs, and fairness increasingly an issue in the private realm of close relationships. As a result, the girls' descriptions of unfairness and not listening come to be linked; the imperative to hear or respond comes to form the core of the girls' concepts of fairness, and the sense that it is only fair to hear comes to form the core of their concepts of listening.

This chapter will attempt to trace the process whereby concerns with unfairness and not listening converge in Emma Willard girls' experiences. It will attempt to show the wide divergence between concepts and experiences of unfairness and not listening for girls at lower grade levels, and the gradual integration of concepts and experiences of unfairness and not listening for girls at higher grade levels. Finally, the chapter will attempt to suggest both the new visions and the questions that the experiences of the Emma Willard girls pose for a model of girls' moral development. For while the imperative to hear or respond instills in these girls great moral strength, it also introduces within them a new dimension of moral ambiguity. As girls feel compelled to hear or respond to disparate perspectives in a situation, they often express uncertainty over the nature and possibility of a fair solution. They thus raise the important question of how listening complicates fairness.

The convergence of unfairness and not-listening contexts

Thirty-four Emma Willard girls answered questions about experiences and concepts of unfairness and not listening. Namely, for unfairness: Can you tell me about a situation in which someone was treated unfairly? What made it unfair? What would have been the fair thing to do? For not listening: Can you tell me about a situation in which someone wasn't listened to? How did you know s/he wasn't being listened to? What would have made it possible for him/her to be heard?

The broadest indicator of the convergence between concerns about unfairness and concerns about not listening over time is the convergence that occurs in the settings of these experiences. Thus, among 9th and 10th graders, unfairness predominantly occurs in the public context of school, while not listening predominantly occurs in the private contexts of family and friendship. A typical 9th grader's description of unfairness is: "The gym teacher put all the worst kids on my team," while a typical situation of not listening is: "When I try to talk to one of my friends . . . and she is all over the place." Conversely, among 12th graders, a majority describe not listening in relation to public authority figures, such as teachers, while a far greater proportion describe unfairness in relation to peers. A typical 12th grader's description of unfairness is: "My friend went against my trust by not keeping a secret," and a typical example of not listening is: an administrative decision "was not representative of the community." These shifts in the settings of unfairness and not listening suggest that for Emma Willard girls over time, responsiveness becomes an increasing concern in the public domain, while reciprocity becomes an increasing concern in the private domain.

The convergence of unfairness and not-listening experiences

The central developmental phenomenon that appears to underlie an increasing relatedness of unfairness and not listening experiences over time in Emma Willard girls may be described as an increasingly psychological approach to both moral and interpersonal experience.

At lower grade levels the concrete focus of responses about unfairness and not listening is striking. The majority of 9th graders and 10th graders, in exemplifying unfairness, cite failures of equality and reciprocity, such as "getting cut from the soccer team," "the fact that freshmen have to go to bed earlier than everyone else on campus," "my parents didn't let me go out for the tech crew for the plays," and "my mother gave my brother a stereo and not me." Adults in these situations, typically authority figures, such as teachers or parents, are viewed as powerful agents of distributive justice. More important, girls tend to base their claims to fair treatment at this stage on what they observe others getting or on what is spelled out in a rule. Ninth and 10th graders typically protest the unfairness of unequal treatment or violation of rules, such as "when things do not come out even, . . . [when] faculty kids would never get in trouble, but the rest of the school would," "when someone else does something and you get blamed for it," "[when] in *Fine Print* it says freshmen are supposed to go to bed at 10:30, and the houseparents put them to bed at 10," "when I am not allowed to do something that I want to do, and somebody else gets to do it."

Also at lower grade levels a corresponding concreteness is evident in girls' examples of not listening. Nearly all of the instances of not listening described by 10th graders, and some by 11th graders, focus on the basic psychological need to have one's existence and reality acknowledged by others. These responses describe the importance of securing that acknowledgment, of getting others' attention. Listening is thus typically viewed literally as the experience of being physically heard or literally understood, which affirms the reality of one's self for others. Not listening most frequently occurs in situations where the experience of being physically heard is obstructed, and girls dwell on signs of nonrecognition, such as "not attending," "interrupting," "not making eye contact," "looking the other way," "not giving any sign of recognition." The imagery of neglect and nothingness in many of these responses reflects a pervasive sense of vulnerability; the girls feel as though they are "not there as another human being," "talking to the wall," "nothing's happening," "[someone is] completely oblivious of me and I felt like a worm on the sidewalk or something." Many girls imagine that only drastic actions will compel others to listen, such as "grabbing someone by the neck and shaking them five times," "pulling out a knife and saying, 'If you don't listen, I'll kill myself!' " The girls do not express moral indignation in these early not-listening responses, but instead focus on action—their dramatic, semihumorous strategies for being heard.

These concrete illustrations of unfairness and not listening, at lower grade levels, create the discrepancy noted between them: Questions about unfairness tend to elicit explicit moral indignation, while questions about not listening tend to elicit observation or implications of psychological need. Moral injunctions are not attached to failures of emotional responsiveness, and the desire for responsiveness is not linked to moral imperatives. The discrepancy between girls' experiences of unfairness and not listening at this stage can be seen by comparing pairs of responses in individual girls, as in the accompanying pairs of excerpts from three 10th grade girls. In these excerpts, language emphasizing the thematic difference between descriptions of unfairness and not listening is highlighted.

Table 8

Unfairness and Not Listening Responses— 10th graders*

Unfairness

My parents didn't let me go on the tech crew for the plays. . . . I didn't think that was fair, because they did all this for my brother. Like he would stay after school to work on the newspaper, and . . . they would pick him up, but they wouldn't pick me up . . . *He got to do what he wanted and I didn't get to do what I wanted.*

Not Listening

I think in the student center . . . because someone turned up the radio . . . I go J—! J—! *She doesn't notice. . . . She didn't react at all. . . . Nothing's happening. (What would have made it possible to be heard?)*

You grab them by the neck and shake them five times, are you there? You do something really silly to get their attention, and then you talk.

—Marianne

Unfairness

I was in typing class . . . and the teacher started to yell at me . . . and [if he] picked on someone else they wouldn't have stopped . . . and *that wasn't fair I thought.* . . . He should have said, "when I am talking there will be no typing," instead of *picking on someone who hadn't started it in the first place.*

Not Listening

Before I came here, I wasn't listened to by the kids I was going to school with. . . . *I wasn't there as another human being.* . . . They couldn't appreciate even the very little things . . . just to listen, to know that I was there. *(What would have made it possible to be heard?)* I don't know. . . . They didn't want to accept me. . . . They just couldn't get through that barrier.

—Jocelyn

Unfairness

My mother bought a stereo . . . for my brother and I . . . and he took the stereo [to college] and it wasn't fair, because . . . it wasn't either of ours. I don't think it should have been given to anyone. *[My mother] should have bought another one, or just didn't give it to either of us.*

Not Listening

I used to call my mother to tell her how much I hated it here . . . and *she never picked up on it* or really listened to it. . . . She would never say anything like "do you want to come home?" *(What would have made it possible to be heard?)* When I am home, I usually yell at her . . . but on the phone, yelling is not going to do anything because *she can hang up on me,* or whatever.

—Tamara

*10th graders were the youngest girls who answered listening questions. Italic face indicates language demonstrating thematic differences in unfairness and not listening responses.

The responses of girls at higher grade levels, however, present a different picture. Older girls attach moral claim to responding to people's needs and feelings, which have no other sanction than their psychological validity. Their responses express a concept of fairness based on inner, not outer, standards, regardless of external rules and practices. Further, their responses express an experience of listening as no longer a fleeting affirmation of one's reality for others, but a reliable feature of both private and public relationships enduring in time.

At higher grade levels, girls describe unfairness and not listening in ways that reflect an intermingling of moral passion with a concern with responsiveness in relationships. As a result of this convergence, the content and tone of unfairness and not-listening responses at higher grade levels grow similar. Both sensitivity to needs and moral passion pervades both types of experience. Most specifically, the intersection of unfairness and not-listening concepts is demonstrated by a girl's description of the same situation as exemplifying both unfairness and not listening, and the ways in which concerns of unfairness and not listening come to define one another.

The convergence in tone and content of girls' responses to questions about unfairness and not listening at higher grade levels are well-illustrated by pairs of responses from 11th and 12th graders. In the first excerpts, Rita expresses moral indignation both about the denial of black students' rights—"It is unfair to expect black people not to want a voice in this student government"—and about the disrespect shown in not listening to her—"that woman was being unfair . . . I deserve a certain amount of respect." Both unfairness and not listening are "unfair." In the second examples illustrating unfairness, Susan expresses moral indignation about bureaucratic insensitivity to a classmate's emotional needs—"I don't think they cared"—and about the unfairness of an administrator's meddling in her example of not listening—"I don't think that was fair. . . . I don't think it was any right of hers to say what she said."

Table 9

Unfairness and Not Listening Responses— 11th and 12th graders*

Unfairness

Something I think is unfair ... is a proposal in CREW that black students would get the voting representative taken away from them. ... It just really, really made me angry. ... I don't think they should have to blend themselves with the non-black students. Black students have certain rights. ... *It is unfair to expect black people to not want a voice in this student government.*

Not Listening

The thing with my math teacher last year ... People were completely on the side of that teacher, and people weren't listening to me saying *that woman was being unfair.* ... She was not being respectful of me and I don't care if I am younger; *I still deserve ... a certain amount of respect.*

—Rita, 12th grade

Unfairness

We had three final assignments ... [and] knowing that the students were feeling very burdened ... it was unfair of her [the teacher] to contribute to that. ... *I don't feel as if she was listening to the class* and that it was something we were really feeling. This is really too much. ... This is not something we feel we can handle and still do a good job at it.

Not Listening

She didn't seem terribly moved by how the class was feeling. ... She was just looking at it as a last ditch attempt to get out of an assignment which really wasn't how we were feeling. ... If she had even acknowledged the fact that I understand that this is a real problem for you. ... But that didn't even come through. ...

—Barbara, 12th grade

Unfairness

The fact that the United States backs counterrevolutionaries in Nicaragua, that's unfair. ... The United States was built on a revolu-

Table 9 continued

tion. . . . Nicaragua was under the control of a dictator and they had a revolution to get out of that whole situation . . . and [we] try to undermine that revolution . . . and that's unfair. . . . If we want them to do something, but we don't do it ourselves, that's hypocritical.

Not Listening

I don't think the people in Nicaragua are being listened to by Reagan, by the news. . . . I have gone to meetings, [and people say] we just had a revolution against our horrible dictator, you've got to help us. . . . [Reagan doesn't say] "I know what you are going through, but you have to see our point of view" . . . he says that they are horrible people to have a revolution and that they are just being ridiculous.

—Maria, 11th grade

Unfairness

A friend of mine last year was kicked out because . . . she had a friend of hers who got 600s on her SATs go in and take them. . . . I understand punishing her, but I don't think that her life should be ruined. . . . It makes me angry. I think they should have had her come back here, because I think being at home is really messing her up. . . . I don't think they cared; I don't think they want to deal with people like that.

Not Listening

We were going to spend a weekend at a boys' school next to here . . . and [the dean] said I understand you are going to do some drinking this weekend. . . . I was just so mad. . . . I said, "I will follow the rules" . . . but she didn't listen. She just wanted to get her point across. . . . I didn't like her getting involved in my plans, because *I didn't think that was fair*, and I don't think it was any right of hers to say what she said.

—Susan, 11th grade

* Italic face indicates intermingling of unfairness and not-listening language.

In all four of these response pairs, the imperative to care is at the core of the unfairness situations, and a sense of moral protest at the core of the not-listening situations. The concerns with care and justice, although distinct, interact very closely. This closeness is graphically demonstrated when the same situation is named as an example of unfairness and of not listening, as in the bracketed pairs of excerpts. In these responses, the meaning of unfairness and not listening is so closely connected that the girls easily shift from describing a situation as an example of unfairness to describing it as an example of not listening. For example, Maria easily shifts from discussing Reagan's double standard regarding the Nicaraguan contras as an example of unfairness—"If we want them to do something, but we don't do it ourselves, that's hypocritical"—to discussing his failure of empathy as an example of not listening—"[Reagan doesn't say] I know what you are going through, but you have to see our point of view." Likewise, Barbara shifts easily from discussing a teacher's knowing infliction of too much work as an example of unfairness—"knowing that the students were feeling very burdened . . . it was unfair for her to contribute to that"—to discussing the teacher's insensitivity as an example of not listening—"if she had even acknowledged . . . 'I understand that this is a real problem for you' . . . but that didn't even come through. . . ."

The differences in unfairness and not listening responses that can be seen in comparing the responses of older and younger girls can also be seen in comparing individual girls at different ages. A sample of these responses appears in Table 10.

Yet the interconnection of fairness and listening themes is made most explicit in responses of older girls when the two concepts are defined in terms of one another, when fairness is defined *as* listening or listening *as* fairness. This occurs several times, as when the unfairness of denying representation to black students is described in terms of silencing a voice ("It is unfair to expect black people not to want a voice in this student government"); when the unfairness of a teacher's behavior is explained by her not listening to student's feelings ("it was unfair [because] I don't feel as if she was listening to the class, that it was something we were really feeling"); and when an administrator's not listening is portrayed as an unfair violation of rights ("I didn't like her getting involved in my plans, because I didn't think that was fair . . . [that] it was any right of hers to say what she said"). Moreover, even when listening and fairness are not linked explicitly through language, one may see the girls as often

Table 10

Longitudinal Cases

Time III: 10th grade—Jennifer

Unfairness

[My houseparent] said go clean the alcove . . . that was really unfair to me . . . that she blamed me for making a mess . . . when it wasn't me. . . . She had no right to yell at me, because I wasn't involved.

Not Listening

I guess situations with friends . . . maybe somebody listens to what I am saying, but you don't really know. Because they are not being attentive and they are looking the other way. . . . I could have yelled . . . and said everybody shut up . . . [or] I guess I could have waited

Time IV: 11th grade—Jennifer

Unfairness

The thing with the fraternity . . . where I can't go over there . . . obviously I had a reason; I have a serious boyfriend. I wanted to see him . . . but it's a rule and they are not going to give in.

Not Listening (same incident)

All she [the dean of students] wanted to do was stick to the rules. . . . She wasn't going to make any exceptions for me and she wasn't going to listen to my side of the story. . . . She wanted her way and that was that.

Time III: 10th grade—Myrna

Unfairness

When you have something that you should be allowed to do but you can't do it for some strange reason . . . [like] in Fine Print it says they [freshman] are supposed to go to bed at 10:30 and the houseparent puts them to bed at 10.

Not Listening

When my Dad and my sister fight . . . my Dad doesn't listen, he just tells her no, you are not doing this. . . . He wasn't considering her ideas . . . he was only talking about his. He just gets more momentum and keeps on going.

Time IV: 11th grade—Myrna

Unfairness

There was this girl who got expelled last year and she didn't get the second chance everyone else got . . . and that was really unfair. I mean they followed her around and did everything for her . . . [another girl] stayed here under the recommendation that she get counseling . . . [but] they didn't give her a chance, they just expelled her. It was awful.

Not Listening

There was another girl here who wasn't being listened to. . . . She wanted to get attention somehow, so she threatened to kill heself . . . and this year she has gotten into drugs which is even scarier. . . . I don't think she is being listened to the way she wants to, because I think she would stop if she got the attention she wanted.

Time III: 11th grade—Laura

Unfairness

My brother and I had the same curfew and he is two years younger than me. And that made me so mad . . . when I was in 8th grade I had to be in at 8 o'clock and now he is in 8th grade and he doesn't have to be in until 10 o'clock. And the age difference and having the same type of rule there, that is frustrating.

Not Listening

In situations with my brother again. (If I say) you know, it would be smart if you put the dish in the bottom part of the dishwasher, he won't listen to me, he will walk out and small things like that.

Time IV: 12th grade—Laura

Unfairness

It was unfair [of my friend to go] against my trust and my wishes to her, and not keep a secret . . . because she confides in me as well. . . . It's a trust being broken or a friendship being broken or something.

Not Listening

Oftentimes I am not being listened to in the whole conversation, like with my boyfriend, he said uh huh. It's frustrating. . . . Wednesday night he fell asleep on the phone so I knew he wasn't listening . . . just from being ignored.

Table 10 continued

> ## Time III: 11th grade—Cindy
>
> *Unfairness*
>
> If a teacher expresses favoritism to a student . . . because they are all in the class together, and they all want to learn the same thing and they all want to do well. . . . [You should] try as much as you can to treat all the students equally.
>
> *Not Listening*
>
> If you are talking to someone while they are watching television or listening to their favorite song . . . and you have to say their name over and over again to get their attention . . . they weren't replying.
>
> ## Time IV: 12th grade—Cindy
>
> *Unfairness*
>
> Last year . . . a real general consensus, overwhelming consensus was to keep the trimester and now we have semesters. . . . They asked for our opinion and *I don't think they listened to it.*
>
> *Not Listening (same incident)*
>
> That was basically not being listened to, because their decision . . . was just not representative of the community.

defining the two concepts in terms of each other—in the sense that fairness is defined in terms of responsiveness to needs, and listening is defined in terms of showing respect. Such implicit definition is illustrated when Susan comments about her friend who got expelled—"I don't think it is fair . . . that her life should be ruined. . . . I don't think they cared. I don't think they want to deal with people like that"—implying that the school authorities neither "heard" nor respected her friend's emotional need.

The complication of fairness by listening

The convergence of concerns with fairness and listening in older girls, for the most part, gives rise to a moral stance of depth and power. The compassion, clarity, and strength of moral outlook are palpable in many of the girls' responses. And yet along with the strength that accompanies their converging concern with fairness and listening comes a subtler difficulty. This difficulty arises when the imperative to listen or care mandates listening to many voices in a situation, which may not be in harmony. In such situations, described by girls at higher grade levels, a new sensitivity to disparate voices or perspectives leads to a new difficulty in judgment and in action as girls struggle to hear and reconcile conflicting perspectives in the determination of a fair or good solution. Lacking a simple standpoint, their efforts to arrive at fair solutions can become painstaking or problematic, often reflecting tension and ambiguity over what a fair solution would be.

This problematic attentiveness to diverse perspectives in a situation is illustrated by several excerpts from 12th grade girls. For example, when asked what a fair solution would be in the case of a friend who got expelled from school for cheating on her SATs, Susan struggles to reconcile the perspective of the school authorities with her perspective as a caring and knowing friend: "I don't know, I think they thought they did the fair thing. But I think they should have had her come back here, because being at home is really messing her up." Susan understands the school's perspective—"I can understand punishing her"—yet she also has a different vantage point: "I just don't think it is fair that her life should be ruined. . . . I don't think they cared." There is ultimate tension and doubt in her view that the fair solution is not fair. Similarly, in the case of the teacher overburdening the class, Barbara observes: "It is hard not wanting to tell her how to run the class, but letting her know that this is not something we all feel we can handle and still do a good job at it. It is hard to say when the decision is not yours." Barbara's sensitivity to both the teacher's and students' perspectives thus introduces ambiguity as to what the fair solution would be.

The clearest example of how listening complicates the determination of a fair solution is described by Hannah, who talks about losing a lead part in the school play to the acting teacher's daughter. Hannah shows how sensitive consideration of each person's perspective in the situation leads only to uncertainty about what a fair solution would be: "I don't know [what the fair solution would have been]. I think for Alison to be interested in the theatre at the same school where her mother is a theatre director, is a bad situation. Because from Alison's point of view, . . . she can't very well say she is going to turn down the part because her mother gave it to her. At the same time . . . if my parents were in charge . . . they would put me last as a matter of principle. . . . [But] Mrs. [x], she is hired to be the director for this school and so from that point of view, she should do things objectively . . . but as a parent I guess it is impossible, so . . . I think it's a bad situation to start with that she should be there."

Hannah clearly illustrates how an empathic understanding of conflicting perspectives in a situation renders determination of a fair solution problematic. She thus raises the question, is the imperative to listen or respond to varying needs in a situation a source of vulnerability or strength in girls' moral reasoning? Is a hesitation to pronounce as fair solutions that do not adequately reflect or respond to all perspectives in a situation a sign of moral weakness or maturity? As Hannah and other Emma Willard girls strive to integrate an imperative to listen in their approaches to moral problems, they compel observers of their experience to ponder how this imperative might be integrated into new models of moral development. Concern about not listening, initially separated from concerns about unfairness, are seen by 12th grade to underscore for some girls the limitations of blind or deaf justice. The moral domain has then become a psychological domain, and moral problems become problems of human relationships, which require seeing and listening for their resolution.

This transformation of the moral domain from a domain of rules to a domain of relationships integrates concerns about unfairness and concerns about not listening as two kinds of concerns about relationships. The question "Is someone being treated unfairly?" joins with the question "Is someone not being listened to?" generating thoughts and feelings about what would be fair and also about how to listen or be heard. Approaching moral problems as problems of relationships leads to an overriding concern with listening and responding. Not listening then comes to be labelled "unfair," and problems of fairness come to be seen in psychological terms as relational problems.

Methodology

Sample

Analyses of unfairness and not-listening responses were conducted on thirty-four Emma Willard girls who answered unfairness questions for at least two consecutive years and questions on not listening for at least one year. Only these girls were studied because they allowed for a modest longitudinal component to the analysis. The reduced size of the sample relative to the larger Emma Willard sample resulted from the fact that questions of unfairness and not listening were introduced, respectively, in the second and third year of the study, preventing many girls who graduated during the study from meeting the criteria. The sample is composed of three subgroups, each spanning a slightly different developmental sequence: nine girls who answered unfairness and not-listening questions between 9th and 11th grade, seven who answered them between 10th and 12th grade, and eighteen who answered them between 11th and 12th grade.

Questions

Questions pertaining to listening were added to the research interview in year three, after many responses to questions of unfairness from the previous year suggested a connection between experiences of unfairness and not listening.

Questions on listening were asked immediately following the fairness questions in the research interview. While this sequence suggests that girls may have been biased toward linking the two concepts, it is all the more striking that girls at lower grade levels failed to make the link, suggesting that linkage between the concepts was an authentic phenomenon and not an artifact of question sequence.

Design

The Dodge Study as a whole was designed to permit both cross-sectional and longitudinal analyses. The possibility for longitudinal analysis of responses on unfairness and not listening, however, was limited both by the small number of girls who answered unfairness and not-listening questions for two years (N = 10) as well as by the absence, spanning more than two years, of unfairness and not-listening responses for individual girls. Despite this, unfairness and not-listening responses of the ten girls for whom there is some longitudinal data show developmental tendencies confirming cross-sectional patterns.

The Body Politic
Normal Female Adolescent Development and the Development of Eating Disorders

CATHERINE STEINER-ADAIR

Editors' Note: *An earlier version of this essay appeared in the* Journal of American Academy of Psychoanalysis *14, no. 1 (1986) 95–114.*

Until recently, research concerning the etiological origins of anorexia nervosa and other eating disorders has focused almost entirely in one of three areas of investigation: psychodynamic, family systems, and organic theories. Yet none of these theories can explain the increase of eating disorders at this time in history or why it initially, almost exclusively, affected middle and upper class (primarily Caucasian) women and is now spreading into broader class and ethnic groups. The inability of the predominant etiological theories to explain the current epidemic has led researchers to conclude that there may be sociocultural influences that make today's young females vulnerable to problems related to dieting and eating at this stage in the life cycle. Historians have shown that in the nineteenth century, hysterical behavior in women and girls was oftentimes related to that era's cultural imperative and to physicians' notions of what constituted normative female behavior. It is equally possible that there are repressive cultural forces in the later twentieth century that are developmentally disabling to young females and, along with individual and familial experiences, are producing the current eating-disordered symptomatology. In other words, it may be that certain sociocultural influences make anorexia nervosa, bulimia, and anorexic-like behavior a seemingly adaptive response to the developmental demands of growing up female in certain populations at this time in history.

If one compares recent research on normal female adolescent development and research concerning the psychodynamics of eating disorders, a curious and striking paradox occurs: What is put forward in the cultural ideal of physical and mental health for contemporary female adolescents is tied to the emergence of psychopathology in the form of eating disorders. Research in female adolescent development indicates that it is normal for girls to be excessively concerned with their bodies and to have difficulty with the separation-individuation process. Concerning the preoccupation with thinness that is the hallmark of anorexia (Bruch 1978), recent research in normal female adolescent development suggests that it is both normal and socially adaptive for girls to diet, regardless of any health-related need to lose weight. In the clinical literature, Goodsitt (1979) proposes that anorexia develops in girls who are unable to accept their bodily imperfections as they reach adolescence; in the developmental literature, Rosenbaum (1979) suggests that female adolescents are socialized to be unaccepting of their bodily imperfections. The conceptualization of eating disorders as a failure to separate and individuate requires critical analysis, for current research on female adolescent development suggests that it is appropriate for a girl to "continuously experience herself in issues of merging and separation" (Chodorow 1978, 166). In contrast to males, for whom identity development is the outcome of increasing experience of separation and gained autonomy, the female personality develops through attachment to others (Chodorow 1978; Gilligan 1977; Marcia 1980). Perhaps a clue to the etiological mystery concerning the current phenomenal increase in eating disorders can be found in further analysis of the bridge between normalcy and pathology, when theories of normal development are viewed in a cultural context.

Separation-individuation and female adolescent development

Theories of psychodynamic object relations and family systems describe the core problem in anorexia as a failure to separate and individuate, and to gain a sense of autonomy. The bias that defines autonomy as the goal of development exists in a fundamental way in our culture (Rothchild 1979) as well as in theories of developmental and clinical psychology. Yet recent research has challenged the applicability and validity of this bias in female development and has demonstrated that separation, individuation, and autonomy per se are not central to female development in the same way that they are central to male development (Gilligan 1982). In contrast to boys, for whom masculine identity is confirmed through separation (Erikson 1968), attachment and relationships are critical issues in female identity formation (Gilligan 1982). In a review of the applicability of research concerning the reemergence of individuation-separation issues in adolescent development and the identity status approach, Marcia concludes that if researchers are going to look seriously at female adolescent development, then "the areas around which crises and commitment are to be determined should be those around which women are expected, initially, to form an identity; the establishment and maintenance of relationships" (Marcia 1980, 9). However, research in eating disorders seems to overlook the central role of maintaining relationships in female adolescent development and continues to suggest that separation and individuation are of primary importance. The bias toward autonomy is evident in the current construction of the problem; the pathology of girls with eating disorders is written and defined in terms of excessive dependence in relationships and a failure to achieve autonomy.

In one of the initial attempts to research possible differences between male and female adolescent development, Douvan and Adelson (1966) interviewed 2,005 girls ages eleven through eighteen and 1,045 boys ages fourteen through sixteen and concluded that identity for the girl is achieved "through a process of finding and defining an internal standard in the individual through attachment to others" (Benedek 1979, 10). Concerning the theoretical emphasis toward separation and autonomy, Douvan and Adelson found no evidence of an intense need among girls, as there was among boys, to break familial bonds. While a preoccupation with developing independently derived internal standards was prognostically a strong indicator of ego strength in boys, the quality of interpersonal relationships related to ego strength in girls.

More recently developmental psychologists have shifted the paradigm of female adolescent development from the male-based traditional model, which emphasizes detachment in movement toward autonomy, toward a model that presents the identity process for adolescent females as one of self-differentiation within the context of relationships; in other words, females develop their identity as they experience themselves through attachment in relationships.

In examining the validity of the oedipal configuration for boys, Chodorow (1974) found that girls never have to separate totally from their primary caretaker in order to gain gender identity as boys do. Because of the unique primary identification with a caretaker of the same sex, the girl will "continue to experience herself in issues of merging and separation, and in attachment characterized by primary identification and the fusion of identification and object choice" (Chodorow 1978, 166). Thus, the identity process for the adolescent female becomes one of self-differentiation within the context of relationships—in other words, to have a distinct sense of self but still be connected to others (Gilligan 1982).

Much has been written about the large extent to which girls with anorexia "rely solely on acceptance from others as the criterion for positive self-evaluation" (Garfinkel and Garner 1982, 24). Since females develop a sense of identity in the context of relationships, girls are naturally more dependent on and vulnerable to external references impacting on their sense of identity. While viewed solely as a disturbance in the clinical literature, research in normal female adolescent development reports that girls are socialized to rely heavily on external acceptance and feedback to inform their identity.

Girls are encouraged to remain fluid and ambiguous between their self-definition and external confirmation in self-definition; girls are oriented toward an external audience for a sense of self, for making judgments, and for signs that will confirm self-esteem (Douvan and Adelson 1966). Kagan (1964) also found that girls at puberty got their self-concept from the relative success or failure that their social skills brought them, making them again dependent on the external audience.

Minuchin (1978), among others, has written about the loyal and peace-keeping familial role of the girl who develops anorexia. Family systems theory describes girls who are vulnerable to eating disorders as girls who avoid creating conflict within the enmeshed family system. Interestingly, the literature on adolescent development points to a striking sex-role difference concerning self-initiated family conflict by an adolescent. Adolescent boys are encouraged to make independent life decisions, which often lead to crisis and conflict within the family and with outside authorities; for a boy, the experience of himself in conflict with "others" is often an identity-confirming event. In contrast, for the adolescent female (who is socialized to be proficient in interpersonal relationships) to create interpersonal conflict by initiating a decision or disagreement can be experienced by her as a disconfirmation of the success of her identity formation (Marcia 1980, 179).

As Chodorow observes: "In any given society, feminine personality comes to define itself in relation and connection to other people more than masculine personality does" (Chodorow 1978, 187). The socialization of girls directs them to be involved with and concerned with others (Chodorow 1974, 51); and where girls are brought up to nurture and assume interpersonal responsibility, boys are brought up to deny involvement and connection. In analyzing games children play, Lever (1976) found that the games boys play prepare them to take a role of the generalized other and to detach themselves from individual connections and, simultaneously, provide them with the organizational skills necessary for coordinating activities involving large and diverse groups of people. In contrast, girls' games did not teach girls to compete, to lead large groups of people autocratically, or to take a more distrustful view of participants. Girls' games taught girls empathy, sensitivity, and how to take the role of the particular other. By adolescence, girls have been clearly educated through home, school, the media, and the culture at large that compliance and dependency and interpersonal sensitivity are expected of them (Kagan and Moss 1962; Weitzman 1975).

One of the major challenges that the adolescent female faces is to confirm the worth of her interest in relationships and in so doing to develop a sense of her own self-worth as an individual (Gilligan, 1982). It follows, then, that the negative or positive value with which any culture regards relationships will affect the developing female identity. There is no doubt that girls are socialized to value relationships; the significant question is: Are girls also socialized to value the values they are given for relationships?

In the last twenty years, a shift in cultural values toward women has led to a situation that is perhaps confronting today's teenage females with a developmental double bind. By adolescence, today's girls have simultaneously been socialized to devalue the importance of relationships and to value independence and autonomy, toward which males are socialized. In evaluating the qualities that adolescents attribute to stereotypically masculine and feminine identities, Broverman and Broverman (1972) found that by the time youngsters reach adolescence, their sex-role stereotyping concerning typically female and male identities is firmly established. When asked to rate personality strengths, boys and girls (and mental health professionals) both listed typical male characteristics (strong, competent, fearless, dominant) as positive and typical female characteristics (weak, incompetent, anxious, passive) as negative. Men were valued for being rational and emotionally controlled; women were devalued for being overly emotional, sympathetic, and dependent. To be a valuable human was equated with being male, and masculinity was defined as being independent. While it is clear from previously cited findings that adolescent girls are primarily concerned with the establishment and maintenance of relationships, neither they themselves, their male peers, nor the current culture at large condones and supports their concern. How can the female adolescent value parts of herself that society suddenly teaches her to devalue?

Body image and normal female adolescent development

A similar difficulty confronts female adolescents as they struggle with the challenge of accepting and integrating their bodies at adolescence. Clearly both sexes experience some degree of anxiety, body preoccupation, and dissatisfaction (Hamburg 1974) during the dramatic physiological changes that accompany adolescence. Yet, the sociocultural influences concerning body image differ dramatically in their impact on teenage boys and girls. The processes of identity formation and body ownership seem to occur simultaneously for girls as a major catalyst for ego development.

While numerous psychodynamic interpretations have been generated concerning the anorexic's inability to accept her body as it is (Galdston 1974; Masterson 1977; Bruch 1979), the recent literature on normal female adolescent development suggests that girls are socialized to be unable to accept their bodies (Rosenbaum 1979). On the one hand, adolescence presents girls with the challenge of coming to terms with their biological bodies; at the same time, society judges girls according to their looks, and the culture encourages girls to struggle to change their bodies to fit a narrowly defined beauty ideal.

The "unrelenting pursuit of thinness" identified by Bruch (1978) as the primary symptom of anorexia nervosa seems, in part, to have its origins in the culture's transition toward a thin beauty ideal over the last twenty years (Schwartz, Thompson, and Johnson 1982). While the preoccupation with thinness in anorexia is recognized in the clinical literature as "an exaggeration and distortion which the patient has applied in a self-destructive manner" (Garner et al. 1982, 13–14), the literature on normal female development affirms that there is some reality to the emphasis girls with anorexia place on thinness, and that the symptomatic self-destructive dieting behavior is culturally supported. The tendency of clinical psychologists to view "the patient's dependence on cultural ideals for feminine body shape" (Garner et al. 1982, 37) as a pathological dependency must be reexamined in light of the cultural influences that create the female's dependency on a rigid cultural beauty ideal.

Exploring the impact of cultural standards on adolescent girls and boys, Wooley and Wooley found that the girls are more influenced by and, therefore, more vulnerable to mandated cultural standards of ideal body images (1980). Bar-Tal and Sax (1976) found that our culture places a higher value on physical beauty in the evaluation of females than males.

Fisher (1975) found that self-esteem, self-confidence, and anxiety levels fluctuate more in women depending on their body image than in men. Elder (1969) found women to be more harshly punished and judged on the basis of their bodies then men, and Clausen (1975) found a direct correlation between female adolescent body build and actual positive and negative evaluations, prestige, and relationships. Where boys are given social approval for academic success and achievement, girls are most rewarded for being slim!

Girls know that beauty is "skin deep." By age five they have been socialized to hate obesity (Wooley and Wooley 1980) and to accept a cultural standard for thinness that is dangerously close to the minimal required weight for reproduction. Rosenbaum found that where boys tend to brag more about their bodies, girls worry more and are more critical and comparative—and self-conscious. The disabling effects of the importance placed on physical appearance in females, combined with a rigid and fixed definition of beauty, can be seen in the numerous studies that demonstrate a higher amount of anxiety and discomfort experienced by female teenagers toward their bodies than by male teenagers (Clifford 1971).

As a result of this, "the adolescent female has been trained to be insecure about her body yet expected to spend some time on her appearance in a way that encourages narcissism" (Benedek 1979, 5). Rather than value what is unique and natural to the female adolescent, the culture punishes her; this is reflected in the psychology of female adolescent development, which as recently as 1970 suggests this solution as an adaptive response to menarche:

> Perhaps if girls clearly and consciously connected changes in their feeling stages to the fact of menstruation, they could at least isolate the feelings associated with premenstrual tension and define them *out of the self concept* [emphasis added]. They could say: I am not myself at this point, since I am about to menstruate and am powerfully affected by changes in my body system, this behavior *is not part of the self that is really me* [emphasis added]. (Douvan 1970, 34)

Rather than help the girl relate to her body, own her body, and live in her body in a creative way that honors the cyclical nature of women, this example magnifies the pervasive cultural reaction to females, which teaches them to deny the validity and reality of who they are as young women. In other words, it is not "healthy" or socially adaptive or rewarding for a girl to accept her body; in fact, society tells adolescent girls that to compromise on their looks is pathological.

Based on the literature on normal female development, it seems plausible to speculate that any culture that does not support the relational component of female identity development jeopardizes the healthy development of its female population. In contrast to the psychodynamic and family systems research that casts the problem of eating disorders as a failure to attain autonomy, the hypothesis explored in this research is that eating disorders have erupted in this culture because of an unhealthy and unrealistic overemphasis on autonomy in women. This hypothesis suggests that eating disorders are tied to girls' perceptions of cultural values that make it difficult for girls to integrate and value relationships.

Sample and procedure

The conflict between the relational aspects of female identity and the cultural image of the independent and autonomously achieving woman was explored through a study of thirty-two girls, ages fourteen through eighteen, attending Emma Willard School. The sample was randomly selected from a well-functioning population. The goal was to identify nonsymptomatic indicators of eating disorders. A twenty-minute semistructured clinical interview was completed, and three weeks later the participants filled out two pen-and-paper diagnostic measures.

Measures

Three criterion variables were used: the clinical interview, the Eating Attitudes Test (Garfinkel and Garner 1982), and an abbreviated version of a questionnaire developed at Wellesley College by Surrey (1982).

The twenty-minute semistructured clinical interview was part of a longitudinal study being conducted by Gilligan et al. The interviews were administered by a team of researchers who were blind to the hypothesis. The questions focused on the girls' perceptions of cultural values and cultural and individual images of women. The clinical questions did not mention anything associated with food, dieting, or eating disorders. A coding system was developed to analyze responses.

Three weeks after the clinical interviews were completed, the girls were asked to complete the Eating Attitudes Test (EAT). The EAT was chosen as the most currently reliable available psychodiagnostic measure for objective self-reporting screening for eating-disordered behavior in a nonclinical sample. "The EAT has an alpha reliability coefficient of 0.79 for anorexia nervosa patients, and 0.94 for pooled anorexic and normal controls, indicating a high degree of internal reliability" (Thompson and Schwartz 1982, 52). The EAT has recently been used by Button and Whitehouse (1981) and Thompson and Schwartz (1982) in a college setting to screen for eating-disordered behavior. Although the EAT alone is not a valid diagnostic measure for eating disorders, it may be "successfully used in a nonclinical setting to indicate the presence of disturbed eating patterns" (Garner et al. 1982, 7).

The Wellesley questionnaire was designed to assess the nature and severity of eating disorders in a random sample of normal female college freshmen. An abbreviated version of the Wellesley questionnaire (AWQ) was selected to provide additional self-reported information concerning the role of food, eating, and weight concerns among the sample. Construct validity has not been established on the AWQ; it was used as a backup to the EAT.*

Results

Clinical interview

Two distinct patterns of responses emerged in the Emma Willard girls' answers to questions concerning perceptions of societal values toward women, cultural ideal images of women, and individual ideal images of women. Sixty percent of the sample responded in the pattern labeled Wise Woman. The Wise Woman pattern involved a sequence of (1) being aware that there are new cultural expectations and values toward women and then identifying specifically the new societal values of autonomy and

---

* A coding system was established with face validity and intercoder reliability for two patterns of responses to the clinical interviews. Responses that were too brief for coding were discarded. A coding system was developed for the clinical interviews using a presence-absence analysis. Interrater reliability was established using Cohen's kappa; a mean of 83 percent coefficient of agreement was established on the two patterns.

Fisher's Exact Probability Test was chosen to compute significant differences in eating attitudes and behavior between the two patterns. Pearson product-moment correlations were computed between the EAT scores and selected AWQ items to see whether the two measures were tapping similar and related dimensions of self-reported behavior. The correlation was computed to test for consistency in self-reported data.

independent achievement in career and looks; (2) identifying the societal image that embodies these values and challenging or rejecting the image; and (3) differentiating one's own ideal image of women from the societal image and making a choice of an ideal that is self-defined and self-oriented (see table 11). Wise Women responses are marked by a clear recognition of the new societal values and expectations of autonomy, independence, and success for women and an ability to take a stand *apart* from these values and to maintain conflicting or different values that focus on the importance of interrelatedness. Inherent in the process of being able to take a stand apart from the culture is the capacity for reflective thinking about the self, which comes through in an emphasis on self-awareness.

Forty percent of the sample responded in a pattern labeled the Super Woman pattern (because of the girls' frequent use of the term "Super Woman"). The Super Woman pattern consists of (1) not identifying exclusively the new cultural values of autonomy and success in women but rather attributing to society the more traditional values of caring and sensitivity toward women and sometimes mentioning some of the newer values; (2) identifying the independent and autonomously successful Super Woman as society's ideal image; and (3) identifying *with* the societal image of the Super Woman as their own ideal image (see table 12). The primary quality that makes the Super Woman superior is her total independence from people. She is a "self-made" woman. Part of being a self-made woman in this ideal image includes remaking the body to fit a rigid beauty ideal. The image of the Super Woman is most often associated with a tall thin body, a briefcase, and a high level of independent achievement. Relationships are described more as accomplishments or appendages: For example, "She has a lover but she *doesn't need* him." Missing from the Super Woman pattern is a reflective perspective enabling the self to comment upon and criticize social convention and values.

The key difference between the two patterns centers around their visions of adulthood and what will be fulfilling. When asked to imagine their lives in the future, Super Women used a lot of superlatives: a *famous* actress, *fabulously* wealthy, a corporate *president*. This is very different from Wise Women, who talk about the future in terms of *self*; "self-fulfillment, self-satisfaction, believes in herself." Wise Women, who reject the cultural image of the Super Woman, are able to envision an ideal of adulthood that makes connectedness to self and others central. It is a vision that supports maturation. Super Women, who identify with the cultural image of an autonomous, independent woman, are unable to hold for themselves a vision of adulthood that integrates the relational aspect of themselves. For them, maturation becomes a process of loss, not gain.

EAT and AWQ

All of the Wise Women girls scored in the noneating-disordered range on the EAT, and eleven of the twelve Super Women girls scored in the eating-disordered range on the EAT. The one Super Woman girl who did not score in the eating-disordered range, scored in the anorexic-like range identified by Thompson and Schwartz (1982). The AWQ results suggest that the average student was within five to ten pounds of her ideal weight. Wise Women were significantly less concerned about their ideal body weight (m = 3.06 on t-tests) or how weight affected their self-image (m = 3.11) than Super Women (ms = 4.08 and 4.33, respectively). For example, significant mean differences were found between Wise Women and Super Women on being preoccupied with being thinner (t = 2.61, p = .05) as well as being preoccupied with fat on their bodies (t = 2.97, p = .01). Wise Women also report eating significantly less diet foods than Super Women (t = 3.04, p = .05) as well as engaging in less dieting behavior (t = 2.22, p = .05). Furthermore, Wise Women less frequently reported comparing how they look to others (t = 2.25, p = .05) and worrying about how they looked (t = 4.63, p = .001) than Super Women. Overall, Wise Women reported only marginally significant less concern with their eating habits, however, (m = 3.17) than did Super Women (m = 3.91).

The central finding of this research is that girls who are able to identify contemporary cultural values and ideal images of women that are unsupportive of core female adolescent developmental needs and who are also able to reject these values in choosing their own female ideal image are not prone to eating disorders. Girls who are unable to identify the societal values that are detrimental to their developmental needs, and who identify with the ideal image that is projected by these values, are at risk for developing eating disorders.

This interpretation highlights a sequence in which cultural values are perceived as influencing eating behavior. Although it is equally possible that values resulting from eating disorders could affect girls' perceptions of cultural values, this interpretation will focus on the possible influence cultural values have on eating disorders.

This data can begin to address the theoretical question of whether a continuum exists between normal female adolescent development and the development of eating disorders. The results confirm the findings reported in the literature—that it is normal for today's female teenagers to be concerned with their weight. However, the consistent differences in responses of Wise Women and Super Women to questions about eating behavior indicate that when thinness and dieting become associated with an image of women that is based on autonomy and that is not relational, girls become increasingly at risk for the development of eating disorders. In other words, Wise Women are concerned about their weight and looks but not in a way that leads them to eating-disordered behavior. It seems safe to speculate that their concern is more directed toward boys and the social arena and is thus linked to psychosocial development. In contrast, Super Women seem to associate thinness with autonomy, success, and recognition for independent achievement, which represent a specific cluster of new cultural values toward women. It is a vision of autonomy and independence that excludes connection to others and a reflective relationship with oneself. This preliminary study suggests that a continuum from normal female adolescent development to the development of eating disorders may exist when thinness and normal dieting becomes symbolically tied to autonomous career achievement and a denial of the importance of and need for interpersonal relationships. In this light, it is possible that eating disorders emerge at adolescence because it is at this point in development when females experience themselves to be at a crossroads in their lives where they must shift from a relational approach to life to an autonomous one—a shift that can represent an intolerable loss when independence is associated with isolation.

The body politic

In order to speculate further about the association between thinness and autonomy, it is useful to consider some research from the field of comparative anthropology. Contemporary psychology portrays the current preoccupation with thinness, self-starving, and bingeing and purging as a unique, wholly contemporary explosion of a modern psychopathological problem. Anorexia, meaning lack of appetite and absence of hunger, was first described by Gull and LaSegue in 1873. However, anorexia nervosa is a misnomer, for the syndrome is not marked by an absence of hunger or a lack of appetite but rather by a willingness and desire to deny one's appetite and stomach-hunger in order to *fast* for a prolonged period of time. Once labeled anorexia nervosa, the connection between anorexic behavior and fasting gradually disappeared. As a result, the psychological theories that have explored the motivations for anorexia through a clinical and pathological lens have been time-, race-, and class-limited and disconnected from the extensive universal history of individuals and large groups of people fasting and starving themselves willfully. By only focusing on the individuals and their families, the clinical psychology literature has obscured from itself the culture that gives meaning to fasting (weight loss) and feasting in females.

Similarly, the "unrelenting pursuit of thinness" (Bruch 1978) that symbolizes anorexia has been virtually unexplored beyond the obvious connection to the fashion industry. It is insufficient to say we are a culture obsessed by thinness and to accept passively the fashion industry as the sole cultural context from which eating disorders spring. It is essential that possible underlying psychological, political, and cultural motivations that produce the fashion industry and foster the cultural obsession be further explored by looking at the past and the present.

There is nothing new about the image of a wasted body; nor is there anything new or totally unusual about individuals or groups of people starving themselves. Remember Gandhi's "fasts unto death," the Irish Republican Army prisoners' hunger strikes. Whether for magical, spiritual, social, agriculture, or political reasons, "man has been and continues to be willing to renounce foods which are pleasant and agreeable to him at all ordinary times, in order that he may prevent certain contingent results following upon his indulgence in them" (Hastings 1912, 760). A unique feature of today's widespread fasting is that it began among females who are often financially comfortable and well-educated, as well as females who appear to be marked for success.

There is an intriguing connection between the emphasis on the relationships found in the literature on normal female adolescent development, and the symbolism associated with the female body in the field of comparative anthropology. Universally, the rounded female body has symbolically represented the value of relationships in life, the interrelatedness and interdependency of people (Neumann 1955).The most obvious symbol is that of the full-breasted, wide-hipped, and pregnant "Great Mother."

Using the body as a "body politic" to make a political, social, or spiritual statement via fasting and self-starving behavior (including the use of emetics and laxatives) seems to be closely connected with the human condition. By body politic, I mean the use of the body as a political statement, promoting a policy via the body: for example, fasting for a hunger strike, the long hair on men in the 1960s, homosexual men piercing an ear.

If we look at the collective phenomenon of starving young middle- and upper-class girls in this culture as a body politic instead of a body pathology, the emaciated females become a symbol of a culture that does not support female development or the value of relationships, which is central to the adolescent girl's identity. The image of the adolescent as a mirror of societal imbalances is not new (Gilligan 1982). "To view the elements of society to which the adolescent must adjust is also to view the problems of adolescent development" (Erikson 1968, 128). In the culture that denies and devalues the principles of sharing, caring, and interrelatedness—what Gilligan has labeled "The Different Voice" (1982)—that are symbolically associated with the rounded female breasts and belly, the adolescent girls collide with the cultural norm and deny developing these symbolic parts of their body. In this context it seems possible that anorexia nervosa is a natural outgrowth of a culture that outcasts that which is most important to its female population and does so in a symbolic idealization of thinness in women. And it is a form of protest adopted by the adolescent who finds, for whatever reasons, that her voice is silenced.

Looking at today's large-scale fasting in light of the traditions and universal purposes that have motivated people to fast throughout time, it appears that eating disorders, which affect a particular population at a specific developmental era, closely resemble fasting undertaken by adolescents at a period of initiation. The prolonged fasting, which prevents the initiation and transition into young adulthood, further resembles a hunger strike undertaken by a group who have a vision of impending calamity and danger.

On a cultural level, these adolescent truth tellers may be carrying a critical vision—some literally dying to communicate it—about the impoverishment of a culture: a culture that does not nourish itself by valuing interrelatedness. Our culture has a mythic image of independence that does not include interdependence. This is most frighteningly clear in our government's proposal of an independent and isolated nuclear war that would theoretically not endanger America. From looking at the universal symbolism associated with the female body, and from numerous conversations with adolescent females who have various kinds of eating-related problems, a consistent picture has emerged: On a personal level, in their familial relationships, these girls have suffered from the kinds of unempathic, emotionally distant, and simultaneously enmeshed family relationships described in the clinical literature (Bruch 1978; Geist forthcoming). Equally important to them and as profoundly disturbing is each girl's vision of how her family situation is a miniature reflection of an equally disturbed culture. It is important to emphasize in stressing the pathology of the culture with respect to female development and in suggesting that it is difficult to explain the current rise in eating disorders without considering cultural factors that this chapter does not imply that eating disorders are simply the result of cultural forces. Rather, it indicates how pathological patterns of experiences within the family and pathological values in the culture join. It is precisely because the family and culture mirror each other that the Super Women have difficulty finding a critical perspective. In an enmeshed family system, growing up is often associated with betrayal and isolation; for the girl with anorexia nervosa, such differentiation from mother and father is often feared as a loss of connection, a paradigm that parallels the cultural bias that defines adulthood in terms of independence and not interdependence.

Girls with eating disorders have a heightened, albeit confused, grasp of the dangerous imbalance of the culture's values, which they cannot articulate in the face of the culture's abject denial of their adolescent, intuitive truth; so they tell their story with their bodies. Perhaps, on a *cultural* level, theirs is a story about the enormous difficulties of growing up female in a culture that does not value the feminine "voice," which speaks about relationships and the importance of interdependence. The girls will not break their fast until they are sure they can gain adulthood without the loss of their relational values.

Table 11

Wise Woman Responses

(Thinking about our society today, what do you think society values in women?)

Oh, well. This is I think the eighties. In the early eighties and the late seventies, they have developed the idea of the superwoman. And now this woman, she's incredible. Not only does she have a gorgeous husband, but she also has three beautiful children who attend nursery school; she is beautiful herself. She's in perfect shape, and at the same time, she is making $50,000 a year.

(What is society's image of the ideal woman?)

By society's standards? *(Yes)* A liberated woman who's not like all-the-way liberated, like Gloria Steinem and pro-ERA, like a rally-type person, but like independent. A working woman who's gone to college and has a good job and like doesn't need a husband or someone to support them, but like, have or want one. *(What does she look like?)* Like pretty perfect. *(What would make her perfect?)* Well, not in my standards, but what seems more on society's standards, sort of the type person that is sort of tall, skinny, and like long hair, whatever, short hair, bobbed hair, and pretty. Whatever ... society is more concerned with how they look on the outside than how they really are, and if they are really happy or not.

(What is your own image of the ideal woman?)

I guess what would be important to her, like relationships with other people, and I guess, you know, partly what decisions she makes. How is that going to affect other people, and not society, but people you are close to. The inner person is important to her, not what people look like.

Table 12

Super Woman Responses

(Thinking about our society today, what do you think society values in women?)

I think they value their ability, their gentleness, and their soft-spokenness.

(What is society's image of the ideal woman?)

All right, she would be successful in something, like a doctor or lawyer, something that really has status or something like that. And she has to be really beautiful, which means being slim and tall, and she would be married and maybe have children, I'd say, and I can just see her breezing into the office, or having a business meeting and just being very put together and knowing what she wants. The most important thing to her is being successful in everything—being successful in her marriage and her work and being beautiful—it all has to be.

(What is your own image of the ideal woman?)

The way you see models and everything . . . maybe the person you wish that you could be. The gorgeous lady that had perfect grades in school and went to all the right schools and knew all the right people and just had the best job and did everything right. And I think that is a real honest picture.

Sources

Bar-Tal, D. and Saxe, L. 1976. Physical attractiveness and its relationship to sex-role stereotyping. *Sex Roles* 2:123-133.

Benedek, E. P. 1979. "Dilemmas in Research on Female Adolescent Development." In *Female Adolescent Development*, edited by M. Sugar. New York: Brunner/Mazel.

Broverman, I., P. Broverman, S. R. Vogel, F. E. Clarkson, and P. S. Rosenkrantz. 1972. Sex role stereotypes: A current appraisal. *Journal of Social Issues* 28:56–78.

Bruch, H. 1979. "Anorexia Nervosa." In S. Feinstein and P. Giovacchini, *Adolescent Psychiatry*. Vol. 5 of *Development and Clinical Studies*. New York: Jason Aronson.

———. 1978. *The Golden Cage: The Enigma of Anorexia Nervosa*. Cambridge: Harvard University Press.

Burdwick, J., E. Douvan, M. Horner, and D. Gutman. 1970. *Feminine Personality and Conflict*. Belmont, Calif.: Wadsworth Publishing.

Button, A. J., and A. Whitehouse. 1981. Subclinical anorexia nervosa. *Psychological Medicine* 2:509–16.

Chodorow, N. 1974. "Family Structure and Feminine Personality." In *Women: Culture and Society*, edited by M. Rosaldo and L. Lamphere. Stanford, Calif.: Stanford University Press.

———. 1978. *The Reproduction of Mothering: Psychoanalysis and the Sociology of Mothering*. Berkeley: University of California Press.

Clausen, J. A. 1975. "The Social Meaning of Differential Physical and Sexual Maturation. In *Adolescence in the Life Cycle*, edited by S. E. Dragastur and G. H. Elder, Jr. New York: Halstead.

Clifford, E. 1971. Body satisfaction in adolescence. *Journal of Perceptual and Motor Skills* 33:119–25.

Crisp. A. H. 1980. *Anorexia Nervosa: Let Me Be*. New York: Academic Press, Grune and Stratton.

Douvan, E. 1970. "New Sources of Conflict in Females at Adolescence and Early Adulthood." In *Feminine Personality and Conflict*, edited by Burdwick, et al. Belmont, Calif.: Wadsworth.

Douvan, E., and J. Adelson. 1966. *The Adolescent Experience*. New York: John Wiley.

Ehrenreich, B., and D. English. 1979. *For Her Own Good: 150 Years of the Experts' Advice on Women*. New York: Anchor Books.

Elder, G. H. 1969. Appearance and education in marriage mobility. *American Sociological Review* 34:519–33.

Erikson, E. 1968. *Identity, Youth and Crisis*. New York: W. W. Norton.

Fisher, S. A. 1975. *Body Consciousness*. New York: Jason Aronson.

Freud, A. 1968. "The Role of Bodily Illness in the Mental Life of Children." In *The Writings of Anna Freud* Vol. 4. New York: International Universities Press, 260–79.

Galdston, R. 1974. Mind over matter: Observations on 50 patients hospitalized with anorexia nervosa. *Journal of the American Academy of Child Psychiatry* 13:246–63.

Gallatin, J. 1975. *Adolescence and Individuality: A Conceptual Approach to Adolescent Psychology*. New York: Harper and Row.

Garfinkel, P., and D. Garner. 1982. *Anorexia Nervosa: A Multidimensional Perspective*. New York: Brunner/Mazel.

Garner, D. M., P. E. Garfinkel, and K. M. Bernis. 1982. A multidimensional psychotherapy for anorexia nervosa. *International Journal of Eating Disorders* 1:24.

Geist, R. Therapeutic dilemmas in the treatment of anorexia nervosa: A self-psychology perspective. Forthcoming.

Gilligan, C. 1985. Female development in adolescence: Implications for theory. Unpublished manuscript. Harvard University.

———. 1986. Remapping development: The power of divergent data. Forthcoming.

———. 1977. In a different voice: Women's conceptions of the self and of morality. *Harvard Educational Review* 47: 481–517.

———. 1979. Woman's place in man's life cycle. *Harvard Educational Review* 29(4).

———. 1982. *In a Different Voice*. Cambridge: Harvard University Press.

Goodsitt, A. 1979. "Narcissistic Disturbances in Anorexia Nervosa." In *Adolescent Psychiatry*. Vol. 5 of *Developmental and Clinical Studies*, edited by Feinstein and Giovacchini. New York: Jason Aronson.

Gray, S. 1977. Social aspects of body image: Perceptions of normalcy of weight and affect on college undergraduates. *Journal of Perceptual and Motor Skills* 45:1035–40.

Gull, W. W. 1873. Anorexia nervosa (apepsia hysteria, anorexia hysteria). *Transactions of the Clinical Society of London* 7:22–28.

Hamburg, B. 1974. Early adolescence: The specific and stressful stage of the life cycle. In *Coping and Adaptation*, edited by G. Coelho, D. A. Hamburg, and J. E. Adams. New York: Basic Books.

Josselson, R. 1973. Psychodynamic aspects of identity formation in college women. *Journal of Youth and Adolescence* 2(1):3–52.

Kaufman, M. 1965. *Evolution of Psychosomatic Concepts: Anorexia Nervosa, a Paradigm*. London: Hogarth Press.

Kagan, J. 1964. "Acquisition and Significance of Sex Typing and Sex Role Identity." In *Review of Child Development Research* Vol. 1, edited by M. L. Hoffman and L. W. Hoffman. New York: Russell Sage Foundation, pp. 137–67.

Kagan, J. and H. A. Moss. 1983. *Birth to Maturity*. New Haven, Conn.: Yale University Press.

Kohlberg, L., and C. Gilligan. 1971. The adolescent as a philosopher. *Daedalus* 100.

Lasaque, C. 1873. "De L'anorexie hystérique." In *Evolution of Psychosomatic Concepts: Anorexia Nervosa, a Paradigm*, edited by R. M. Kaufman and M. Heiman. New York: International Universities Press.

Laufer, M. 1968. The body image, the function of masturbation, and adolescence: Problem of ownership of the body. *Psychoanalytic Study of the Child* 23:114–37.

Lever, J. 1976. Sex differences in the games children play. *Social Problems* 23:478–87.

Masterson, J. F. 1977. Primary anorexia nervosa in the borderline adolescent: An object-relations view. In *Borderline Personality Disorders: The Concept, The Syndrome, The Patient*, edited by P. Martocollis. New York: International Universities Press.

Marcia, J. 1980. "Identity in Adolescence." In *Handbook of Adolescent Psychology*, edited by J. Adelson. New York: John Wiley.

Minuchin, S., B. Rosman, and L. Baker. 1978. *Psychosomatic Families: Anorexia Nervosa in Context*. Cambridge: Harvard University Press.

Neumann, E. 1955. *The Great Mother*. Princeton, N.J.: Bollingenin Foundation, Princeton University Press.

Rosenbaum, M. B. 1979. "The Changing Body Image of the Adolescent Girl. In *Female Adolescent Development*, edited by M. Sugar, pp. 234–53.

Rothchild, E. 1979. "Female Power: Lines to Development of Autonomy. In *Female Adolescent Development*, edited by M. Sugar, 274–96.

Schwartz, D., M. Thompson, and C. Johnson. 1982. Anorexia nervosa and bulimia, the socio-cultural context. *International Journal of Eating Disorders* 1:20–36.

Sherman, J. A. 1971. *On the Psychology of Women: A Survey of Empirical Studies*. Springfield, Ill.: Charles C. Thomas.

Steiner-Adair, C. 1984. The body politic: Normal female adolescent development and the development of eating disorders. Ed.D. diss., Harvard Graduate School of Education.

Sugar, M. 1979. *Female Adolescent Development*. New York: Brunner/Mazel.

Thompson, M. and D. Schwartz. Winter 1982. Life adjustment of women with anorexia nervosa and anorexic-like behavior. *International Journal of Eating Disorders*.

Weitzman, L. 1975. "Sex Role Socialization. In *Women: A Feminist Perspective*, edited by J. Freeman. Palo Alto: Mayfield Publishers.

Wooley, S. C., and O. W. Wooley. 1980. "Eating Disorders, Obesity and Anorexia." In *Women and Psychotherapy*, edited by A. Brodsky and R. Hare-Mustin. New York: Guilford Press, pp. 135–59.

Competencies and Visions
Emma Willard Girls Talk about Being Leaders

NONA P. LYONS, JANE FORBES SALTONSTALL,
AND TRUDY J. HANMER

Editors' Note: *In 1983, at the request of some members of the Emma Willard faculty and with the support of the Helena Rubinstein Foundation, a special study of leadership was conducted with a small sample of girls, including both leaders and nonleaders at the school.*

When psychologist David McClelland was putting together a study of power in human relationships, he tried to develop a way of measuring people's power needs and their ways of using power, as previously he had measured people's need for achievement (McClelland 1975). But when McClelland found that women, unlike the men of his sample, clustered in one place on a scale—indicating, according to the psychological measure, less "maturity" about power than men—he questioned if something was wrong (wrong, that is, with the measure—not with his subjects). Redirecting his analyses and constructing a new instrument, one incorporating women's experiences, McClelland ultimately concluded that there were differences in the ways men and women thought about and used power. McClelland's work suggests at least two things: that how people think about and use any competence may vary in important ways and that there is a need to be attentive to how psychological categories of analysis and interpretation are developed and to ask if the experiences of girls and women are included in them.

This chapter reports on a study of leadership in Emma Willard girls carried out as a special exploration of the Dodge Study at Emma Willard School. The purpose was to identify how a sample of adolescent girls think about and act as leaders. Twenty-two students at Emma Willard School, girls in actual leadership positions, participated in the study, along with twenty-six nonleaders. Through a semistructured, open-ended interview, girls responded to questions about leadership, including: What does leadership mean to you? What is the best thing a leader can do? the worst thing? When you think about voting someone in this school into a leadership position, what kinds of things do you consider? Girls in leadership positions answered additional questions, identifying typical conflicts they encountered as leaders and describing in detail how they actually dealt with them. In analyzing these data, two tasks were primary: to describe girls' ideas about leadership; and, then, to begin to categorize them. In particular, competencies of girls holding leadership positions were identified and examined.

This way of proceeding seems appropriate given the cautions from McClelland's work and state-of-the-art studies of adolescent girls as leaders. Remarkably, at a time of increased numbers of women in the work place as well as in leadership positions, leadership studies of girls are few (Nichols 1984; Winterbottom 1988) as are systematic studies of women leaders (Kotter 1982; Carroll 1984; Kellerman 1984). Further, Nichols (1984) found that most available studies of school leaders focus not on the experiences of students as leaders but almost exclusively on the relationship between leadership and such factors as birth order, academic achievement, and so forth. In the best and most extensive study of adolescents—by Douvan and Adelson (1966)—leadership was not included. In all, Adelson's assessment in a review of research on adolescent girls seems starkly accurate, that is, that: "Adolescent girls have simply not been much studied" (Adelson 1980). Descriptive studies of girls as leaders are urgently needed so that categories of interpretation drawn from girls' experience can be created.

Recent research on adult leaders supports this approach. It argues that one way to understand effective managers and leaders is to document their actual practices (Argyris 1976; Drucker 1982; Burns 1978; Levinson 1978; Stogdill 1977; Kotter 1982). Fewer prescriptions and more descriptions of leaders are needed, Burns asserts (1978). Boyatzis, a colleague of McClelland's, analyzing several studies of what managers actually said and did as leaders, developed a model that defined the competencies they used in their day-to-day functioning (Boyatzis 1980; Klemp 1982; Huff, Klemp, and Winter 1980). This method of deriving competencies from the practices of acting leaders served in this work as a guide to delineating Emma Willard girls' leadership competencies.

In the analysis of Emma Willard girls' responses to questions about leadership, a set of ideas emerged around two different conceptions of leadership, referred to here as leadership modes. Each mode points to different values and assumptions about leadership, and each has a set of related competencies—goals, strategies, and skills. These modes—called the leader as interdependent and the leader as autonomous—present two ways of being a leader, each with its own logic. Each uses a range of similar competencies but expresses them with different emphases. And while these leadership modes are not mutually exclusive, each describes a characteristic way of being a leader derived from girls' ideas. Here the two ideas of leadership are presented through girls' reports of their leadership experiences so that the connections between girls' ideas about leadership and their actual behaviors may be made explicit.

This chapter does three things. It first describes Emma Willard girls' ideas about leadership and presents the two leadership modes. Then, using case studies of actual situations of conflict reported by Emma Willard leaders, these modes are examined and explored, especially as they indicate approaches to conflict negotiation and problem solving. A model of the two leadership modes with their competencies, skills, and interpersonal processes is presented. Finally, this essay discusses the implications of this work, especially for thinking about the education of girls for leadership. In this discussion, Emma Willard student leaders and leaders in other high schools are compared through reference to new research modeled after the Emma Willard leadership study (Garrod et al. 1988). In particular, competencies of school leaders are compared.

The leader as interdependent

Some people say they are doers and others are just talkers, and the leaders, they listen to what other people want and then they go out and do it. That's what I think a leader is.

Thus characterizing what makes someone a leader in her view, a young high school student, Sarah, begins to identify her ideas about leadership. Focusing on the leader as a "listener," Sarah talks first about how listening plays a role in her conception of leadership. When asked, What is the best thing a leader can do? she elaborates:

I guess to be open-minded, like listening. . . . You don't want to be following one thing, you want to see other views . . . because there is no one way, there is no one opinion, there is no right thing. And everyone has different opinions and that is the most important thing for a leader, she has to take that into account.

Seeing that there is "no one opinion" or "right thing" to do, the leader must acknowledge differences. It follows for this student that the worst thing a leader can do would be:

Not listen and not do what her group members want her to do, or to do what she thinks is best for them. . . . She [would be] doing it for herself . . . not for the other members. And that is why she is there, to work for them, not for herself.

When the interviewer urges her to elaborate, to explain what you learn from listening to someone, Sarah—herself a school leader—responds, revealing what is at work for her when a leader is listening:

I think I learn how to become open to new ideas. And I think I learn the importance of talking to people and of communication and of representing other people and of making people happy or something. Not making people happy but making people feel like something has been accomplished and like they have done something and not just one person has done it, but everyone has done it together. Because every opinion has been taken into consideration and everyone has helped and everyone's perspective and views are taken in. . . . Because every idea, everyone gives in ideas and you don't take a single idea completely. You take bits and pieces of every idea and you incorporate it into one big idea that people can still recognize. Like, they will see something and [think], I thought that, I gave in that idea. Even if it is not completely whole they still know their partial thought is there.

Learning from listening seems to involve "seeing" as well. Sarah continues:

Since we are used to our own ways, it is so hard for other people to change us; and listening and seeing and just watching other people—listening to other people's opinions—we get to see two sides to them.

Here, Sarah identifies a set of interrelated ideas that present a logic of leadership. The leader, assuming differences among people and by listening and talking to others, takes in "the bits and pieces of everyone's ideas" to incorporate them into a new plan—one, however, recognizable to its contributors. Such a leader is there to work with others. Although attentive to others' ideas, this leader must also strengthen and expand her own ways of seeing things. This conceptualization of leadership will influence a number of interpersonal and decision-making processes. Other Emma Willard students expand these ideas.

For example, listening to people is not simply a way of being polite. Rather, it becomes the basis for decision making. As another student declares: "You listen to what other people have to say and take all those things into regard and decide then what is going to happen."

In decision making such a leader is someone who needs another skill—patience. One girl explains:

> You have to be patient because you have to listen to what everyone thinks before you make a decision. And it takes a lot of time for things to get done, and what you thought was something that everyone would immediately like, there are a lot of people who won't like it, who want to discuss it. And even though you think this is such a wonderful idea, you start to listen to their reasoning.

This activity of listening engages, too, an intellectual process: following the reasoning of another. And for those leaders who follow this style of building goals and visions by listening for others' ideas, it is demanding in another way: It is time-consuming.

In this idea of leadership, the leader is not quite the representative of others in the sense of one deputized to act for another. Rather, the leader stands with others, acting as the integrator of their ideas, facilitating their working together. The leader must, as this student suggests, see herself as part of "we":

> I think that the best thing a leader can do would be to involve herself in the group that she's leading and when she talks to them not to say "you" but to say "we" and not make such a separation between I'm the leader and you're the followers, just that it's we. . . . Because if someone stands up in front of a group of people and says: 'You should be doing this' and 'You should be doing that,' they are going to resent it and then it is going to be harder to gain respect. You have to have people's respect to get things done, because people won't listen otherwise. The worst thing a leader can do is to say You—to make that separation.

The idea of facilitating people's working together can turn into a leadership goal when it is enabling of a leader's vision. For example, a class president reports:

I just had certain goals for the class to be at by the end of this year.
Just to be more of a class, everybody to know each other, to have
raised a certain amount of money. . . . I think that by senior year,
when you are a senior, that drives the class together by itself. But
I think [in] the classes here, it is important to be able to work with
people your age and get things accomplished. And it just adds
another aspect to the school, to have classes that are closely knit. . . .
Not necessarily everybody has to be friends with each other, just
that when we have class meetings that everybody gets a chance to
say something and everybody listens to other people, and that everybody knows each other. . . . the senior class has to get a lot of things
done, such as put on seniors-in-concert, certain dinners for juniors,
and things like that. And it just makes it a whole lot easier if
everyone knows each other.

Similarly, this leader deals with exclusion:

A leader is someone who listens, who . . . doesn't exclude anyone.
The worst thing a leader can do is shut out other people, not listen,
do only what they want . . . not what the people [they] are working
for want.

In a mode that prizes "listening" and collaborative decision making,
these strategies become, in turn, criteria for voting for school leaders. In
response to the question "When you think about voting for someone in
this school, what kinds of things do you take into consideration," one
girl says:

I mainly base it on, I see it as: She listens to people, she is not
narrow-minded, and—those two, I think, is what I base it on . . .
and a good sense of humor, I think. If they are really going to work
hard. If this is something they really want to do. And, you know,
if they are willing to listen to others. . . .

Thus a logic is evident that extends from a set of ideas about leadership
to goals, assumptions, and skills. The fundamental assumption is of
differences—that people are likely to be different and to hold different
opinions. Plans of action emerge from the careful encouragement of a
group's participation in articulating and "voicing" these differences and

their ideas. In that process, listening is an activity of competency—following the reasoning of people, weighing ideas against other ideas, including one's own, and developing new options. This way of thinking—which has been identified as characteristic of divergent thinkers (those who think tangentially, not first converging on one line of reasoning)—is just one of the intellectual skills required of this mode. At work, as well, are other competencies: diagnosing and recognizing different components of ideas; interpreting discrete ideas so that they can become part of larger plans of action; synthesizing the ideas of others; and perhaps most importantly, having a stance toward the self that allows the leader to hear and encourage others, not at her own expense, but with a special sense of relation to them as a leader. This model of leadership is termed the leader as interdependent.

Strengths and vulnerabilities

While there are strengths within this mode of leadership, there are also potential "vulnerabilities." One issue explored here is how to interpret girls' leadership choices. Although not fully articulated in these data, the questions of how and for whom one is a leader need to be better understood. For example, comparing what it is like to be a class officer with being a proctor, one young Emma Willard student, Alison, articulates why she would like to change her leadership role from class officer to hall proctor:

> I decided that I really don't like the politics of the school, or maybe I don't like politics in general. I have never been involved in politics, so I don't know, but it's just, everything is so harsh, and people's feelings just, they don't get considered, when you work with the administration and there are so many rules. . . . And so it gets very frustrating. . . . It also gets frustrating to work with one hundred people at a time, because when you work with one hundred people, it's hard to reach people individually. And so . . . it's almost artificial when you are standing up there in front of a hundred people and telling them things and trying to get everybody's opinions, because you are not going to get everybody's opinions. And so I thought as a proctor, I would have to work with twenty people at the most, so it would be much more individual. And I wouldn't have to . . . although I am going to have to worry about rules on the hall, they are not major rules of the school. They don't have to do with

academics and units and graduation and all that. And it's more involved, when someone has a problem now in the class, it is usually about money or something like that. But being a proctor, the problems you are faced with, other people's problems, are usually personal—like friendship and things—and so I would rather work like individually.

In her analysis, Alison rejects one position of leadership for another, opting for an "individual" way of working rather than the schoolwide one. While one interpretation of her choice is some fear of the power and politics of a large-scale leadership role, (Horner 1968), there is also another interpretation: that is, that this young woman is not rejecting leadership, rather she is deciding how she will lead and with whom she will work (Sassen 1980). Working in a smaller, face-to-face role might enable her to enact a way of being a leader she values. In this light, Alison's decision stems from a sense of her own set of values and efficacy. Seen in this way personal preference may well be a matter of judgment, a young woman's "political" judgment. But most important is understanding more fully just how girls think about politics and power.

The leader as autonomous

I would consider someone a leader, not that takes the trust of people, but that people will put their trust in. . . . Leaders serve a purpose . . . either to accomplish something for the group of people, that one person has to maneuver something or manipulate something or do something. I mean a leader as opposed to anarchy, that kind of thing. . . . If you would take control, or allow them to give you control of the situation or the project, you would then be able to tell them the reasons why you are doing it, in a way that they will understand.

In contrast to the mode of leadership already described, the leader as interdependent, there is a second idea of leadership present in the ideas of Emma Willard girls: that is, the leader as "autonomous." While sharing, in part, many concerns of leadership that echo those of the "interdependent" mode, there are within this second mode different emphases. These emphases suggest different underlying assumptions and values. This mode of leadership is not found as frequently in the voices of this sample of adolescent girls as is the interdependent one, the predominant mode identified within the Emma Willard group. However, it is possible to sketch the autonomous mode, holding for future research the task of fully articulating and elaborating how both modes overlap or interact.

In the "autonomous" mode of leadership, the leader characteristically is one who acts or is delegated to act for others. Emphasis is on the autonomy of a leader. There is in this mode attention to task, to the achievement of a goal or purpose, or the solution of some problem. Attention can focus on the role or job or the responsibilities of the job as well as the individual. The best thing a leader can do is achieve some goal of the people she represents and by so doing to represent well. As one girl explains:

> Whether it be a small situation or a big situation . . . if you look at friends, sometimes there is a person that will—and I don't include aggressiveness or pushiness—there is often a person that people will kind of place some kind of trust in. [I would define trust as being] willing to give some kind of responsibility to . . . feeling comfortable giving some kind of responsibility to somehow.

In the psychology of this mode of leadership, the leader is one who can "handle the responsibility," but also "delegate responsibility" and mobilize people and events to get things done. As one student puts it:

> Someone who is a leader is someone who can take the responsibility for themselves and others and make decisions that would be in the best interests of the group of people and themselves in a way that lets people see what's right and gives them a direction to go with those ideas.

In part, the best thing this leader can do "is to make her constituency feel that . . . something has been changed, or solved. . . ." Similarly, in the logic of this mode, the worst thing a leader can do is:

> Just be a bad leader, be ineffective. And even if there are many times here when leaders take matters into their own hands and say 'I don't give a damn what the whole student body thinks, this is what I think and this is what I am going to do,' and that's fine. . . .

As another student, Terry, emphasizes, there is a particular way of thinking about the self for this kind of leader. She sees the self as effective. Terry describes this:

> The worst thing a leader can do is just be ineffective. . . . You've got to at least do things on time, hand things in on time, even if there are things only you believe in and nobody else does. You owe it to yourself, because obviously . . . usually leader positions are elected positions, and so you owe it to the people who voted for you and you yourself to be at least effective and do things on time even if those things don't represent the opinions of who you represent. . . .

For Terry, then, organization and efficiency must be valued as well as the individual's independent decision making. The worst thing a leader can do is:

> Be ineffective. I mean that strictly in the clerical sense. I mean just getting notices on time and putting things in mailboxes . . . because [if you are not efficient] then the whole structure falls apart. If you don't get the minutes of the last proposal typed up, then the whole thing is rendered inoperable. . . . Even if you have a proposal that not everybody else agrees with, I mean, that doesn't make as much difference as if there [were] no proposal, no minutes, no nothing, you know. [If] you didn't reserve this room for a meeting at 3 o'clock, then there is no place to meet. And I have seen people who have no charisma and personality as leaders, who do things that a lot of people don't like, but they get things done. And for that, their organization works.

In part, as one girl says, "leadership quality is organization," but it is also "being able to get [people] together and have [them] get interested in [you]" and your assessment of what to do. The leader is one who can take control of a situation and deal with it. For example, as one leader explains:

> If there is a group of people involved, to make them first stop and then look at what's going on and make them understand where you stand and why you think that's the way it should be. And to

organize something that would benefit them or solve their problems, or bring about a solution to the situation, or a new situation.

Those students who represent the autonomous mode of leadership believe that the leader is one, too, who has a vision: "They have wanted to do something for their community and have gone out of their way to make it happen." What "happens" may, in part, be a factor of the goal of the individual leader or her ability to be an entrepreneur:

> One of my friends, she made up a group, the [x] club here and she elected herself president of it, because she wanted it to happen. Because she was interested in it, she organized it as a club.

This leader has a purpose in knowing how to deal with people, for in this model the leader stands in a special relationship to her constituents. She often needs certain interpersonal skills, for example, to be persuasive:

> And if you know how to deal with different kinds of people and you know basically how different people think, or just watch the way they think, then you can make them understand what you are trying to get across. And it would be easier for them to follow you, if you would take control or allow them to give you control of the situation or the project. You would be able to tell them the reasons why you are doing it, in a way that they will understand.

Within this mode of leadership it is not surprising that there is concern, too, for the use and abuse of power. The interviewer asks, What makes someone a leader in your eyes? A student leader responds: "Someone that can handle the responsibility, that can deal with, that can hold an office and not go on a power trip."

Another student echoes similar ideas. She wants a leader to "make sure that they are actually leading the people that they are representing and not just carrying out their own whims or whatever."

The worst thing a leader can do is to "respond to their personal interests." The leader must "remember that he/she is no better than anybody else," and similarly a leader must not "forget who elected you and why and what for."

In this mode, the values one places on leadership become, as well, the criteria for voting others into leadership positions. The interviewer asks, When you think of voting for someone in this school into a leadership position, what kinds of things do you consider? A student responds: "How responsible they are, how would they fit in this job."

Another student differentiates job competency from personal charisma:

> I would vote for who I thought was best qualified. . . . I would say even though she is a schmuck, she will get things done. So I will vote for her. You know, rather than someone who is very charismatic and everybody likes and who I may like personally but they don't really do a very good job as a leader . . . because I have seen friends who I elected into leadership roles, and I kind of realized when I voted for them that they weren't really the best people for that role. . . . and I have seen them really mess up and there are girls whom I haven't liked . . . but who would have done a good job. . . . [So, I will vote for them.]

The logic of this leadership mode, then, emphasizes the individual as responsible, representative, skilled in organizational ability, and—demonstrating competencies necessary in the execution of leadership—being efficient and creative. There can also be an emphasis on strategies:

> . . . I like to listen to people and I find that the more I curb myself from going out after hearing people—going out and running into the administration's doors and pounding on them and saying, I have this and this to say—but keeping cool is one of my, I think, biggest assets as a leader. I am very willing to compromise . . . I will compromise to all ends of the earth to get anything accomplished. And when the administration gives me an argument . . . I will listen to them and I will say, I can see your point, and I will try to see their point.

Compromise is just one kind of leadership strategy. While it is important to stress that this strategy does not exhaust those possible to this mode, it is a strategy that is identified in these data. The use of compromise suggests an assumption about differences: that there are differences, but some must be given up to be effective, to achieve an end. The leader can best make this decision.

Strengths and vulnerabilities

As there are strengths to this mode, there may also be vulnerabilities as well. One student suggests the vulnerability she has felt in holding this idea of leadership as the only model of leadership in her thinking. Saying that "I don't like to be in positions of leadership sometimes," she goes on:

> I think that a lot of times with friends and groups of people I often end up being a leader and I don't really want to be. . . . I have always been the kind of person that decides what a group of people are going to do. I have never really liked it very much because I feel like I don't want that because it is, there is a stereotype in our society of someone who controls or is aggressive with a group of people. And I don't feel that way about myself and I don't like feeling that I am the person deciding where we are going to go or what we are going to do.

While this student did not elaborate her fears of leadership as "control," it would be interesting to know what nurtured these concerns and what it might take to have this young woman see herself in a more positive way as a potential leader. Perhaps this concern stems from not finding a more suitable mode of leadership. The student gives some clues:

> I don't think of myself as a leader. I think of myself as a person. I would hope that most people don't think of themselves as leaders. I don't like that at all. . . . I guess it is again that I don't feel any need to compete with people or things like that. . . .

A leadership model

Ideas presented here identify two leadership modes: the leader-as-interdependent or the leader-as-autonomous-in-relation-to-others. These modes of leadership have been conceptualized as a way to capture distinctions heard in Emma Willard girls' interviews. While these two modes are not considered mutually exclusive, they do represent a set of ideas that cluster in clearly identifiable patterns, termed here as "priority" competencies. The logic of each mode, evident in the data, suggests that for each there are different assumptions about leadership that are then manifest in characteristic goals and visions and other competencies: interpersonal processes, decision making, and related skills.

For example, while each of the leadership modes include decision making, each suggests that different things will be emphasized in the decision-making process. The "interdependent" leader will make sure everyone's ideas are included in a larger plan of action, which the leader has synthesized and then brought to her group. In this process an actual decision may be the last step in a series of smaller "decisions" already achieved by the act of listening to everyone's ideas. In contrast, for "autonomous" leaders the burden lies in an accurate identification of a problem and in offering a unique and fitting solution. The decision itself is a kind of test of both the leader's analysis of the problem and the prescription for its solution. In the moment of decision making for the autonomous leader, the emphasis will be on persuading one's constituents that both are right.

Because of these differences in interpretation and the processes of leadership, words come to have different meanings. For example, while each of these leadership modes values creativity, each is creative in different ways. For the interdependent leaders, creativity comes from the conceptual integration of others' ideas. For the autonomous leader, creativity comes from being an idea generator.

To examine how these ideas and modes of leadership can be manifested in the day-to-day experiences of student leaders at Emma Willard School, two Emma Willard students offer their ideas about leadership, decision making, and conflict negotiation. Through their experiences it is possible to examine how a set of ideas relate to actual behavior. In particular, their processes of seeing and resolving conflict offer models of more general ways of problem posing and problem solving.

Looking at adolescent girls as leaders: two case studies
of decision making and conflict negotiation

Asked to say what leadership means to them, two student leaders, one an editor, the other a proctor, respond. Becky, the proctor, begins:

> A leader is someone who can gauge what their constituencies' feelings seem to be, someone who can hear a bunch of people and say: This seems to be the problem. . . . There seems to be something wrong here—and being able to kind of pinpoint and generalize it. So that is the most important leadership quality someone can have: to be able to see what is going on and suggest a kind of definite action or at least say this seems to be the general problem.

The second student, Jane, the editor, says:

> The best thing a leader can do would be to have everyone in their

group involved in what is going on, to know everyone's involved in things that are going on . . . because, as a leader, things shouldn't be a one-person show. It's not your time to be in the limelight and glory. Your job as a leader is to get the people organized so that they are doing their work, as a group effort. I think as a leader you are more an organizer. You get the whole group working, rather than 'I am the leader' and 'I am going to do it.' How can I explain it? . . . It is important that everyone is involved so they get to know what is going on, learn how to do different things, learn some responsibility so that other people's ideas are in there. It's always important to be sharing. . . .

For Jane, the editor, leadership involves approaching something jointly, identifying as a group what needs to be done, involving everyone in a solution, and getting "the whole group working." As leader, Jane is the organizer, the facilitator of others, eschewing the "limelight" and "glory" and working to help others know what's going on and to share in the doing.

For Becky, leadership involves a different idea: gauging the problem, identifying and articulating it for others, and then "suggesting a kind of action" or finding a solution. In Becky's view, the leader is autonomous. In Jane's, the leader is interdependent. Each idea of leadership involves both a different conception of self and a different way of interacting with others. These assumptions will, in turn, present each student with a different kind of conflict as a leader, revealing particular kinds of logic at work and subtle differences in the expression of a set of competencies both share.

Responding to an interviewer who asks each of them to tell about a conflict she has faced, the two adolescent leaders reveal situations that caused them conflict. The conflicts they present pertain to their leadership duties. Jane begins by identifying a situation she faced when a member of her editorial staff failed to carry out her job. Describing the situation and her problem, Jane says:

I had a problem with a . . . girl whom I would tell her that I needed her to get something done and I would tell her two weeks ahead of time and then I would go remind her . . . and she would kind of act like I was nagging her about it. So I wouldn't say anything to her and then when I needed whatever she was supposed to have done, she hadn't done it. And this went on for about two months.

It took me a long time . . . I felt like I really knew that I needed somebody else to be doing the job and, yet, I felt that whenever I would talk things over with her, she would say, 'Yah, I really want to do it and I want to be able to help.' It's like I kept feeling torn between should I get someone new and say you are fired, or should I just keep waiting. I guess I finally decided that I looked at things she was doing. . . . I wasn't really sure, partly I wasn't sure if I should be dealing with her or I should ask my faculty adviser to go speak to her so I wouldn't have to get involved. I finally decided that it was probably better if I talked to her, because it was really a problem between me and her and the faculty adviser wasn't involved.

Becky, the proctor, in one of the school's dormitories, responsible for some ten students in her hall, reveals a situation of conflict that occurred for her:

This year as a proctor I am supposed to mark people off. And at the beginning of the year, I was very concerned with really doing, being a straight arrow and doing a good job. And somebody once asked me—one of the three musketeers, one of my good friends, who I lived with—asked me if she could sleep through Morning Reports [assembly], which is never supposed to be done, because I am supposed to mark her off if she is there. And that was hard, because I was caught between choosing between a friend and what was right.

Asked to specify the conflict, Becky goes on:

It was the difference between choosing, doing what the rule said, what the rules dictated and choosing between maintaining my friendship with this girl, at least as I saw it, to maintain my relationship with this girl.

While both girls could have invoked the authority of their position to resolve the conflicts they report, they did not. Becky, for example, could have told her friend, No, you can't sleep in. Similarly, Jane could have said, Have your assignment in by Friday or I will have to replace you. And while the conflicts they report could have been cast quite similarly —I had a problem in doing my job—they are cast with different emphases. While these differences may at first appear subtle, they are none-theless identifiable (see table 13 on page 200 for a comparison of the problems the girls saw, indicating in each student's own words how the problem was construed and the considerations each brought to its res-olution and to the evaluation of the resolution).

The contrast between these students reveals different elements in prior-ity. For the proctor the challenge of rule versus friendship is cast as an issue of hierarchy: the priority of her friendship versus her authority in maintaining the rules. For the editor the conflict is twofold, both wanting to honor the girl's desire to keep the job on the school journal and having to confront her when she fails to do her assignments. It is not just that different kinds of conflict engage these young women, but that each girl frames the conflict differently and different actions follow.

A careful examination of the specifics of these situations shows certain features and patterns to each girl's thinking. For Jane, the editor, a hes-itant questioning is her first response to the situation. Maybe she was being unreasonable, unclear. Maybe she hadn't made "it clear to her the things I needed her to do." As she ponders what she actually considered in thinking through what to do, at work is this same questioning: ". . . I wanted to yell at her [but] couldn't look at my situation as the most important thing." Seeing what else is going on in the other girl's life, stepping into her situation and context, forces Jane to stop. By taking on the work of the other girl, she comes to recognize, too, that she is hurting herself. There is no good solution in doing the work herself. Similarly, she recognizes that other people—in taking up the slack and doing added work—were finding it too much for them. Ultimately she decides she must decide for herself, confront the girl, and, when she does, is amazed to discover that the girl is not upset to give up her job.

Categorizing aspects of Jane's thinking, several features can be iden-tified. As a leader, she

is tentative and questioning (questions if she is right);

is context oriented (looks to see the other in her situation and contexts and listens to her construction of the problem);

tests her reading of the conflict with those involved and seeks under-standing of self and other;

uses dialogue with others to assess the problem and find a solution; and deliberates more about solving the problem than any other aspect of it.

Table 13

Analysis of Two Kinds of Leadership Conflicts: Considerations
Used in the Construction of the Problem, the Resolution, and
the Evaluation of the Resolution

Conflict 1: Jane, the editor

1. I didn't really want to confront her and I knew I had to.

2. I didn't know if I was being unreasonable in things I was asking her to do; maybe I didn't make it clear to her the things I needed [her] to do.

Resolution

1. Part of me wanted to yell at her, but when I would see her upset about things that were going on in her life or just other things that she was busy with, I couldn't just go and say, "You know, why aren't you doing this. . . ." I just couldn't look at my situation, that this is the most important thing because I realized there were other things going on.

2. One of my decisions was taking on the work that she hadn't done and not really dealing with her. . . . I guess I could have conceivably kept her on and her never really doing the work and . . . [But] I would end up feeling bad about it because I did.

3. I also talked to some other people about it on the staff [asking] "What do you think?" . . . So I was passing it off like "Do you know why she isn't doing this?"

4. And everyone else was sort of doing her job and it was getting to be too much work for other people. I guess I had to decide, me decide.

Conflict 2: Becky, the proctor

1. It was a difference between choosing what the rules said—what the rules dictated—and . . . maintaining my friendship with this girl.

Resolution

1. I considered that she knew my job, she knew what kind of pressure I was under and if she was going to sit there and pressure me, what kind of a friend was she, and if I said "No" to her over morning reports and she decided this was the end of our friendship, maybe we didn't have that much of a friendship.

2. I was at a point where I needed to assert my authority as a leader and she needed some limits set for her.

Evaluation (Was it the right thing to do?)

1. Yeah. I think looking back on it, I do. In some ways because I knew she really wanted to do it and in the beginning I felt bad. I could say, "Yeah, she really does want to do it." But I feel now that it was the right thing because obviously she wasn't upset by what happened in the end. It was more upsetting when there were problems going on.

Evaluation (Was it the right thing to do?)

1. Sure, yeah, because it's important at the beginning of the year to draw, at least to start with, a hard line because then it makes it a lot easier to ease up later. And I didn't want to start easy and then have to tighten up.

2. At that point in time, I was at the point that I needed to assert my authority as a leader and she needed some limits set for her too, because she was at the period where she was testing me out to see what I would do . . . because it was new in the year. She had known me as somebody who fooled around the year before, I mean by being late to study hall and not regarding the rules as a sacred cow and saying, "That is a stupid rule and I am going to violate it because I don't feel it has a lot of merit." So she was testing me out to see what kind of an authority figure . . . I was going to be and I needed to say to her, "Hey, you are not going to be able to use our friendship as a tool to push me around with."

3. I realized that you can do what is right and at the same time not sacrifice relationships. As my friends have gotten older they have an ability to do that too. . . . I believe this is right and the world is going to die unless this happens and she believes something else very strongly and we are able to argue about that. In fact we are able to fight a lot and still get along, and our friendship still works. And [because] that can work, I have discovered that I can still do the right thing and not sacrifice a relationship.

One might say in the end that Jane, as a leader, learns something about the girl and herself; it was more upsetting living the situation than confronting the person—a kind of psychological knowledge of the interactions between individuals.

Similarly, in characterizing aspects of Becky's thinking as a leader, several features are revealed. She

is assertive and self-referencing;

is oriented to seeing the problem in terms of how it meets a standard she holds ("If she were going to pressure me, what kind of friend was she . . . maybe we didn't have that much of a friendship");

seeks understanding of self by others ("She knew what kind of pressure I was under.");

casts the problem as if within a hierarchy ("choosing what the rule said or maintaining my friendship.");

fits the problem to a general situation ("I needed to assert my authority as a leader, and she needed some limits set for her, too . . . she was at the period where she was testing me out to see what I would do."); and

deliberates more about how she evaluates her decision, that is, how she justifies her actions.

In the end, Becky learns something about friendship and herself: that she can keep to her standards, do the right thing, and still have a relationship. It is a balancing the individual can achieve—a psychological knowledge of the self about relationships.

The logic of the leadership models presented here offers an interpretation for the two kinds of conflict Jane and Becky experience. For Becky, a leader characterized as "autonomous," a high premium must be placed upon acting as an "authority." In a mode that marks the leader as problem-identifier and prescriber, individual authority must be maintained. Any threat to that authority is a potential conflict. Similarly, for Jane, the student editor characterized as "interdependent," what will be most challenging as a conflict may well involve the line between "was I being unreasonable in the things I was asking her to do, trying to be nice to someone, and really doing all the work myself." If this interdependent mode values the participation and contribution of others, it seems that conflict may emerge around those issues. How far one goes in supporting participation of others can, indeed, become a difficult decision.

Through girls' articulation of their thoughts and actions in day-to-day leadership activities, their assumptions about leadership are revealed that, in turn, influence their interactions with their constituencies and fellow workers. The logic revealed in these ideas and behaviors has led to the identification of two leadership modes (see table 14 on page 204). The implications of these discoveries when fully developed will enhance the understanding of leadership and the ways of educating student leaders.

Implications

Recently, when researchers Blum and Smith examined the place of women in corporate America's executive and management positions they discovered some unexpected results. Using census and other data, they found a clear and dramatic increase of women in the work force, from 18.5 percent in 1970 to nearly 36 percent in 1985. However, the actual situation of women was more problematic, so much so that they argue:

> The politics of optimism, which stem from the widely accepted image of women's upward mobility in the business world, exaggerates both the actual extent of women's integration and opportunities available in managerial ranks. (Blum and Smith 1988)

For although the rate of increase of women in management positions has been great, the proportion of women employed as managers is still quite small, increasing from 3.6 percent of all working women in 1970 to only 6.8 percent in 1980. And while it is younger women who are making it into these positions, Blum and Smith raise some troubling yet important issues in thinking about the education of women for leadership.

For example, Blum and Smith point to the two most influential studies of women in management of the last ten years—the work of Henning and Jardim (1977) and that of Rosabeth Kanter (1977)—and characterize them as decidedly too optimistic. Both offered explanations for why women were not yet sharing leadership and management positions equally with men and both were widely acclaimed. Arguing that women are socialized to be passive and less aggressive than men, Henning and Jardim suggested that women should emulate those masculine characteristics necessary for success. In contrast, Kanter pointed to the structure of the organization and posited that women would advance when the structure of the organization changed: that is, when there was less hierarchy and

Table 14

Modes of Leadership Related to Priority Competencies: Goals, Processes, and Skills*

Leadership Mode	Goals/vision	Interpersonal skills
1. Interdependent-in-relation-to-others	Goals/plans derived from listening to people, being open to new ideas, and then making a plan from people's suggestions in order to get things done. Although leader enters her own ideas, acts more as idea synthesizer.	Listening to others, synthesizing ideas, facilitating interactions. Worst thing a leader can do is make a separation between self and others. Motivation for people to work together comes from people who know each other and get along.
2. Autonomous-in-relation-to-others	Goals/plans come from leader using her own judgment. As representative of others, leader puts forth a plan in order to get things done/to solve problem. Although leader will modify her ideas for others, acts as idea generator.	Developing and presenting people with ideas/plans. Worst thing a leader can do is be ineffective or misuse power, that is, go beyond what the group or structure allows. Motivation for people to work together comes from structure/organization and efficiency of leader—being on time, getting things done, having agendas, etc.

Decision making; leader makes decision	Related skills
Takes into account all things people have said and then decides.	Listening; eliciting ideas and information from others; being patient.
Considers individuals in their contexts and situations.	Synthesizing, conceptualizing, idea synthesizer; creativity is in integration.
Tests a reading of conflicts with those involved.	
Leader makes decision— even if everyone has not always been heard—in order to move forward.	Being organized, being efficient, being persuasive, conceptualizing, idea generator; creativity is in development of new/ different ideas.
Uses standards, principles as guides in decision making.	

*Competencies are termed "priority" for each mode to stress that they are not necessarily mutually exclusive between modes of leadership, but rather within a mode are patterned in a particular order of priority. But it should be stated too that the particular logic of a leadership mode shifts meaning of words, for example, decision making, being creative, etc. (Lyons 1985) a greater integration of roles across organizational levels, including those of women. Thus, each suggested different agendas for the education of women for leadership positions.

For example, the work of Henning and Jardim offered a rationale for assertiveness training and a "dress for success" imperative. Kanter, focusing on women's subordinate status rather than individual personality traits, looked for new roles in a new organizational ideal—the integrated rather than segmented organization. And while Henning and Jardim saw success in women's determination and will, Kanter saw it in the number of slots available within organizations. But it is with both models that Blum and Smith see undue optimism and, ultimately, disappointment for women seeking gender equality.

While it is not the purpose here to elaborate the work of Blum and Smith, it is sobering to consider. They alert us to the realities that may be in the future for girls who seek leadership in the workplace. They also help us to conceptualize how we think about the education of girls for leadership.

For example, what realities about organizations, power, and leadership are girls educated to? It seems a delicate balance is necessary: permitting some discussions of career opportunities, ones that reveal the complexities of jobs yet are not discouraging. High school internships that rotate students through several different kinds of jobs might offer girls useful experiences in providing a variety of career suggestions and in presenting opportunities to explore organizational structures and varying needs of women actually working in different organizational settings.

Similarly schools need to think as well about how they support and encourage the development of young women—and men—as leaders. What kinds of experiences do they provide? What kinds of models of leadership are inherent in the positions and roles open to students in schools? What are the assumptions, goals, skills implied, taught, or encouraged by the leadership roles schools ask students to fill? In exploring leadership in Emma Willard girls there emerged evidence of two ideas of leadership. The stability and frequency of both remain questions for future research. And, these issues need to be examined in different contexts—in other public and private schools and in single-sex and coed settings. For this work points to implications both for considering a new model of leadership and for thinking about educational practices in school settings.

For example, although similar qualities and leadership terms are mentioned and discussed by girls of both leadership orientations, the same word was found to carry very different meanings. When talking about the leadership qualities they look for in the candidates, girls of both modes spoke about candidates that they could "respect." But in the "interdependent" mode, respect is a characteristic of a leader who "relates to the constituency and creates a mutual understanding." This understanding allows the leader to know what the constituency wants and to carry out these mutually understood goals. Respect is gained through the leader's ability to cull from the group its goals and desires. In the autonomous mode, respect is defined as the "leader's ability to gain and hold the confidence of the constituency and to create public appeal." In this mode a leader is respected for his or her ability to convince the voters that he or she is capable, strong, and forceful; that the constituency is in good hands; and that it is led by a person who has good ideas and can act on them. The same words may carry different meanings suggesting different underlying logics of leadership and thus different actions. As one student suggested, it is important to have an idea and put forth a plan, any plan, in order to mobilize the group and get things done. In contrast, another student says: "Listening to the group may be more important than having an idea."

The different behaviors implied by the two logics of leadership can also be identified in different emphases in interpersonal skills and interactions. In the interdependent mode one can hear the goal of "personal interaction and understanding so that everyone involved in the running of the organization understands and grows." Each person contributes equally and the importance of the individual's involvement is judged in terms not only of contributions but also of the involvement of each member. The greater involvement, the greater strength. In the autonomous mode "working well together" means "carrying out an assigned role efficiently and quickly." Focus is on executing a part, doing the job. Like a well-run machine, each part is essential to the main goal of getting the job done efficiently and well. Strength is gained through the effective assignment of tasks.

In evaluating the two leadership modes, it is clear there are strengths and weaknesses of each. For effective leadership, a balance and flexibility in both modes may be necessary, especially considering the context of leadership. Although recent management literature has begun to assign high priority to collaborative and interdependent skills, the predominant and still valued mode in our highly competitive society is the more autonomous orientation. However, in this sample of adolescent girls, the predominant mode is the "interdependent" one; this may explain the tension that girls can experience as they look for a way to act on their own styles. Some girls will choose to be proctor instead of class officer or to deny their role as leader because they "do not want to be separate but want to be a person." Possibly the nonvalidation of this interdependent mode and previous lack of understanding and elaboration of it is perceived by adolescent girls, causing some to drop out of leadership positions or to move into other types of roles that more easily fit their interdependent orientation.

Affirmation of the girls who use this mode seems a first step for these students. Similarly, in the expectations for the autonomous leader, there is an implied notion that the leader should already possess the qualities necessary for leadership when she comes to the position. The leader must have previously proven herself and "must be able to get people's attention and get people moving." There is no room for rehearsal; a polished performance seems required from the beginning. But leadership is learned. Helping students become more reflective about their personal assumptions about leadership may help both the interdependent and autonomous leaders to avoid the pitfalls of their mode of leadership and to value its strengths.

But what about the school itself? Do schools tacitly value one set of leadership qualities more than others? Or one set for boys and another for girls? Recent research modeled on the Emma Willard leadership study offers some perspectives (Garrod et al. 1988).

In a study conducted at a private coed day school and at a public coed high school with some twenty students from each school matching Emma Willard students in social and economic background, Garrod et al. developed a model describing leadership competencies based on the boys and girls he studied. An analysis of Emma Willard data carried out by a coder trained in the same method—one based on McClelland's ideas —revealed a similar set of competencies. Twenty-five competencies were identified in five categories for Emma Willard student leaders (see table 15 on page 209).

A comparative analysis of leadership competencies of students in Garrod's study and Emma Willard students revealed that student leaders were matched in competencies at all three schools. Some differences appeared, however, among the boys and the girls. On some leadership competencies, boys and girls tended to emphasize different aspects. For example, in defining responsibility boys in both schools focused on com-

Table 15

High School Leadership Competency Model: Emma Willard School Leaders

1. Basic values
concern for people's welfare; responsibility; authenticity; integrity

2. Personality factors
autonomy; strong self-concept; sense of identity as a leader; introspection

3. Cognitive competencies
systems perspective; foresight; human insight; empathy; objectivity; relational thinking

4. Achievement related competencies
sense of purpose; desire to do one's best; self-confidence; initiative

5. Power/influence related competencies
concern for influence; need for recognition; self-control; political awareness; skillful use of influence; communication skill; presence

mitment "to upholding the specific terms of [their] leadership roles," while girls focused on "feeling responsible for fulfilling the expectations of their constituents." Girls were more concerned with their constituencies than with their roles.

The Garrod study also showed that there was a considerable difference in the attitude of students in one school to leadership roles of girls. In brief, boys at that school did not expect girls to be competent leaders and stated this openly to girls and to their teachers (Garrod et al. 1988). In the tradition of its founder, Emma Hart Willard, Emma Willard School is committed to the education of women for leadership roles. What difference, then, do these school attitudes or goals make in supporting women in developing leadership abilities?

Clearly, these issues need to be explored further. Other research, especially Lee and Bryk's, points to several important results, including a positive sense of self and higher academic achievement by girls in single-sex institutions (Lee and Bryk 1986). Hall and Sandler (1982) and Krupnick (1984) identify specific classroom behaviors—in particular, the quantifiably smaller number of classroom responses by girls in coed settings—that suggest some benefits to young women in single-sex institutions but indicate a need to monitor and evaluate classroom practices in both single-sex and coed settings. Good practices in educating girls for leadership need to be identified.

It seems, then, considering the findings of the Emma Willard leadership study as well as the life contexts of today's world that adolescent girls in schools might be well-served in their development as leaders by the following:

Being affirmed: Girls need to be affirmed in their leadership skills, interests, and emerging styles. Before asking girls to change a way of doing things, it might be well to understand what they see themselves as trying to bring into being.

Participating in leadership experiences: A range of leadership experiences ought to be available to students in schools and perhaps in outside organizations, places where girls cannot only act in real positions but also see women in their work environments and discover the realities of the world of work, power, and leadership.

Reflecting on practice: Girls will benefit from opportunities to discuss and examine the experiences they are having, to reflect on their own responses to them and contrast them with the real-life experiences of other women.

This work began with an interest in assessing how adolescent girls thought about and acted as leaders in one school setting. While there is clearly a need to broaden this sample to include a systematic study of girls and boys at public and other private schools, this work does offer descriptions of two leadership modes associated with different competencies and raises new questions:

Do the leadership skills and competencies of adolescent girls and boys change over time? Is there, for example, a way of thinking about and being a leader during adolescence that is connected developmentally to ways of being a leader as an adult?

How does school climate or school setting—private, public, single-sex, or coed—make a difference in developing leadership ability? In the kinds of leadership modes encouraged?

How reflectively aware of their own modes of leadership are students? Should they be?

How reflectively aware of different approaches to leadership are adults who advise students?

Talking about the best thing a leader could do, one student suggested that leaders could just "further the people themselves so that they become more like leaders." This seems an appropriate goal for educators to consider as they think about supporting the development of adolescent girls for leadership and citizenship in the world that they will enter as adult women.

Methodology

Leadership interview

Introduction:

What leadership position do you hold and how did you come to it?

Looking back over the time since you came to your leadership position, tell me how it has been for you as a leader? What stands out for you or stays with you?

Leadership:

What does leadership mean to you?

How would you describe yourself as a leader? Is the way you see yourself as a leader different from the way you usually see yourself? If so, how? Why not?

What is the best thing a leader can do? What is the worst thing a leader can do?

Conflict and Decision Making:

Can you tell me about a situation you faced in your position where you had to make a decision and you weren't sure what was the right thing to do? Where you had conflict and weren't sure what was the right thing to do? Could you describe the situation? What was the conflict for you in that situation? In thinking about what to do? What kinds of things did you consider? Did you think it was the right thing to do? Did you consider this situation a moral conflict? What does morality mean to you?

Being a Leader:

When you think of voting someone into a leadership position in this school, what kinds of things do you consider?

If you were to advise someone who is going to be in your position next year, what would you say?

To categorize girls' ideas about leadership, three procedures were used. First, a coder trained in the McClelland method of deriving competencies analyzed the interview responses of student leaders and derived a competency model indicating a range of twenty-five competencies. Second, data from all interviews ($N = 48$) were scrutinized for responses to the question, What does leadership mean to you? and to the questions, What is the best thing a leader can do/What is the worst thing a leader can do? In this analysis data were examined to identify girls' ideas about leadership. Third, competencies of actual leaders were identified and elaborated from data drawn only from those students who were actual leaders at the Emma Willard School: that is, students in elected or selected leadership positions, such as class president, editor of the newspaper, proctor, head of weekend activities. Results of these procedures revealed the two modes of leadership (see table 13, in which each mode is shown having what may be called "priority" visions and goals, strategies for decision making, and other related competencies).

Sources

Adelson, J., ed. 1980. *The Handbook of Adolescent Psychology*. New York: John Wiley.

Argyris, C. 1976. *Increasing Leadership Effectiveness*. New York: John Wiley.

Blum, L., and V. Smith. 1988. Women's mobility in the corporation: A critique of the politics of optimism. *Signs* vol. 13, no. 3.

Boyatzis, R. E. 1980. *The Competent Manager*. New York: John Wiley.

Burns, J. MacGregor. 1978. *Leadership*. New York: Harper and Row.

Carroll, S. J. 1984. "Feminist Scholarship on Political Leadership." In *Leadership: Multidisciplinary Perspectives*, edited by B. Kellerman. Englewood Cliffs, N.J.: Prentice-Hall.

Douvan, E., and J. Adelson. 1966. *The Adolescent Experience*. New York: John Wiley.

Drucker, P. 1982. *The Changing World of the Executive*. New York: N.Y. Times Books.

Garrod, A., et al. 1988. Psychological skills of adolescent leaders. Unpublished manuscript, Dartmouth College.

Hall, R., and B. Sandler. 1982. "The Classroom Climate: A Chilly One for Women?". Washington, D.C.: Project on the Status and Education of Women, Association of American Colleges.

Henning, M., and A. Jardim. 1977. *The Managerial Woman*. New York: Anchor Press.

Horner, M. S. 1968. Sex differences in achievement motivation and performance in competitive and noncompetitive situations. Ph.D. diss. University of Michigan.

Huff, S., G. O. Klemp, and D. G. Winter. 1980. "The Definition and Measurement of Competence in Higher Ed." In *The Assessment of Occupational Competence*, edited by G. O. Klemp, Jr. Boston, Mass.: McBer and Co.

Kanter, R. 1977. *Men and Women of the Corporation*. New York: Basic Books.

Kellerman, B. 1984. *Leadership: Multidisciplinary Perspectives*. Englewood Cliffs, N.J.: Prentice-Hall.

Klemp, G. O. 1982. *Assessing Student Potential: An Immodest Proposal.* Boston, Mass.: McBer and Co.

Kotter, J. 1982. *The General Managers.* New York: The Free Press.

Krupnick, C. 1984. Sex differences in college teachers' classroom talk. Ph.D. diss. Harvard University.

Lee, V. E., and A. S. Bryk. 1986. Effects of single-sex secondary schools on student achievement and attitudes. *Journal of Educational Psychology* 78.

Levinson, D. 1978. *The Seasons of a Man's Life.* New York: Knopf.

McClelland, D. 1975. *Power: The Inner Experience.* New York: Irvington Publishers.

Nichols, M. 1984. Retrospective reports of adolescent leadership roles. Ed.D. diss. Harvard University.

Sassen, G. 1980. Success anxiety in women: A constructivist interpretation of its source and its significance. *Harvard Educational Review* 50:13–24.

Stogdill, R. M. 1977. *Leadership Abstracts and Bibliography, 1904 to 1974.* Columbus, Ohio: Ohio State University.

Winterbottom, N. 1988. Gender differences in adolescent career decision-making: The study of one high school population. Ed.D. diss. Harvard University.

Racial Identity Formation and Transformation

JANIE VICTORIA WARD

Editors' Note: Dr. Ward participated in all four years of the Emma Willard School study as an interviewer. In this chapter she discusses issues of racial identity formation of a group of young minority women who were participants in the study. Because the author, a black woman, interviewed nearly all of the minority women, a same-sex, same-race match between interviewer and interviewee was achieved.

In a recent study of black adolescents' self-concept and academic achievement, Signithia Fordham presents an analysis of the tension felt by some students between group identity and academic success. She asks if racelessness, the tactic adopted by a number of high achieving black students, is a "pragmatic strategy or a Pyrrhic victory" (Fordham 1988; see also Fordham and Ogbu 1986). She describes students torn between an individualistic ethos encouraged by school officials and a collectivistic ethos promoted by peers. For some black students, doing well in school is equated with "selling out" or becoming nonblack; thus for them, "the burden of acting white" was too high a price to pay for academic success.

This chapter presents a very different relationship between group identity and adolescent development. Listening to the voices of a small group of academically successful black adolescent women exploring the meaning of race in their lives reveals how racial identity formation, personal commitment, and academic achievement can successfully converge during the high school years. This chapter has implications for understanding the psychosocial development of black adolescents, particularly black females, and for creating positive and nurturing educational environments for minority students in racially isolated settings.

Between the years 1981 and 1985, when this research project took place, a minimum of thirty-eight and a maximum of fifty-one minority students attended Emma Willard School. Of this number approximately twenty-four were from American ethnic and racial minorities. These children were primarily black American, but several originated from other countries, including the Caribbean Islands and Africa. Over the four-year period a total of seven minority girls were interviewed.[1] From these seven girls, twenty interviews were generated, and they provide the data analyzed in this paper.

The minority students received the same interview questions as the majority students. Both groups were asked self-description and morality questions. In addition the interviewers asked the students to explore their significant relationships and solicited their opinions about growing up female. Following the formal interview, which usually lasted from one to two hours, the interviewers asked the minority students the following questions regarding their racial identities: What does it mean to you to be a black woman? How has the meaning changed for you over the years? What do you think being black will mean to you in the future?

With very few exceptions, discussions of race and race-related topics presented themselves throughout the entire interview session. However, data analysis of the girls' reflections on the meaning and role that race plays in their lives were mentioned primarily in response to the afore-mentioned specific queries.

Background information was not collected on the young women, although some information was shared during the interview sessions; thus data about socioeconomic status and factors related to individual family histories are incomplete. The purpose of this chapter is to focus not on individual cases, but on general themes that seemed to recur in the data when racial identity and race-related events were discussed.

Although specific data were not compiled, two major background factors affecting the lives of the young black women should be acknowledged. First, several girls grew up in family settings with ethnic origins other than black American (including Caribbean, Hispanic, and biracial families). Often these students volunteered comparisons of their past experiences with those of black American students they knew, pointing out both similarities and differences. Studies of black family life have focused on the life-styles, beliefs, and practices of black American families, and most of the research cited in this paper reflects this orientation. The early developmental paths followed by Emma Willard's black girls may have differed slightly given their multiculturality and subsequent intraracial differences in family socialization.

A second commonality in the girls' backgrounds was attained anecdotally. Very few of the young women grew up in predominantly black neighborhoods. Many described themselves as suburbanites in black spill-over communities; most had spent at least part, if not all, of their childhood in mixed, or predominantly white, neighborhoods. Previous schooling reflected this fact as well. Only two students recalled attending an academic institution with large numbers of black or other minority students. In conversations with these girls, this aspect of their childhoods stood out. Although they were in small numbers at Emma Willard, their "minority" status (in terms of numbers) was by no means new to them. All of the young women had previously experienced racial isolation either in their integrated communities, where there might have been two or three other black families, or in their schools, in which more than two black children per class was rare. Therefore, for this group growing up and being educated in racially isolated settings was the norm. The choice to send a child away to boarding school is difficult for any family and is perhaps harder still for families in which minority of color is involved. It would seem that these earlier "minority" educational experiences helped to prepare both parent and child for what was later to come.

The seven black girls interviewed at length over the four-year study represent both the diversity and similarities evident in the nation's black communities. Several were children of immigrants, and a few were born outside of this country. For two students, Spanish was the primary language spoken at home. However varied the life experiences of the past, strong commonalities exist among members of the black diaspora. This is manifest most clearly in the fact that blacks residing in the United States must all share the common social experience of racism and discrimination. In this nation, the visibility of one's skin color and of other physical traits associated with socially devalued groups marks individuals as "targets" for subordination and discrimination by members of the white society. Thus the most striking commonality among blacks is the oppression they share based solely on the meanings attributed to the color of one's skin.

The research presented in this paper provides empirical evidence from a small sample of black female adolescents of what some psychologists have called the developmental process of black identity formation. The research seeks to illuminate how young women integrate their race-related experiences of the past with their present-day reality. The connections between patterns of family socialization, beliefs, attitudes, and values developed and adopted over time—and the girls' own subjective understanding of the role that race plays in their lives—will be made more clear.

Brief theoretical overview

This work is placed within two existing bodies of literature: First, the exhaustive research explicating the process of identity formation for adolescents in general and second, the current understandings of racial identity formation and its significance and implications during the adolescent years.

Erikson's concept of identity formation has been central to the literature on adolescent development (1950, 1956, 1968). He states that adolescence has as its most fundamental task the establishment of a sense of identity. To understand development, one must understand the context in which one lives. The process of identity formation is psychosocial, which refers both to the continuity of self over time and to one's relationship to society. Central to the experience of adolescence is the cognitive ability to take the self as object and to reflect upon the relationship between self and society. The adolescent is thus able to see the self as the self is seen by others. Erikson ties identity formation to ideology, that is, a necessary simplification of beliefs. Adolescence is a period of renegotiation—of social relationships and power dynamics—and often demands a redefinition of the self. Standing at the threshold of adulthood, the interplay between who I am and what I believe may lead the teen to reject the prevailing truths of childhood, constructing in its place new truths that affirm the emerging sense of one's identity and one's status in the world.

The effort to understand identity formation in black adolescents is incomplete without an appreciation of the concept of racial identity. Psychologists argue that a stable concept of self both as an individual as well as a group member (black) is essential to the healthy growth and development of the black self (Comer and Poussaint 1975; Cross 1971, 1978, 1980; Ladner 1978). Through racial identity, the group's way of organizing experience is transmitted to and internalized by the child (Barnes 1980). While so often neglected or confused in the literature, this integration of the individual's personal identity with one's racial identity is a necessary and inevitable developmental task of growing up black in white America.

During adolescence, the need to identify strongly with a sense of peoplehood or a shared social identity is heightened by a consciousness of belonging to a specific group that is characteristically different from other groups. Black teens often begin to question the relevancy of using a white norm for self measurement. To be black takes on new and powerful meanings—meanings that hold social and political significance to who one is and who one believes one should become.[2] As the black child sees herself as others see her, she knows that she is viewed in this society as a member of a devalued group. Transmitted daily to black children are messages that black people are undesirable, inadequate, and inferior. Therefore, if she is black, she is undesirable, inadequate, and inferior. In the face of glaring contradictions between the black experience as non-blacks believe it to be, and the black experience that the black adolescent knows it to be, the task becomes one in which the black child must unravel the faulty and dangerous attacks upon her identity, both individual and group. While some black children fall victim to these attempts to demean and destroy a positive sense of self, many studies show that blacks do not believe the negative stereotypes about themselves nor do they believe that they are inferior to whites (Powell 1982).

This movement beyond an internalization of racial subservience to racial pride begins first with a conscious confrontation with one's racial identity. Resolution of the so-called identity crisis of youth requires that all adolescents proclaim "I am not" as the first step to defining what I am. To the initial stages of the identity process the black adolescent, all too familiar with the demeaning stereotypes held about her and her racial group, must add "I am not what you believe black people to be, *and I am black.*" Herein lie the necessary statements of repudiation and affirmation. The black adolescent must reject white society's negative evaluation and must construct an identity that includes one's blackness as positively valued and desired. For blacks, identity formation is a necessary rebirth in one's own terms. If this process of positive identification with the black reference group, despite its devalued status, is not completed and internalized, identity formation will be at risk. The process of repudiation, a casting off of the racially based negative perceptions of others, lays the groundwork for the formation of a positive self-concept.

Growing up black dictates the necessity to negotiate discriminatory and oppressive conditions. It means having to face daily injustice inflicted simply on the basis of skin color. And it means having to live among and interact with people who may seek to hurt you. Some psychologists argue that black children who enter an alien, isolating environment with their self-esteem intact, should have little trouble withstanding the assaults against their budding personality. Yet being and becoming black is seldom an easy experience.

The racial identity interview

It is not surprising that all of the young black women at Emma Willard remembered and shared past personal experiences where they had been made painfully aware of themselves as racially different from whites. Many years have passed since a brownie troop leader, upon discovering a parent of one of her brownies was black, dismissed the girl from the troop, justifying her decision on the child's lack of "brownie spirit." And the recollection of a teacher who made her resentment of a little black girl's academic achievement very clear, although it has long since lost its initial sting, remains sharp memory. "There was a time [when] I said, Gosh, it would be so much easier if I were white," explained Ann as she remembered the name calling and teasing she was forced to endure. She could still recall the psychic energy required to be always on the defensive, trying desperately to find words to fire back that would make her attacker feel as bad as she. As she grew older, resentment turned to understanding, and her anger to pity and resignation. Numerous incidents similar to these were now an acknowledged part of the girls' personal histories and served to lay the foundation upon which their racial identities were built.

To no other question in the racial identity interview was there a more uniform response than to the question, What does it mean to be a black woman? "It means it's going to be hard" was a prediction echoed by all. Even the sheltered experience of Emma Willard was not enough to convince the young women that life after Emma would be anything similar to life in the school. For a few of the girls, the impact of the consequence of being black and female evolved over time: ". . . now I see that sometimes you really are knocked down just because you are black, and I have come to accept that and learn to deal with it." For others the focus on diligence was projected into the work world, where these black women could already imagine obstacles to be overcome. As one says, "I will always have to work harder. I would have that pressure, and I would be watched, you know." Explained another: "I will have to be better than another, say, a white woman who is, who would be my equal in terms of qualifications. I will have to do something that will be one step better than her . . . because you've got two strikes against you: You're a woman and you're black." This awareness of double jeopardy, because of the additive effect of gender and race, served to heighten levels of introspection and self-examination. In the process, some young women uncovered personal fortitude beneath the struggle.

I really think you have to understand who you are better, because there are going to be experiences that are really going to try your strength as a human being. And I think you need a very strong inner strength. [But] we have always worked, and we have always had to be strong. And I think that is a historical strength. . . .

Psychologist Diane Slaughter concurred when she wrote. "Black women must see [their liberation] through an assessment of what the black experience in this nation and abroad has been." This historical analysis is crucial to the black woman's sense of self and empowerment.

Expressions of racial pride were also repeated from interview to interview. Maria represented these sentiments well when she proclaimed:

There's a lot of heritage and culture behind all of that. I have to be very proud of that, and I'm not saying you have to fight for it . . . but you have to be willing to make your stand. It's a very important part of any culture today, and it shouldn't be just brushed aside.

The articulations of racial pride and proactive orientation toward racial barriers heard from Emma Willard's young black women align with Bowman and Howard's study of socialization and achievement in black youth. In their study differential patterns by gender were noted, suggesting that within black families there is a greater emphasis on racial pride in the socialization of girls. This contrasts with a greater emphasis on racial barriers for boys (Bowman and Howard 1985). The young black women at Emma Willard spoke often of feeling both good about their race and personally strengthened by their racial status.

Most of the women interviewed seemed to have brought to Emma Willard the skills necessary to survive and flourish in a predominantly white academic setting. The strong family background of each of these girls was instrumental in preparing the adolescents for what they would encounter.

What lessons are learned and what role do black families play in helping their children negotiate the persistent dynamics of racism and discrimination? Many researchers have attempted to elucidate a theoretical framework for describing black families. Given that black people are not a monolithic group in either their attitudes or their ways of expressing them, and given that there are a variety of ways of adapting to the American system of race relations, the functional approach to studying black family life suggests that families possess a distinct culture and strength that enables them to survive in racist America.

Through socialization the child learns what she needs to know about the world, how things are, and the skills necessary to cope and succeed. The task of the black family has been to provide a sense of identity and historical continuity by instilling in its offspring a sense of racial purpose and pride, thereby preparing its children to live among white people without becoming white people (Ladner 1971, 1978). Black families socialize their children to acquire the attitudes, values, and appropriate patterns of interaction conducive to their social and political environment. These include age and sex roles (which historically have been necessarily flexible in the black community), as well as the racial roles of resistance, suspicion, and caution (Nobles 1980, 1981). If power is the ability to define phenomenon, then the black family and community play a crucial role in the interpretation of race relations and in the invention of strategies necessary to prevail. What one chooses depends on the way that one perceives the problem, and how one perceives the problem depends on where one stands. Black families prepare black children for the onslaught of negation they must endure by providing the positive feelings and self-confidence underlying what it means to be a black person and a member of the black race.

Whether they were being teased or being painfully ignored, all of the girls who had reported past experiences of discrimination also reported that they brought the incidents home for discussion. Parents had the task of interpreting the incident for the child, explaining the confusing and painful aspects of being singled out and demeaned. Learning to live with the heartache of being discriminated against and the knowledge that such events could and would occur again is not easy. These are very difficult lessons to be transmitted to the black child.

Nearly all of the girls interviewed acknowledged that the information they received about how to deal with race came from within the family. "Our family talks about it [racism] . . . and how to deal with it" was the most common response. One girl elaborates:

> Like sometimes when something happens and it really bothers me, I'll talk to my mother or my sister and say: 'Somebody said something and I'm trying to decide whether they meant it or if they didn't know what they were saying and it just came out.' So we'll talk about it then. But its the type of thing where my whole family . . .

like we know it's there. And if somebody had trouble dealing with it, then we talk about it and try and help them. Otherwise it's just like, whoa, you just ignore it and do the stuff you can.

Parents also have the responsibility of interpreting race-related incidents for children who don't yet fully understand these dynamics. Several students described family discussions of racial events in which sensitive subtleties of racial content were carefully dissected and reviewed. This served a dual purpose. First, it gave the child criteria for determining malice, and it helped the child determine what action was then appropriate for retribution or reconciliation. Finally, students described sophisticated coping techniques that were developed to help the child make sense of painful personal attacks and maintain self-worth and value. Rose recalled that her father would say, "We all know the reason behind this. But don't dwell on it, just forget about it." Thus when messages of white society say "you can't," the well-functioning black family and community stand ready to counter such messages with those that say, You can, we have, we will.

To understand the formation and transformation of racial identity in the young black women of Emma Willard, one must understand the context in which they were living during the four-year study. At any given time they represented less than twenty percent of the student population. During the years of the study there were never more than two black faculty members employed at the school at any given point. Thus, should a race-related event erupt on campus, black students rarely have adult blacks to help negotiate its outcome. Two-thirds of Emma Willard's students, the boarding population, live, sleep, and eat with one another, (including all of the young women in this sample), and although from time to time tempers may flare, the close proximity of the setting forces the young women to become adept at interpersonal understanding and conflict resolution. The black women interviewed all expressed great satisfaction with their choice to attend Emma Willard and most spoke fondly of the friendships they had forged with both white and black students. Learning about race and race relations did not stop just because the young women had left their families and communities behind. The education continued on Emma's campus, in the classrooms and in the dormitories.

Black students learned a great deal about themselves and the meaning that race would play in their lives through their interactions with white students. "I'm a comfortable black friend," Vera noted ironically, describing how her background, articulateness, and even lighter skin color made her very acceptable to white friends (see Okazawa-Rey, Robinson, and Ward 1987). Susan repeated this observation, "If you are a light black person, people will react differently to you than if you are my color." She told the author, "It's as if they can see you more clearly . . . ," suggesting that the closer blacks look and act like whites, the easier they can be imagined as equals. Susan acknowledged that she falls victim to similarly narrowed perceptions herself: "I think I see myself as a black person in a predominately white school, just because I don't know the people. They come off first as white and then I get to know them and then the color disappears." A number of students mentioned their awareness of differences between themselves and their white counterparts, citing most often family financial status, differing tastes in music, and differing childrearing practices, particularly those involving discipline. Nevertheless for the most part, the young black women described themselves as very similar to their white friends in terms of goals, attitudes, and desires. At the same time they all acknowledged that the color of their skin created for them a different reality than for whites. The philosophy of Emma Willard is to promote and encourage individuality, Alice explained, yet when a problem occurred black students received a very mixed message from whites in school. In her view: "We're always on display . . . always being watched and when one of you slip up, they say that the black community slipped up. . . . We are all looked at as one large grouping." This double-talk—you're different, but you're the same—was unsettling to the young women interviewed, and it reinforced their belief that in the minds of white America, the blacks' individual identity and group identity would always be enmeshed.

Because the girls were interviewed at different ages and at differing stages of maturation and self-awareness, their comments offer an interesting array of perspectives regarding specific incidents in which white students, letting their guard drop, allowed their true feelings to show. In these moments of insensitivity, black students learned who their friends really were and whom they could trust. Overall the most striking indictment was a shared observation that their white friends were lamentably ignorant about racial differences. Some incidents were merely annoying, such as when white students would ask questions about how black women groom their hair. ("Come back someday when I'm hyperactive and need something to talk about and I will tell you," was one interviewee's exasperated reply.) Other stories describing comments heard from white students speaking about race from outdated and stereotypic notions of black American behavior, reflected a much deeper level of unenlightenment, and the young black women interviewed expressed shock and anger that such misinformation was allowed to persist.

Accurate racial knowledge, they felt, was terribly onesided, where black students knew far more about their white friends than the whites knew of blacks.[3] Attempts to educate were met with uneven success. According to the black women interviewed, part of the problem was the general hesitation white students expressed when discussions of race would arise. Explained Rose:

> Some of the girls are afraid of discussing . . . racial differences for fear that either they will offend me . . . what they don't understand is . . . I won't get upset if they are speaking out of pure ignorance . . . I will enlighten them. But I guess people are very afraid to face differences here. And what it could mean to them. It's a very fragile status quo. They guard it with their lives, just don't want to discuss it.

Maria added: ". . . they still think you might rob them in the night sort of thing, they are not comfortable with you yet. [They wonder], Did your brother mug me on the subway?" Distrust, fear, and apathy were cited as major factors preventing honest communication between the races. By virtue of being the color of the majority, white students could afford to make race a less significant aspect of their existence. The black students, however, knew that they live in a society that causes different outcomes for blacks and whites, and this simple fact had forged a wedge between the young women, which for some could not be overcome.

At a time when defining one's self-concept is crucial, integration reinforces the notion that black children are different. One black looking back on his student days recalls: "At that age you want to fit in with people around you. The last thing you want to do is stand out. The trouble is you do stand out. The education you get makes you stand out" (Perkins in Anson 1987, 41). Social integration and affluence can separate minority children from the racial ties, extended kinship networks, and folklore of ethnic culture and these must be replaced with something of equal value (Powell 1982). When peer acceptance is dependent upon how white-like one is, says psychiatrist Gloria Powell, then education becomes a subtractive process, a relinquishing of cultural self-identity. Black students in predominantly white settings are often living biculturally, straddling at least two worlds: black and white.

During adolescence, it can become increasingly difficult to separate one's own values and identity from those of the majority culture. Sometimes blacks and whites view the same circumstance from entirely different perspectives, causing a perceptual clash that begs for one's position to be affirmed. For several of the young women interviewed, Emma Willard's minority student population totaled more black students than they had been exposed to in the past. Barbara reflected, "I was always in such a white man's world. I thought maybe there was something more." At Emma Willard, Barbara was able to find more young women like herself, and to her particular delight, more high-powered ambitious young black women to whom she could relate. Barbara explains, "Most of them hold powerful positions in the school. They are not just back in the distance and everything." Eventually Barbara became one of those powerful black students, rising through the years to hold a key position in the school's black student organization (BSEW).

Black student organizations often fulfill the need to come to terms with racial and ethnic differences, by way of self- and group identity. Often such organizations can provide needed social support as the adolescents struggle with the complicated issues of identity, inclusion and exclusion, and intragroup differences. Many times it is in these settings that black students learn the most about themselves and about other blacks. When Emma Willard's black students came together in their group, they described a discovery of self through mutual recognition and connection. "I found a part of myself at BSEW," Mary recalled as she looked back on the day she first decided to join the group formally. In listening to Mary and others it was clear that the black women in BSEW shared tremendous affection and concern for the welfare of one another. During the years of this study, along with their formal activities, BSEW brought the girls together to help one another negotiate the Emma Willard way of life, to share beauty tips, to discuss racial incidents, and to talk about boys.

Male companionship is of course important to Emma Willard's young women, but issues around dating and relationships with men can be particularly perplexing for black women growing up outside the mainstream of their racial community. Along with never-ending conversations about young men, intraracial differences and similarities were often the topic of all-night discussions. Not everyone made sense of racial concerns in the same way, and, the girls discovered, not everyone was up to the challenge of being black. Black students learned a great deal about the many ways in which one can be a black woman from other black students.

The neighborhood "oreos," black people who were ashamed of their heritage, were analyzed, criticized, and summarily denounced. And the occasional student who adopted a "blacker than thou" stance toward the others was similarly rebuked. Students described BSEW as safe and supportive, a place where confidence was kept, where students could feel free to share thoughts, feelings, and fears in an atmosphere of acceptance, camaraderie, and understanding.

Finally, BSEW provided an environment in which young black women could have the opportunity to recognize and participate in leadership activities. Two of the girls interviewed eventually held leadership positions at Emma Willard (in either BSEW or the school government), of which they spoke fondly and with tremendous pride. Ultimately these organizations figured prominently in the young women's development. First, students learned the difficulty and tremendous responsibility of leading others. "Dealing with people of your own race, you always expect them to somehow be behind you, and still it is the same amount of work and the same amount of hassle," Helen exclaimed. In large part, education is the process of helping students gain a degree of control over their lives in the present and in the future. Through her activities with BSEW, Helen was offered the chance to make a difference in her social environment. While the results of her efforts are unknown, the satisfaction she expressed and the lessons she learned about interpersonal negotiation, diplomacy, and tact were invaluable. Effective leadership demands that decisions regarding direction and purpose are made carefully. She explained:

> I think the black community really [must] have a sense of why am I here. What can I be doing, what is our purpose? We really have to put maybe a little more thought [into it], because whatever you go into may be that much harder for you, and you are going to have to make sure it is what you really want and what you really want to do. It's not easy to back away sometimes.

Even more revealing from the discussions of leadership was the manner in which service to others affected the young women's developing sense of self. Several students discovered that through community activities, whether they be on campus with BSEW or school government, or off campus with, for example, the local Big Sister organization, they could express their newly formed sense of social commitment. These students saw themselves as having a role to play in improving the lives of others, and especially in the development and the strengthening of black communities. It is not surprising that the young women who took on these extracurricular activities were the same girls who spoke most passionately about oppression, discrimination, and the desire for a better society. Most of the black students interviewed acknowledged the sacrifice (economic and otherwise) made by their parents in order for them to attend Emma Willard. An education at Emma Willard was indeed a privilege and, these young women believed, with that privilege came an obligation to give something back in return.

It has been said that to be born black and female is to start with two strikes against you. The convergence of these two gender and racial identities has been assumed to create an overwhelming dilemma not easily overcome. Yet from this data it is evident that the process of being and becoming black provides young women with three essential opportunities for growth. First, there is an opportunity for role negation—the repudiation of both race- and gender-based stereotypes. Second, there is an opportunity to create a new and personally defined identity in one's own terms. And third, when opportunities for leadership are provided, there's a chance to effect change in one's social environment by developing and pursuing one's personal commitments.

Implications

The purpose of this essay was to illuminate the formation and transformation of racial identity in a small group of black adolescent females attending Emma Willard School. Most of the focus was on the psychological experiences faced by these young women. The path that their development followed, however, was greatly influenced by the social context in which it was unfolding. Sometimes educational institutions, in the effort to assimilate minority students, follow a norm of promoting sameness, thus ignoring differences. This posture may encourage minority students to reject their ethnic identity and the unique qualities of being black. When education is seen as an estrangement from who one is, or is seen as an effort to disconnect the student from where she came, neither education nor integration will be served.

Predominately white educational institutions, such as Emma Willard, may strive to be aware of and respectful toward racial differences. As is clear from these data, the implication of these differences for the psychological and social development of minority adolescents constitutes an important focus of research. While teachers and administrators of the school may not share the same cultural perspectives as the families of minority children, the school has a clear role to play in the developmental process. Teachers and administrators seeking to be supportive of this venture toward identity development and self-understanding can help students make sense of who they are and where they are going. In particular, they can help students make sense of what they see in the world; specifically the major social inequities in the United States and the evidence of racism and sexism. These are important educational lessons for children of all colors, but even more critical for black women. Research suggests that for females, issues of attachment and connection are of primary concern (Gilligan 1982), and for black females, the orientation toward racial pride and continuity begins early in life. Here, too, adults in predominantly white school settings have a role to play in helping minority students aspire while still maintaining connection with their racial and ethnic communities.

Ultimately, the young women interviewed over the four-year period ended up feeling that rather than being overwhelmed and disheartened by the double burden of being black and female, they felt fortunate to have an opportunity to reject negative stereotypes of black women, and to create and sustain in its place a positive racial identity. The process of racial identity formation encouraged them to decide upon who one is and what one will stand for. Especially through the pursuit of leadership opportunities, the young black women of Emma Willard gained a sense of personal efficacy and a commitment to acting in the public sphere. This serendipitous finding is indeed intriguing and suggests directions for future research.

Notes

1. The interviews of the seven minority students occurred in the following manner. Two were interviewed only once, one was interviewed twice, one was interviewed three times, one was interviewed four times, and two were interviewed five times. While all of the black women were interviewed at least once by the author, two were interviewed by other (nonblack) interviewers on three occasions. In all cases, even when the girls were interviewed by someone else in the Harvard Group, the questions about racial identity were posed and discussed with the author. Most of the quotations used in this paper come from responses to that category of question; however, the questions about self-description and

leadership generated a number of usable comments. Following the interview sessions, only one tape was determined to be inaudible and unusable. The data presented in this paper comes from twenty interviews, the total of transcribable interviews of all the minority students.

2. Elsewhere I have analyzed five separate models of what psychologists and psychiatrists have described as black identity development (Ward 1984). These theoretical interpretations include a psychodynamic approach (Grier and Cobbs 1968), a developmental model (Thomas 1971 and Cross 1971), a racial/cultural group orientation model (Nobles 1980) and a longitudinal, in-depth interview and analysis approach (Ladner 1971).

3. Jean Baker Miller, in *Towards a New Psychology of Women* from the Beacon Press in Boston, 1976, offers an excellent discussion of sociopolitical knowledge—black/white, male/female, subordinate/dominant relationships.

Sources

Anson, R. S. 1987. *Best Intentions: The Education and Killing of Edmund Perry*. New York: Random House.

Barnes, E. 1972. "The Black Community as the Source of Positive Self-Concept for Black Children: A Theoretical Perspective in Black Psychology." In *Black Psychology*, edited by R. Jones. New York: Harper and Row.

Bowman, P., and C. Howard. 1985. Race-related socialization, motivation and academic achievement: A study of black youths in three generation families. *Journal of the American Academy of Child Psychiatry* 24 (2) 134–41.

Comer, J. and A. Poussaint. 1975. *Black Child Care*. New York: Pocket Books.

Cross, W. July 1971. The Negro to black conversion experience: Towards a psychology of black liberation. *Black World* 20, no. 9, 13–27.

———. 1978. Models of psychological nigrescence: A literature review. *Journal of Black Psychology* 5:13–31.

———. 1980. "Black Identity: Rediscovering the Distinction between Personal Identity and Reference Group Orientation." New York: Africana Studies and Research Center, Cornell University.

Erikson, E. 1950. *Childhood and Society.* New York: W. W. Norton.

———. 1956. The problem of ego identity. *Journal of the American Psychoanalytic Association* 4:56–121.

———. October 1964. A memorandum on identity and Negro youth. *Journal of Social Issues* 10:4, 29–42.

———. 1968. *Identity, Youth and Crisis.* New York: W. W. Norton.

Fordam, S., and J. Ogbu. 1986. Black students' school success: Coping with the burden of acting white. *The Urban Review* 18: 3, 176–206.

Gay, G. May 1978. Ethnic identity in early adolescence: Some implications for institutional reform. *Educational Leadership*, p. 649–55.

Gilligan, C. 1982. *In a Different Voice.* Cambridge, Mass: Harvard University Press.

Grier, W., and P. Cobbs. 1968. *Black Rage.* New York: Basic Books.

Jones, R. 1980. *Black Psychology*, 2nd Ed. New York: Harper and Row.

Ladner, J. 1971. *Tomorrow's Tomorrow: The Black Woman.* New York: Doubleday.

———. 1978. *Mixed Families: Adopting Across Racial Boundaries.* New York: Doubleday.

Nobles, W. 1981. "African-American Family Life: An Instrument of Culture." In *Black Families*, edited by H. P. McAdoo. Beverly Hills, Calif.: Sage Press.

———. 1980. "African Philosophy: Foundations for Black Psychology." In *Black Psychology*, edited by R. Jones. New York: Harper and Row.

Okazawa-Rey, M., T. Robinson and J. Ward. 1987. "Black Women and the Politics of Skin Color and Hair." In *Women, Power and Therapy: Issues for Women*, edited by M. Braude. New York: The Haworth Press.

Powell, G. 1982. "School Desegregation and Self-Concept Among Junior High School Students." In *The Afro-American Family: Assessment Treatment and Research Issues*, edited by B. Bass, G. Wyatt, and G. Powell. New York: Grune and Stratton.

Slaughter, D. February 1972. Becoming an Afro-American woman. *School Review*, 299–318.

Thomas, C. 1971. *Boys Know More*. Beverly Hills, Calif.: Glencoe Press.

Ward J. January 1984. Racial identity formation and transformation: A literature review. Unpublished Qualifying Paper, Harvard Graduate School of Education.

The View from Step Number 16

*Girls from Emma Willard School Talk
about Themselves and Their Futures*

JANET MENDELSOHN

A youth expected to fight for his personal place in a society of well-defined direction is not lost but on his way. . . . Only when each group has its own important tasks, when one without the other cannot succeed, when age provides the direction but youth the leadership and the fighting manpower, is it clearly understood that whether the battle is won or lost depends on youth's fulfilling its all-important share of the total struggle.
—*Bruno Bettelheim, "The Problem of Generations"*

Me, myself, like a young girl at this time, it is like the new generation growing up, of women and what's going to be and each generation, like my little cousin who is two. She is going to be one step above me, each generation I think is getting one step above to, like, being equal or being just the whole. . . . We are a step, and I am, like, step number 16. Our generation is step number 16. It gets you further and further to the front of the goal.
—*Sophomore, Emma Willard School*

This chapter examines conceptions of self and the future in the responses of thirty of the girls interviewed at Emma Willard in 1981 and 1982. These conceptions center on responses to the following questions:

How would you describe yourself to yourself?

Is the way you see yourself now different from the way you saw yourself in the past?

Who is someone you admire?

What does it mean to be a young woman today?

When you think about your life in the future, how do you imagine your life (in terms of work and relationship)?

In looking at responses to questions about how these girls see themselves, how their view of themselves is changing, who and what sorts of qualities they admire, and how they see their futures, it is possible to construct a picture of how they envision their passage into adulthood and maturity. This chapter, then, examines adolescent girls' images of themselves as they project themselves into adulthood.

The first part of this chapter describes in some detail the patterns of response to the questions asked, noting the tone and substance of what emerges as a dominant voice in the interviews. The next part of the chapter examines the apparent assumptions behind this dominant voice, looking at what seems to be meant by the words the girls use to describe themselves and who they are becoming. Finally, there is a brief discussion of exceptions to the rule: those girls whose responses do not fit the descriptions of the dominant group.

The findings here appear to confirm and extend Gilligan's work on the role of relationships in adolescent girls' development. Gilligan found that dependence and independence are not opposed, rather, "dependence is opposed to isolation and independence in the sense of autonomy [is] seen not to exist. . . . Instead, independence is seen as enhancing and enhanced by relationships. . . ." (Gilligan 1982).

In thinking about themselves and their futures, these girls tend to experience little discontinuity between present and future self. They characterize each as both responsible and independent, and use both terms to mean usefully and richly connected to other people.

The findings here also suggest that the perceptions about the future of at least this small sample of adolescent girls are not characterized by the sort of passivity, and the tendency to defer issues of identity, that so many observers of adolescents have seen as characteristic of girls as opposed to boys. The girls interviewed here are active and concrete in their approach to their lives now and into the future.

The third section of this chapter suggests that the particular stance toward the future maintained by these girls is best understood in sociological as well as in developmental psychological terms. Such factors as the social changes attributable to the new feminism, the rhetoric and pedagogy of Emma Willard School, and the diversity of backgrounds from which these girls all come seem to combine in a particularly benign fashion to fill the students with the sense that meaningful work and relationships surround and await them.

A common vision

The thirty interviews demonstrated extraordinary similarities in the responses concerning how the girls describe themselves, what sorts of qualities they admire, and what they believe it means to be a young woman today. Virtually without exception, these girls portray the same ideal (approving these qualities in themselves, striving to assume more of them, or admiring these qualities in others): they admire and seek to become someone who is "responsible," "independent," "outgoing," "understanding," "confident," "striving," "enthusiastic."

> I like being independent. I like it a lot, because I feel that I am very responsible and I feel like I have never been given credit for that before, so it is nice to be able to do my own laundry and things.
>
> I get along really well with most people. I am very open about people and I think that I am very accepting of them. . . . I have become a lot more independent, I can do things for myself. . . .
>
> I like to help other people. I am a good friend. . . . I have found that working a lot harder and doing the best job I can makes a big difference in how everyone at Emma Willard treats you, because I am more responsible and I feel like I have changed a lot since I came here.

There is also general agreement that being a young woman today involves "being responsible," "more aware," "independent." Becoming a young woman also means beginning to experience first hand the problems of discrimination against women in the society and combating this discrimination with "an upright attitude," "striving to do my best."

Caring about and being open to other people commonly emerge in these girls' self-descriptions:

> I like to listen and try to understand other people. It is important to me to see how other people are feeling, and I don't like to make other people feel upset. It really bothers me if I have hurt somebody else.
>
> I am someone who cares about other people and cares about what they think and feel. . . . I try to make [people] feel not left out. . . . I just wish that there wasn't any unhappiness in the world.

Most of the girls interviewed see these qualities as ones they have had for some time:

> I would say that I am a very open-minded person . . . very understanding, always willing to help. . . . *(Is the way that you see your-*

self now different from the way that you saw yourself in the past?)
No, not really. From all the times that I can remember. I mean, as
I have been growing up, the times I can really remember I have
always been basically the same. . . . I have always been understanding and I have always been leading, always striving to keep going.

The sense of striving that this girl expresses is also a common theme:

I am a doer. I like to get things done. I like to work hard.
   I got to where I wanted to go simply because I applied myself.
I like that about me, that I could get to places because I wanted to
do it badly enough, that I made things work and that I *could* make
things work, that it wasn't just some dream of a seventeen-year-
old.

Differences in the self-descriptions tend to focus on questions of how
successful one is at trying hard and at being involved and open with
people. For example, there is some strain apparent in a number of responses, although the terms used are almost identical:

I'd say I have my good times and my bad times and I try to be
outgoing, but there are times I would say honestly that my shyness
would get in the way. Sometimes I procrastinate. I try to do things
for other people. I try to put my best out. I try to be open-minded
for other people.

Another girl, lamenting her shyness, says, "I am very outgoing on the
inside."
   There is also widespread agreement about the influence that Emma
Willard School has had on them. Virtually without exception they see
the faculty and students at the school as having helped them gain confidence, become more responsible, become more open to people, learn
to work more productively and harder, and become more independent.
Only one girl out of these thirty interviews is openly critical of the school:

Here we lead such sheltered lives—it's gross. They say that this is
a college prep school, but it's a bunch of bull. . . . They don't let
you grow at all here. I feel like I am a little paper doll that they
just kind of push around.

One important area in which many girls see their experience at Emma Willard as having helped them gain independence lies in their separation from boys and the accompanying release from looking to boys for approval:

> I think a lot of it is that I am not around boys anymore, and that used to intimidate me a lot. I was scared to death that if I said something wrong, so-and-so wouldn't like me any more. . . . And when you are here they are not even a part of your life, which in some ways is good, because you don't have that pressure to . . . I don't know what the pressure is, I have never been able to confront it, but there is always the pressure I hear from the girls around me; if I don't look nice they won't like me, and if I am not smart they won't like me, and when you get here you realize that it really doesn't matter. If they don't like you because you are ugly or they don't like you because you are stupid, who cares?

The intensity with which some of the girls experience their release from boys' power over their images of themselves is reflected in the black humor of this response:

> My 8th grade year I was totally subservient to boys. Here I regard boys more as objects. It makes me feel I'm getting my revenge. All those times that I was, you know, I'd kill myself for them, now I regard them as inanimate pieces of flesh that you can use and throw away.

The picture that emerges is that each of these girls wants to be responsible, outgoing, mature, independent, understanding, enthusiastic, self-confident, and virtually each of them describes herself as becoming increasingly so, even though some may see themselves as having a longer way to go than others.

These girls also agree overwhelmingly on the basic outlines of a vision for the future. Without exception, the thirty girls say they will work after college and that work will be important to them. They all want to have relationships with men, and most also want to marry and have children. Although roughly half of the girls think they would probably like to interrupt their careers in order to devote themselves to raising children, most see these hiatuses as temporary, and many want to remain "self-supporting" throughout marriage.

A popular strategy for managing career and family is to establish a career or work at a job before starting a family, then leave work for some time. Most do not want to marry "right away," preferring to wait "a long time" (until they are over twenty-five) to marry and have children.

Typical responses to the question, How do you see yourself in the future? included:

> Probably the first half of my life I'd like to have a job and be dedicated to that, but once I started a family I'd like to concentrate on that.
>
> Real skinny, very independent, and working at a real high job . . . devoting myself to my work. Living in an apartment by myself with my dog, and going to work and coming home and fixing my own meals and going on a date at night and just very easygoing, having lots of friends and having parties. . . . I want to stop work to raise my kids, then go back when they're four, then stay home again when they're ten, because I know when kids need parental guidance because I have that all written down in my diary so I won't forget.

Largely unaddressed are the problems likely to be associated either with giving up hard-won meaningful careers for family life, or with obstacles to being able to come and go from work commitments at will in order to raise their own children.

Without exception, the girls interviewed express interest in having careers that would enable them to do interesting work. Most mention wanting to be "successful" as very important to their image of themselves in the future. While most are vague about the particular careers, relationships, and life-styles they envision, there tends to be greater clarity and concreteness concerning their future work than future marriages and families. For most of the girls it is easier to imagine living as an adult with a job than it is to imagine living a married life. In fact, of all the aspects of the future that are considered, marriage itself tends to be the activity that is most vaguely or ambivalently treated. Work and children appear to be more substantial and perhaps more reliable components of adult life than marriage.

One girl responds to the question, How about relationships when you think about the future?

> I imagine . . . it's funny because my friends, we talk sometimes about, Are you going to get married? It used to be what kind of

person are you going to marry, and now we are talking about are we even going to get married at all, and at this point, I don't think I can say I don't think I will get married. I can't say I am definitely going to get married because it all depends if I find somebody I like enough to marry.

At least two factors may contribute to this view: Many of the girls' parents are divorced, giving them and their friends firsthand evidence that marriage may not be satisfying or may well be a temporary status —not something to plan your life around. Second, a feminist critique of marriage appears to be made available to them through discussions with their teachers. Several girls say that they think that marriage cannot be everything for a woman, and they criticize the media and the society in general for perpetuating a myth that marriage is enough and forever. As one says:

A lot of us have realized through the help of our teachers and other people, that in America marriage has been blown up to something, that everything is supposed to be sex and romance, and you have to realize and take into account that a marriage can't be all that. There are going to be bad times, you have to be able to depend on the other person and trust the other person, almost more so than love them . . . If they let you down a lot and then once a year come home with a dozen roses, it shouldn't make everything all better.

While a number of girls perceive marriage as problematic, their feelings about retaining emotional and financial independence differ in interesting ways. Several girls approach this desire for independence within marriage with a sort of pride and explicit awareness that they are very much a part of the feminist struggle:

I think I'll be very independent. I am not going to rely on the husband to make all the money. I'm planning to be, like, a lawyer.

I will work. I don't know what I want to work at. Women don't stay in the house anymore. We go out, we work, we can depend on ourselves. . . .

Others, who seem less zealous, appear to be reacting to what they see around them. They assume they will work because that is what is being done by women these days:

In the past I always thought that I would get out of college, and I was going to have kids, and I was going to live at home, and I was just going to be, I don't know, a stereotypical woman. And when my mother was growing up that is what everyone did, and now that I look ahead, even if I wanted to do that, I could never see myself following my mother's footsteps, because I don't see women doing that any more very often. And it is very important to me to go out and be successful, and I don't think of that as successful at all.

Some others seem to see work as a fallback position, one to be assumed in the face of the unpleasant possibility that marriages may not last forever:

I imagine to have a husband and a family, but yet I don't want to go straight into a family, but working. And I want to be kind of independent by myself, so I would know if anything else happened and I had to live by myself, that I could do it, and I won't be stuck there. . . . I want to have a family.

And, in answer to the question, What is the image of the ideal woman? a girl answers:

Somebody who can have a family and still have a job. *(How would you describe her life?)* Hectic . . . I'm not sure that's what I want for myself, if I want to do both.

Thus, although there appears to be widespread agreement that financial and emotional independence are important, even necessary, for a woman today, this realization is not greeted by most as quite the brave new world but rather as a necessary fact of life.

There is much about these statements that is worth noting in the light of perceived notions of women's development. There is, first of all, the universal expectation that they will work in meaningful jobs and that their careers will play a major role in defining them and establishing their success. This expectation, combined with vivid fantasies of individual achievement and with a flatness of affect in the reporting of fantasies of love and marriage, stands in stark contrast to the work of Douvan and Adelson (1966). These authors compared male and female responses to questions concerning plans for and dreams about the future. They found that in girls' responses, real-world plans focused on occupational choice and were vague and emotionally uninvested, while fantasies tended to concern love and glamour and were colorful and emotionally charged. They concluded that:

> In the boys we find that dreams and plans are either similar in focus or at least appropriate to each other. Girls, on the other hand, show a marked discontinuity between fantasy and reality planning.

There is also an astonishing absence of passivity in the Emma Willard girls' responses. Their active stance toward their lives now and into the future can be seen in the way careers are seen as having ongoing importance; in the way marriage is portrayed as problematic, often transient; in the way relationships with friends are portrayed as having great significance now and into the future, weaving through projected relationships with husband and children. In this respect, there is no sign of the kind of interlude of passivity described by Erikson (1968). Whereas these girls do tend to perceive development as occurring within a context of relationship, their ongoing relationships with friends, family, and teachers form the crucible in which identity is forged. There is no hint of holding identity in abeyance, no suggestion that one has the option of waiting to be defined by an intimate relationship with a future husband.

There is also remarkable activity in the language used to talk about the future, even in the presence of uncertainty about the content of the vision.

Asked, What does it mean to you to be a young woman? a girl replies:

> I am still deciding how I am going to be. I think of myself basically as an adult, a new adult, but an adult. . . . I think there is a lot that is expected of me because I am a female—get married, have kids —and I think that I am going to ignore that and do what I want. . . . And I think, I can't really say, because I don't really know what it is like to be a young man. But I am happy. I really am. And I think I am glad I am female. I don't know why I am, but I am.

Contrast this with the single response that is clearly passive: "I often wonder what's going to happen to me. . . ."

Remarkably absent also are fantasies of romance and rescue. Although several girls want to "marry a gorgeous millionaire," their fantasies are not about being awakened, empowered, changed by the lover. In fact there is little the gorgeous, rich husband really changes. He does not sweep her into a dazzling adult world to which only he has access. Instead, he is a facilitator. His money makes life easier, providing maids to do the housework so the heroine can be free to devote herself to career and children.

It seems clear, then, that these girls do not see themselves as needing to be rescued from the responsibility of making choices about the future.

What is it that gives rise in other girls and women to the need to abdicate responsibility for choice? Gilligan, in her book *In a Different Voice* (1982), says: "To the extent that women perceive themselves as having no choice they correspondingly excuse themselves from the responsibility that decision entails" (P. 67). The girls at Emma Willard apparently perceive a world rife with choices and opportunities. The need to be rescued comes about if one sees no way out, no link between where one is and where one needs to be in order to be safe. When safety was defined as existing only under the protection of a husband, the gap between adolescence and adulthood for young women was, in effect, unbridgeable. There was a chasm across which no woman could walk alone. To be rescued was the only way to grow. Apparently these girls do not share this vision. They appear to see other routes across the divide between childhood and adulthood.

Underlying assumptions: the meanings attached to responsibility and independence

The chapter thus far has sketched common themes running through the content of the girls' responses. What follows looks at what seems like the subtext of this pattern of responses, the psychological underpinnings of these girls' self assessments and their visions of the future.

When the interviewer asks, How would you describe yourself to yourself? a girl responds:

> I'm very responsible, like, I'm trustworthy, too. . . . I think I have a lot of responsibility and I can handle difficult situations and kinds of adult situations. I don't give in to peer pressure, I'm very individual, outgoing, friendly, not shy.

When asked, When you think about the future, how do you imagine your life? she continues:

When I grow up I think I'll be a lot like my mother, in the fact that I will be very independent and I will be responsible like she is. . . . I want to do something rewarding for myself, I want to be comfortable and happy . . . comfortable in mind and body.

Apparent here is a strong sense of continuity between present and future self. This girl sees herself now as very responsible, not giving in to peer pressure, very individualistic, and she looks forward to being a responsible and independent adult. The sense of a continuous line stretching from childhood through adolescence and into adulthood is characteristic of these interviews. In this view, the transition from adolescence to adulthood is not particularly problematic. As one girl expresses the process:

You go from the stage where your mother takes care of you, where you start to get some type of individualism, and then you want more independence, and then finally you are independent and you have to support yourself and take care of yourself.

The fact that these girls see little discontinuity between childhood, adolescence, and adulthood does not mean they see no differences, nor do they think that the changes just happen to a person. The picture they paint is an active one, involving striving within a familiar framework of responsibility and independence. One of them comments:

Childlike is just fooling around—not really seriously—whereas if you are an adult you take things seriously and you understand exactly what you are looking for. You grasp what the world is about. . . . When you grow to start to become an adult, you start to take on more responsibilities.

But what is meant by responsibility? And what is meant by independence? How are these words used and understood? It appears first of all that independence and responsibility exist in comfortable compatibility. There can be no true independence without responsibility and no real responsibility unless it is independently arrived at. This compatibility is made possible because the concepts of responsibility and independence, used rigorously, avoid certain associations and adhere to others. Responsibility is not often seen as a burden; rather, it is the glue that holds the pleasurable aspects of life together—work, children, and friends all demand responsible service. (Interestingly, this upbeat view of adult responsibility doesn't seem to be attributable to a romanticized picture of the future. Certain aspects of women's lives, like having to do housework, are viewed with universal revulsion.)

In this view, responsibility has been rescued from the dreary realm of duty, revived within the context of having choices, now taking on the appealing quality of combining control with a sense of connection, and avoiding the implication of self-denial. Responsibility is not perceived as involving a choice between attending to the needs of others over and above self. Responsibility here seems opposed to both lack of control and lack of connection. Rarely in the interviews does one get a sense that someone is contrasting responsibility with being carefree or adventurous. Control, seen as an important part of responsibility, is itself interestingly used. Asked who they admire, many girls mentioned people who seemed to be in control:

> My sister: She's very pretty, in control of her surroundings, she's got a pretty stable situation, or she keeps herself in a stable situation. She doesn't let things get too much out of control. . . . She always keeps herself in good shape and in good health and seems a stable person.

> My aunt: She's very successful in what she does. She's a person who has a very almost organized life, having a place to be, something you have to do.

Even Brooke Shields is admired, in part because:

> She is the woman who seems to never do anything wrong. She is the number one virgin who has these morals to stand by, and she's so firm on her feet and all that.

Being in control of one's life means being confident, having control over how things go. There is the strong feeling that these things in themselves are pleasurable now and in the future. Speaking of the present, a girl says:

> It's important to me to always be at my best, to look or feel good, feel good about myself. I like to be in good shape. I like to be strong, to be in good health. Hair looking half decent. I don't like it to get ratty or anything. Take a shower everyday. Don't get overweight.

Another reflects on her future:

> Living in an apartment by myself with my dog, and going to work and coming home and fixing my own meals, and going on a date at night and just a very easygoing, having lots of friends and having parties.

There is no indication that being in control might involve having power over other people, nor is control ever equated with being—in the quaint parlance of another era—"uptight." There is no fear of the routines and regimentation that may be associated with living a life guided by self-control. And there is little imagery having to do with the pleasure of abandoning control, cutting loose, or feeling wicked.

Of these thirty interviews, only one reflected deep resistance to the idea of responsibility and control:

> I don't think I can handle a lot of responsibility. I can't see myself doing a job where there is someone telling me what to do . . . I bristle at that. I just—ugh. You can't tell me what to do. But they can! . . . If they are my boss.
>
> I think I am going to have to be free for a long time to get this out of me, before I am ready to settle down. If I do. I have to be in a place where I can be free, where I can laugh at everything or I can take it seriously if I want to . . . just let things flow, not make five decisions every minute.

There is a hint of protest here, I suspect, against a tone that is set at Emma Willard. Apparently this is not a place where one can feel free to laugh or take something seriously as the mood strikes one. Life at the school is seen here as a drill in decision making—"five decisions every minute," each one taken seriously. For the great majority of the girls this approach appears to work well. They feel they are growing in the capacity to do what they want to do—take an active role in shaping their own lives as confident and responsible young women. For this girl and some few others, however, the vision is constraining or exhausting.

As for the notion of independence, the word is used again and again to mean something like confident and self-respecting. It seems never to be used to mean unattached or on one's own, unconnected to other people. Gilligan (October 1982) has pointed out that in answer to questions about relationships posed elsewhere in these interviews, girls tend to stress their feelings of connection to other people by defining dependence in opposition to isolation, rather than to independence or autonomy. What can be seen in their answers to questions about self now and in the future is the use of the word independent as implicitly opposed to passive, timid, childish, clinging to others. But it is also an independence that exists within the context of relationships of love and care. One is independent not of the family but within it, not of relationships with friends but within them:

> I feel so independent. I care a lot about what other people say, and I am not independent in that I don't listen to other people in relationships I really value and trust, family relationships and all that. But I don't feel typical, because everything I do is my own decision.

It is common for these girls to describe themselves as becoming increasingly independent of peer pressure as they become more mature, but not as isolated from the influence of caring people. Many girls welcome the increasing independence they feel at Emma Willard, independence from the judgments of boys and from the pressures, experienced at former schools, to take drugs. Once at Emma Willard they tend to experience others' judgments of them and the pressure to conform to the particular standards of the school as influences encouraging self-enhancement and individuality. They tend to see the school (teachers and fellow students alike) as forces encouraging them to become more their own person, more independent, even though the end result, what they seem to be encouraged to be, sounds so homogeneous. What they seem to be saying is that growing more mature means doing what is expected of one without having to be asked to do it. As one of them puts it:

> I feel I am very responsible. It's nice to be able to do my laundry and things. *(What do you mean by more independent?)* I get mad when people tell me what to do and it is something that I would have done anyway. I want credit for having done it on my own.

An important topic in tracing the progress toward independence is the movement from child to adult within family relationships. Several girls describe the effort to become more mature as initially involving a pulling away from other people, particularly from parents:

Last year I was quiet and difficult to live with, and I was becoming independent from my family, and I was a lot less comfortable with myself last year than I am now. I was changing a lot, from being young and little to being old and grown-up. . . . I was trying to change roles, I was trying to become an adult instead of being a little kid. It involved being rebellious and not listening to my parents, and I wish I had. And hurting them. . . . I like myself better since I've come here.

What seems interesting in this and several other interviews is the time-limited quality of this period of withdrawal and struggle to move out of the family. There seems to be a brief period when relationships, especially with parents, are experienced as constraining, or at least a time when self is defined less in terms of relationships of responsibility and interdependence and more in terms of expanding personal power. Girls who referred to these feelings, however, described them as being in the past. For a brief time some of these girls saw childhood dependence as constraining. Quickly, though, they experience the limitations of this worldview that equates independence with autonomy, moving through that vision to a view of the world that fuses independence with responsibility, which, taken together, produce an interdependent perspective. The view of responsibility changes:

When I was younger, being a woman was having guys go by and whistle when you're on a bike. Now it is more responsibility to your family to mostly everything around . . . like cleaning house and writing letters and keeping in touch and making people feel like they're needed and wanted. Responsibility to your grandmother to let her know that you are still thinking of her.

The girl whose story begins this section of the chapter shows a way in which doing what one is supposed to do is really quite different from still being a little girl. There is a sense of achievement, of a position thoughtfully arrived at. There are real undeniable changes taking place in her self, her position among her friends, and her role in the family. She contemplates these changes:

Like, most of my friends give in very easily to peer pressure, very easily—like, on Halloween everybody went out, and they were all smoking. And I didn't even ask for a cigarette, and everyone was drinking and I suppose if I liked the taste of beer and things, I'd drink it. But everyone was doing it because everyone else was doing it. But I don't give in to peer pressure at all. Like, I wear the clothes that I like to wear. I do what I like to do. I don't try to please everyone in the way that they will think less of me if I don't be like them. I'm like myself. I am very individual.

The rebelliousness represented by drinking and smoking is here seen as the mindless tyranny of peer-group pressure. The route out of childhood for this girl may be seen as a movement into and through peer culture, with peer culture giving her another model for growth that she rejects. But her return to the family is informed by that choice. Having experienced herself as one who can make choices, she is no longer the same child in the family. This awareness that choices are available and have been made may account for the sense of independence that so many girls have even as they model themselves after approved figures in the adult world.

It is also made possible by two other elements: enthusiasm for the prospect of maturation (fueled by the sense that adulthood offers some very appealing features) and a strong preference for interdependence—the sense that one is understood and accepted and, in turn, that one will understand and accept others:

I am not afraid to talk to people and, like, explain something. Like, usually my parents are my best guidelines. I am not very rebellious actually. I'd just as soon have everything happy . . . I'm very good at putting myself in someone else's place . . . I hate being misunderstood. Like my brother, for example: He just got bad grades on his report card, and my mother was very upset and she yelled at him. And he won't explain; he won't sit down and talk to her. I never want something to be thought of me that's not true if I can help it. I wouldn't want my mother to misunderstand me. My brother does that often, like, my mother never sees him study. He does; I see him study all the time. But my brother, just to rebel against my mother, he just studies when my mother is out, and so that when she comes home, he is in front of the TV. And she says, D., do your homework. And he goes, I already did it. And she is, like, You did not. And he goes, I don't care, I am watching TV and aggravates her and won't tell her. He likes that feeling of, you know, he knows he's right and he knows she's wrong, but he won't tell her she's wrong, you know, he just lets her continue being wrong. He's just doing it to get her, you know?

Here is a portrait of two different ways of establishing oneself as an independent person with the family. In order to feel that he has room to make his own choices about how and when to study, her brother pushes his mother away to give himself some room to exercise choice. Rather than be controlled by his mother, he prefers to be misjudged, blamed— this is better than being constrained. His way out of childhood obedience is to create the impression that he is rebelling even if, in fact, he is meeting the responsibilities in question. In contrast, the girl feels able to grow within the family by asking to be heard and making sure she is understood.

Exceptions

The girls discussed in this chapter thus far portray a dominant voice in the interview. Of the thirty interviews, twenty-one seem to fall into this dominant pattern, reflecting the perception of a smooth transition from an increasingly responsible, independent adolescence to a responsible, independent, successful work- and family-oriented adulthood. Nine interviews do not seem to reflect this pattern of response. Characterizing these nine in contrast to the majority further delineates the thinking of the dominant group, rather than presenting a full account of the thinking of these "exceptions." Much more work remains to be done in order to present a full portrait of this group. Although this is beyond the scope of this chapter, it may well be worth doing, since these nine voices are among the most interesting in the sample. They tend to be especially reflective, intense, and original in their thinking.

These nine girls do not seem to constitute a group in any way other than the fact that they perceive themselves and the future differently than do the dominants. Each voice is quite distinct. What they seem to have in common, when compared with the dominant group, is an increased awareness of difficulty, tension, ambivalence, and contradiction in their lives. Yet they are radically different from one another in the way they experience and apply their heightened perception of strain. Two of the girls are politically radical in their views and interested in working toward social change; two appear to have a history of heavy drug use and sexual acting out, which they are now moving away from but which has left them hurt and cynical; two others seem to find it especially difficult to establish emotional contact with people, and they feel lonely and disconnected; the remaining three seem very much like the dominant group, except that they have many more doubts about their ability to perform adequately and more ambivalence about relationships and responsibility.

The increased turmoil and uneasiness experienced by this group can be seen throughout the range of their responses. They speak of discontinuities in their lives, of conflicting expectations from fathers and mothers (most of whom are divorced); and they express a feeling of not belonging anywhere. A portion of one interview reveals this confusion:

> *(What are your parents' expectations for you?)* None . . . maybe . . . my mother wants me to make one hundred thousand dollars a year; my father wants me to be a stable adult. *(How does this affect you?)* It tears me. Because they are very different expectations; one is materialistic, the other is the opposite. And when those pull on you, you are not quite sure what to do because you cannot be totally one thing and totally the other. *(Describe yourself to yourself.)* Lonely. They are all awful, not awful but unhappy things. Sort of torn between two places, here and with the people I believe are, have a pride. And I don't feel like I belong in either facet—or any facet of society that I have been in.

Several speak of doubts about the future, or they have trouble projecting themselves into a concrete future:

> I do have doubts about the future . . . Will I be able to succeed? Will I be able to get it all together? Will I be able to be what I want to be. *(What do you want to be?)* I don't know, but once I decide what succeeding is, I'll feel pretty bad if I don't get there. *(What does it mean to you to be a young woman?)* I feel a little insecure because I am very worried about my future. I don't want to fail— but I don't really know what failing means. When I do decide what I want, I don't want not to have it. I am worrying about not being happy in the future. There'll be all kinds of stress in school, all kinds of pressure to do well so that you can go on and do well in the new things and build on it, and if you don't get the base down, then everything crumbles. I am worried that it will not achieve anything. Or what it achieves will not be what I want to do.

There are fears about their ability to live with and be responsible for children:

Motherhood kind of scares me because you have to be so selfless, and I don't know if I could do that. There are many times I feel strangled, I hate feeling stifled . . . being responsible for another individual is really scary, but I want to perpetuate myself.

I imagine having problems when I have kids. I imagine having problems dealing with them, not as a mother/child, but trying to come across as a friend like my mother has. She does a marvelous job of it, and I am always afraid I will not be able to do that. I am afraid of becoming like my grandmother, who is very hard-nosed. She doesn't feel she needs anybody and that scares me. I see it in me a great deal of the time. The other side of me sees what my mother is, which is a very dependent person, which scares me also.

For these girls conflict is paralyzing because each side continues to assert its claims.

Another tone of voice characteristic of this group and notable for its absence in the dominants is anger. Several of these "exceptional" responses are characterized by images of violence that spring suddenly from an otherwise familiar narrative.

Women don't stay in the house anymore. We go out, we work, we can depend on ourselves, we are strong enough. At some points I think women are stronger to do it than men. I think if we ever came up with war again, I think women could fight better than men. I think we are a lot . . . when women get mad we get mad. I mean men have always taken us as the dainty little things, but if I really had to, I could beat the hell out of anybody, you know. And if someone is coming at me with a gun, I'd blow his head off. That is the way it is, you know. I would wipe them all out. *(What does it mean to you to be a young woman?)* It's excellent. There is so much, there are so many opportunities open to us now. *(If you could change the world, where would you start?)* I'd have females as leaders of the world, that's what I'd do. *(And then what would the world be like?)* Female dominated. The guys would be on their knees to us instead. . . . They are so different and if we could all know about each other, you know, just a little more, I think there would be a better understanding just on the whole—just to put them in our place for one day. I think that would do it. They'd go crazy, I don't think they would be able to handle it.

There also tends to be a certain toleration for ambiguity, inconsistency, and deviance not apparent in the dominants' responses. Two girls respond to the question, Can you think of a person that you admire, and how would you describe that person?

A person I admire? My uncle. I hate him, but he's got to be . . . he's admirable. He's cute. . . . He's devious but he's so good. Like within the next year he is going to be a millionaire. He sold his lamp store just because he wanted to. He said, 'I was sick of it, so I did.' And that is the way I am: I'm sick of it, I won't do it anymore.

It has to be Grace Slick, you know, the Jefferson Airplane. I don't know, I have always loved her voice and she is such . . . she is so talented, and I'd just love to be like her. Last year I had a crush on her because she was so, she was just like my whole world. It was like an obsession and, like, she was on drugs and everything and she was, like, the acid queen of rock and roll. And I was trying to portray her, and that's what messed me up in the first place . . . She seems so free. *(Free from what?)* Free from life. I don't know if you can understand that.

The agitation and confusion in these responses, although atypical of the girls in this sample, recall descriptions of adolescent turmoil familiar in the literature on adolescence. Whether this agitation stems from increased strain in their families, intrapsychic problems, particular sensitivity, or acuteness of perception is an open question. It does seem worth noting that what has been seen as the norm for adolescents in the psychological literature appears as the exception in this sample of girls at Emma Willard. Interestingly, these feelings are experienced individually; there is no attempt to establish an adolescent culture built around turmoil or dissent. Thus, although the responses may be seen as implying a political critique of the dominant vision of adulthood, almost always their doubts are seen as their problem rather than as a valid response to the world as they have experienced it. Like the girl who sees herself as "very outgoing on the inside"—all but three of the girls seem to yearn to share the dominant vision.

Emma Willard and the new feminism

The tone of hopefulness and confidence that pervades the majority of the interviews is striking because of its peculiar mixture of complacency and mission. My sense is that it is a tone of voice that is made possible by a unique moment in the history of middle-class women's consciousness. Rarely before has it been possible to hold socially conservative values while being filled with the sense that one is on the frontlines of a battle for a new social order. The new feminism has laid the groundwork for this, while the solidly conservative values of their parents and Emma Willard's academic mission mesh well with the real pressures and values of the "success-oriented" 1980s. If, in the words of sixties agitator Jerry Rubin, "The 1980s are about success," then Emma Willard School is about women's success.

The legacy of the women's movement of the early 1970s seems to be less its radical critique of the oppressive structures of capitalist society and more its demand for equal consideration for women in existing society. Embedded in this relatively moderate demand, however, is the sense that equal consideration should extend beyond opportunity and salary to the recognition that a female point of view toward experience must also be heard.

These high school girls seem to reflect this new understanding of women's importance now; they combine a sense that they can and are obliged to enter the work force with a good deal of seriousness and with the strong sense that they will bring to their future lives values and styles of functioning very different from those of the male-dominated world. They value relationships and connectedness as much as they do individual ambition. From the women's movement they have gotten the sense that their distinctive voice matters. Whereas it has always been acknowledged that women were different, the particular qualities of difference have only recently begun to be seen as potentially valuable, or at least valid. In large part, because of the women's movement, these girls have a sense that they have something special to contribute to the future. Here the adolescent girl of the 1980s stands in strong contrast both to the adolescent of the 1960s and to male adolescents today.

But if these high school girls see themselves as new women, they seem equally invested in the dominant values of their time. Few of them recoil at any of the implications of growing up in the 1980s. While they express some concern or apprehension about whether they will find a satisfying career, whether they will be able to handle the competing pressures of work and family, whether they will find a balance that is right for them, the vast majority of the girls experience their doubts within a framework of overwhelming acceptance of the values and realities of the adult world. Unlike their counterparts of the late 1960s and 1970s, these children of the 1980s neither fear nor reject the world they inherit. Although virtually all of the girls are concerned about encountering obstacles for women in society, they appear to have the sense that these are vestiges of an old order. They perceive that they will have to struggle against the old ways, but they sense that the momentum of history is on their side. Interestingly, many of the girls see their mothers and their mothers' generation as allies in this struggle. This sense of indebtedness to and partnership with older women extends their tendency to experience their lives as continuous with their mothers' into a political dimension as well:

My mother . . . I can see the difference, the slight difference of me getting a little bit higher. My mother's, like, ahead of her time. Like, when she was in high school, she wanted to do everything that women nowadays do. Like, she wanted to be in the army, a parachute jumper, she would do anything . . . and she is interested in everything, car mechanics, everything. Now they are female-categorized, and if she had been in this generation she could have done everything she wanted to.

The sense of sisterhood in struggle with one's mother, identifying with one's mother's aspirations rather than with her complicity in her own oppression seems like a wonderful gift that the new feminism has given mothers and daughters of this generation.

While the new feminism seems to explain their sense of mission, these Emma Willard girls exhibit a sense of complacency that is harder to place. Virtually all these students are white and middle to upper-middle class. The sense of choice and of limitless possibilities they have is as tied to the privileges of class and race as to the women's movement. They also appear to accept the idea that hard work will bring success and that success in the adult world is worth the effort. Put even more simply, they accept the idea that the adult world itself is worth something. Whether this idea is true or not, it is not one that they share with adolescents of the late sixties and the seventies. Nor do they share the earlier generations' preoccupation with injustice and inequality in the society, except as it may pertain to their lives as women. Thus there does not appear to be the sense that the adult world is hostile, corrupt, alien, routine, empty, hollow, dry. To account for this acceptance of so much of the world as given we probably should look, in part, to the lives their parents, particularly their mothers, are living. It appears that many of their parents have communicated a sense of satisfaction with their lives, and these girls are sufficiently identified with their parents that they do not reject their experience. Second, images in the media support this upbeat view of success in the adult world. Finally, no viable counterculture now exists to provide alternative models for success whatever they may be. But whatever the reasons, the adult world now appears to be experiencing a renaissance in the eyes of these adolescents. The attitude of the girls at Emma Willard is quite different from the adolescent questioning described by Kohlberg and Gilligan in their paper "The Adolescent as a Philosopher," written in 1971. They observed that "The current radical rejection of adult society seems to be the rejection of any adult society whatever, if an adult society means one including institutions of work, family, law, and government." These Emma Willard students seem much closer to Kohlberg and Gilligan's characterization of the teenagers of the 1950s:

> Even when he wanted to know why, the American adolescent seldom questioned the American assumptions of progress and upward mobility, the assumption that society was moving ahead. Rather, he questioned the wisdom of his parents because they were old-fashioned. This questioning was itself an expression of faith in the adult society of the future. . . . (P. 1053)

This acceptance of traditional adult values at Emma Willard can also be seen in the meshing between the stated values of the school and the responses of the students:

> We are interested in the whole girl; in her respect for effort and hard work; her appreciation for self-discipline; her maturity in exercising freedom and accepting responsibility; her intentions toward and commitment to others; her courage and conviction; her honesty and integrity; and the joy she gives to and takes from the school community. (*To Achieve*, Emma Willard School Viewbook, 1983)

> I get along well with other people; I'm very accepting; I have become more independent; I can do things for myself.

I'm an outgoing person; I like people; I'm pretty intelligent. I try to be generous to people. It's important to me to always be at my best, to look or feel good, feel good about myself. . . .

Could it be that feminism has made the adult world viable for these girls? Because they see a place for themselves—not just to sit but to reach for, a place indicated by but not yet achieved by their mothers' generation—the prospect of maturation has been invested with dramatic meaning. In this respect they may be in a far more enviable position than their male counterparts who accept adult success and crave acceptance into the world as given and must worry about finding career openings without the feminist sense of mission and community that appears to energize these girls.

This generation of girls may have been granted the chance to live out the ideal which Bettelheim (1965) describes:

> If the generations thus need each other, they can live together successfully, and the problem of their succession, though not negligible, can be mastered successfully. Under such conditions youth and age need each other not only for their economic but even more for their moral survival. This makes youth secure—if not in its position, at least in its self-respect.

The question remains whether the particular quality of the feminist vision these girls hold is a sustaining one. These Emma Willard girls are now strengthened by their peculiar combination of mission and the puritanical values of hard work and responsibility. As women are increasingly accepted into American society, as the sense of being soldiers on an important mission changes to being defenders of the status quo, will hard work and responsibility be seen to have won empty success?

Sources

Bettelheim, B. 1965. "The Problem of Generations." In *The Challenge of Youth*, edited by E. Erikson. New York: Doubleday.

Douvan, E., and J. Adelson. 1966. *The Adolescent Experience*. New York: John Wiley.

Erikson, E. 1968. *Identity: Youth and Crisis*. New York: W. W. Norton.

Gilligan, C. 1982. *In a Different Voice*. Cambridge: Harvard University Press.

————. June 1982. Problems of adolescent development. Unpublished manuscript.

————. October 1982. Three lectures on the psychology of love: Sins for the sake of loyalty. Unpublished manuscript.

Kohlberg, L., and C. Gilligan. 1971. The adolescent as a philosopher: The discovery of the self in a post-conventional world. *Daedalus* 100:1051–86.

Daughters' Views of Their Relationships with Their Mothers

SHARON RICH

Editors' Note: *The chapter summarizes research findings of the dissertation by the same author.*

The relationship between mother and daughter is typically the child's primary attachment. Adolescence is an especially informative time to look at this relationship. Rapid changes occur in daughters' development, and the effects of these changes on relationships between daughters and mothers are not well understood. Do daughters break away from their mothers as psychologists formerly assumed? What are the struggles and conflicts between mothers and adolescent daughters about? How is closeness experienced between adolescent daughters and their mothers?

This chapter addresses mother-daughter relationships in light of conflicting psychological theories about female adolescence: that adolescence is a time of separation from attachments to parents and that maintenance of relationships is central in female identity. These theoretical contradictions have sometimes led clinicians who deal with problematic mother-daughter relationships to blame mothers for failing to let go of their daughters and/or daughters for failing to separate from their mothers. This chapter systematically explores mother-daughter relationships using data gathered from interviews with twenty-two Emma Willard girls.[1]

These daughters offer perspectives that do not fit into traditional models of parent-adolescent relationships in that girls present an overall picture of enduring connections. Over time, they adapt poorly or well through peaceful communication, conflict, and fighting, or through learning how to live with unresolved conflicts. Responding to interview questions about their relationships with their mothers, the daughters discussed here describe a wide range of mother-daughter relationships. Some girls characterize the relationships as becoming increasingly distant or problematic over time; others describe them as becoming closer. Some girls characterize relationships as being consistently weak, some consistently strong; and others as changing over time. Overall, the interviews suggest how girls' views of themselves relate to their views of their relationships with their mothers.

Attachment

Throughout these interviews, Emma Willard girls describe strong connections with their mothers. Daughters in this sample highly value their mothers "being there" for them, both emotionally and physically: "She's always saying to me . . . she'll always be there;" "I expect her to be there." The girls report that physical presence contributes to feelings of closeness and creates opportunities for conflict. Time apart from each other, when controlled by daughters, is welcomed by some daughters but raises mixed feelings for others. The endurance of the relationship and girls' dependence on support from their mothers are often mentioned. Daughters tell of feeling close to their mothers for a variety of reasons, especially talking and sharing: "I mean that I can tell her what I feel, and she can understand, and I don't have to hide anything from her, if I don't want to, for fear of her looking at me a different way or getting mad at me." Conversely, daughters relate lack of closeness to poor communication, to the presence of major differences, and to inconsistent care from their mothers. Yet, even girls who recount weak connections say that they would like to feel closer to their mothers.

These teenagers describe turning (or not being able to turn) to their mothers for love, care, protection, an understanding ear, and nurturance. They depend on their mothers for material comfort, for emotional sustenance, and for approval, guidance, and role modeling. From daughters' perspectives, dependence—in its various forms—has both negative and positive aspects. One teenager summarizes her appreciation of dependency: "I feel better for my dependency on her, because I know without her, I would be missing something in my personality, and I don't think I'd be as full or interesting a person as I guess I am."

Daughters also tell of "being there" for their mothers: loving, caring, and protecting them—from problems in their mothers' lives, their own lives, and the relationship. At times, mothers' dependence on daughters outweighs daughters' dependence on mothers; this can be troubling for the daughters. The girls depict limits to connection and dependence in the relationship. Some daughters experience intermittent emotional support; others see time limitations to the relationship; and still others tell of the need for mothers to adjust to changes in girls' lives as they form their own ideas and leave home.

Independence

Because mother-daughter relationships are often secure and supportive places, adolescent girls often feel free to explore their own projected adult identities by looking for differences and similarities between themselves and their mothers. And because mothers have been important resources for information and guidance, daughters often try within this relationship to practice their own decision-making skills.

At adolescence, daughters and mothers often speak about one another as distinct and growing people. In adapting to change, relationships that may have once been fairly tranquil can become discordant as daughters and mothers both voice their ideas and struggle to maintain their connection. The two related themes of differentiation (that is, searching for distinct voices) and independence (or making their own choices and taking action on their own)—are found throughout the interviews with these twenty-two Emma Willard girls.

One girl describes the process she feels daughters go through in making independent decisions and seeing themselves as responsible for the actions they take:

> You go from the stage where your mother takes care of you, where you start to get some type of individualism, and then you want more independence and then finally you are independent and you have to support yourself and take care of yourself and see that you are, because otherwise you won't survive. Whereas, when you are a child, you always know that you will survive because there is always going to be somebody there, most of the time, anyway, unless you are an orphan, for me anyway.

At the same time that daughters want mothers to be there for them, daughters also want their mothers to recognize their ability to care for themselves and to trust that ability. They often become frustrated when they feel their mothers fail to see them as responsible people.

Some daughters describe themselves as rebelling—actively going against their mothers' beliefs or directions. Rebellion is presented as being problematic to the relationship, as mothers and daughters renegotiate who controls daughters' lives. Such conflicts often involve decisions in daughters' lives, such as how they use their time, whom they date, how they treat their bodies, and where they live. However, active rebellion may end up contributing to the relationship, because mothers and daughters make new connections as more complex people.

According to the girls in this sample, the move toward independence can contribute to the connection within relationships. But there are limits. Total independence may be related to lack of connection, and daughters want to be able to know that they can depend on their mothers for support even if they do not currently need that support. These daughters describe wanting to be interdependent with their mothers; they know that change and maturation strengthens, rather than weakens, their relationship with their mothers. Take the case of Sally.

Sally: close and independent

Sally, a second-year boarding student describes a continually close and strong relationship over three years. She and her mother can both talk about and live with unresolved conflicts. First interviewed during her sophomore year, Sally is from a white upper-middle class family; her parents are married and live outside of the United States. She is the youngest of the children in her family, having a much older brother and older sisters. In her first year, she describes a moral dilemma of deciding whether to attend boarding school. Sally tells of her concern about protecting her parents from being alone; yet she decides to do what she thinks is best for herself. She receives her mother's support to attend the school. When asked to describe an important relationship, she talks about both of her parents, saying she has a very loving, close, strong unchanging relationship with both of them. She feels closer with her mother, who is "a little more sensitive" than her father.

Sally reports that the members of the family are independent but says she will never be completely independent of her parents. Conflicts exist, "but I am very verbal about them." Yet, she says that she becomes "really quiet" when there are conflicts because her parents "don't deserve anything bad from me." Their connection seems to survive these apparently unresolved conflicts. She tells of a time when she "was really sick of them," and her mother and father were bickering a lot. Resolution came when her parents spent time apart, and Sally had the opportunity to live with one parent at a time.

In the next year's interview, Sally describes a moral dilemma of deciding what courses to take at school. Her parents play a central role: "I feel I want to do what is right for both me and them." During this interview, she does not speak first of her mother when asked to describe an important relationship. Still, she says, as she did during the first interview, "I have always been a very independent person, but my parents and I have a very close relationship. . . . I couldn't live without them, just knowing that they are there." She tells of increasingly being able to talk with her mother but still not talking "that much." As a result of being away at boarding school, she comments, "I just feel that we kind of need each other more; I have grown closer to her . . . I shouldn't take her for granted."

At the interview during her third year, having lived with her parents over the summer for the first time in a long while, Sally describes loving her parents but being too independent to live at home: "It really bothered me that I had that responsibility, that they were worrying about me." Her moral dilemma includes concerns about "breaking away" from what her parents think and "[becoming] just a free person." Still, she thinks her parents will support her decisions.

Sally describes her relationship with her mother as loving, caring, and close. She feels as though she became closer to her mother over the summer because they "talked about everything," including "things that happened to her when I was younger that I never heard about before." One reason she mentions for talking with her mother is to protect her mother's feelings. And they "needed each other more. . . . The need to know that your mother is there, that your daughter is there; the need to know that you still love each other and still care about each other."

She says that at times she openly disagrees with her mother: for example, when she "wants something to change." She explains: "Like, if I wanted to go out and I asked my mother, Can I go out tonight? And she'll say no. I'll say, I disagree, this is why I think you should let me go out." However, Sally says there are not many conflicts: "Conflict comes more from a clash of character that you aren't necessarily going to want to change at all." In other words, Sally tries to accept unresolved differences with her mother when she thinks disagreeing will not help bring about change. For example, she characterizes herself as "avoiding problems," when "it is hard to get her [mother] to change something. . . . I usually avoid problems rather than face them."

The theme of connection between mothers and daughters is strong in Sally's interviews. During all three interviews she mentions protecting her mother, respecting her mother's opinions, their needing each other, and their increasing communication. Her mother is "there" for her, and the relationship continues even when mother and daughter disagree or have unresolved conflicts. Sally discusses her own independence and ability to take care of herself and resentment at having to report in to her parents. Although she says that she voices her opinions, she contradicts herself several times. She says she remains quiet when she wants to prevent pain and harm to her mother or when she believes changing her mother may not be possible. By deciding when to speak up and when to live with unresolved conflicts, Sally has created strategies for dealing with the limitations that exist in the relationship.

Differentiation

The term differentiation describes daughters coming to voice their own views in the relationship.[2] As characterized by the girls of this sample, it involves at least six aspects.

Similarities

The recognition or expectation of similarities can have contradictory effects. It may contribute to closeness in the relationship, making it safer for the relationship to change. On the other hand, similarities may make it challenging for daughters to see how they are different from their mothers and can limit change in the relationship. Similarities in personality, such as mothers and daughters who both are stubborn, may make it difficult to maintain open communication and reduce opportunities for change in the relationship.

Differences

In their portrayals of differences, daughters discuss being physically distinct, living different lives and growing up at different times, having different views, and, in general, being different people. One reflects, "We care about totally different things. Mom is kind of a Shaker . . . , she doesn't believe in comforts too much, just very basic things. Everything I do is extravagant." Many of these daughters express wanting to be different from their mothers or wanting to live lives that differ from their mothers'. For instance, one daughter says, "I would never do what my mother did, getting married at nineteen and not finishing college." In addition, many girls report that their mothers do not see or acknowledge the differences experienced by the daughters.

Six of the twenty-two mention competition with their mothers during their interviews. The competition they describe has three aspects: competition in the relationship for power, competition stemming from different advantages available to daughters, and competition in terms of conventional norms and looks and social success. At times, competition can lead to bitterness between mother and daughter; for example, one daughter says:

> She always wanted to go to a girls' school, a girls' prep school, when she was a kid. And she begged her parents to let her go and they had the money, but they said no. So I guess she's kind of bitter because she sees me doing a lot of things that she couldn't do.

Complaints

During her interview, one girl says, "I think there is a time for every kid when they stop seeing their parents as perfect and start seeing them as human beings." Descriptions of mothers' mistakes and instances of being wrong pervade the interviews. Girls offer complaints running the range from mothers who borrow clothes, to mothers who do not listen and are unyielding, to mothers who are seen as causing pain and harm to daughters and siblings. One says, "My mother, if she gets angry at someone, she will take it out on someone else, not physically, but psychologically. And I can see her taking it out on my sister already. . . . I don't want her [my sister] to go through what I went through."

Recognizing that mothers are imperfect often serves as an intermediary step for daughters between simply noting the differences that exist and realizing that they have their own viewpoints needing to be voiced in the relationship. When daughters transform their perceptions of their mothers, the relationship they share is affected as daughters make new connections with their mothers. One comments:

> I think that by realizing she is a person, that makes us more equal, because I am a person, too. [*When you said your mother is a person, what do you mean?*] When I think of a person—a human being—they have faults, and I have just realized that her faults are human, so that I don't judge them so severely and things.

Another reflects:

I think I see my mother as a woman now and as a person. Before I just saw her, you know, I just saw her as Mom; she always opposed everything I do, what I do is wrong, things like that. . . . I perceive my mother more as a friend and more as a woman with needs of a human being, and you know, I think she is feeling likewise.

Disagreements

Differentiation also involves daughters' disagreements with their mothers. In the interviews, girls recount various ways they disagree with their mothers around such issues as household chores, curfews, homework, and clothing—as well as drugs, finances, sex, dating boys of a similar religion, abortion, and schooling. In other words, this sample reports that they disagree "About everything. About what I should have done, what I did, whether I have done something or not, whether my room is messy or not, whether she wanted me to do a thing and I didn't do it, lots of things, like, little things." This kind of disagreement, although often a source of agony and conflict, may help daughters realize that they have distinct views and values, and that their own perceptions and judgments are important.

Some daughters report that their mothers support them in exploring distinct ideas and acknowledge their daughters as maturing persons. The daughters tell of their mothers listening to their ideas, mothers sharing details about their own lives and feelings, relationships changing as a result of what the girls are saying, and daughters being more willing to listen to their mothers' suggestions. One daughter describes how talking and listening leads to change:

We talk, and I think most mothers talk with their daughters. . . . I guess that is normal just to be able to tell the other person what you feel. . . . If we sit there and argue, it gets nowhere. But if we just sit there and talk, and if I voice my opinion then she will tell me hers. We pretty much work it out in that way.

While some daughters describe their mothers as authoritarian, daughters also describe themselves as unyielding: "We don't want to admit that the other is right. I go, She might be right and I may believe what she is saying, but I won't say it." From their comments, it is clear that these daughters realize that their stubbornness may be unproductive in sustaining the relationship and in getting their own voices heard.

Many of the girls in this sample suggest that relationships between mothers and daughters must in some ways respond to the daughters' discovery of their own values and visions as distinct from their mothers'. The daughters suggest that they need to work out new ways to communicate with their mothers to prevent the relationship from weakening. Thus:

Talking and sharing may increase in relationships when divergent ideas are valued.

Fighting and conflicts may increase when ideas are too divergent for quiet coexistence; when daughters feel they are not being heard; or when individuals compete to be right.

Sharing may decrease when daughters (or mothers) limit their talking because they believe they are not heard or they want to protect their privacy.

Dealing with conflicts

In realizing they disagree with their mothers, daughters come to differentiate between conventional views of relationships—as nonconflicted —and realistic views of relationships—mother and daughter acknowledging, confronting, and working through differences.

Connections between mothers and daughters strengthen or weaken through sharing, fighting, and conflicts. The quality of fights between mothers and daughters vary—from a little yelling to arguments that last all day or all summer. Fighting and arguments do not necessarily result from a breakdown of closeness but rather from the need to engage in and voice differences. As one girl reports, "We usually have big fights, even though we are good friends." Another states, "My mother and I quarrel quite a bit, but it is not that we are mad at each other. We just yell because I guess that is the way we both are unfortunately. My father is going, 'Don't yell at your mother.' And we are not yelling. We are not mad at each other. We are just, like, having heated discussions."

Because change does not always come easily to an existing relationship, daughters may feel that they have to fight in order to establish themselves as mature adults with views and ideas different from their mothers' beliefs. One asserts, "But I think I was fighting to become really independent." Another says, "I don't even like to fight it out, but I have to because I don't always want her to think she's so right when she's not."

Still, even when fights are felt to contribute to a better relationship, many girls can have negative reactions to them. Fights are often seen as upsetting, pointless, and leading to greater unhappiness. Furthermore, fighting does not always result in increased communication but may end up in a deterioration of relationship. This is likely when there is no perceived change as a result of fights, or when misunderstandings are felt to create impasses between mothers and daughters.

Thus girls depict conflicts in both positive and negative terms. Some daughters want to have more conflicts, while others feel that conflicts are useless. Girls describe conflicts as negative experiences when they are perceived as either failing to lead to change or "getting nowhere." When change seems possible, girls describe conflicts as difficult but important experiences, leading to growth within relationships.

Daughters in this sample report that conflicts with their mothers are dealt with by avoidance, resolution, or stalemate. For example, as one girl reports, "We discuss it and usually can decide that somebody is right, yes, of course." Sometimes, conflicts are ended by daughters apologizing or giving in. Quite often, though, girls say that conflicts are left unresolved because communication breaks down and because differences cannot always be eradicated. One notes, "It just doesn't work; we just end up screaming and no one is listening to either side." Whereas resolving conflicts through communication is an important aspect of maintaining mother-daughter relationships, daughters also learn to sustain mother-daughter relationships in spite of unresolved conflicts.

Accepting limitations to relationships

A final aspect of differentiation depicted through the interviews is that of daughters accepting limitations in their relationships with their mothers. For some daughters and mothers, differences are so great that they preclude a close relationship: "Mom and I are not really buddies. We are very different people. We care about totally different things."

According to this sample, mothers who are perceived as being unresponsive to what daughters say harm the relationship. Some mothers seem not to have the time, are not physically present, or are distracted. Some mothers apparently fail to hear and understand what their daughters are saying. Several girls postulate that their mothers are having problems in seeing and accepting them as equal persons instead of as children. "I think she could relate to me a lot more when I was younger than she can do now. . . . I don't want to say that she resents me, but she just, I don't think she likes me knowing and recognizing things, like her drinking and things like that, being able to recognize it, the situation."

Other girls describe their mothers as being poor listeners who do not change in response to what is being said or who react with anger. These girls depict themselves as receiving two messages when they feel their mothers are not listening: Their mothers do not care and are not "there" for them; and their own opinions are not important.

Daughters, in saying that they do not share much with their mothers and that they try to limit arguments, may be attempting through their silence to be taking care of their distinct voices and themselves. In some cases, they may believe or have previously found that voicing their ideas is ineffective. Others may have an untested fear that by sharing and being vocal they will give up part of themselves. Still others may have been directly hurt by sharing or by arguments.

One reflects:

> I sort of feel that I don't want her to know too much about me. I mean not that I'm trying to keep everything a secret, but just that I want to be more myself and less her trying to mold me. And so there are lots of things I don't tell her because I just know what she would say . . . and I don't feel like hearing it.

Yet, in attempting to protect themselves from feeling "terrible," daughters may cut off the primary means for changing the relationship: communication. Many girls decide to be silent because of their fear that the relationship could break apart or from a repeated experience that voicing opinions does not lead to change. For some girls, silence in relation to their mother may be the only way for them to continue to hear and respect their own voices.

Amanda: a changing relationship

Amanda feels open with her mother throughout most of her early adolescence but as she grows older, she comes to experience distance in their relationship. She attributes this to their fighting. Amanda, a boarder, is a sophomore in her first year at the school when she is initially interviewed. She comes from an upper-class white family; her parents are married, and she has a younger sister. In the first two interviews, she describes increased openness with her mother. In her first interview, she tells of an "improved" relationship with her mother "because now we can talk . . . and we were understanding each other more . . . I think my mom saw me as growing up and going away and she didn't like that, but she had to accept it. . . . So I think that we understand each other more now because I'm growing up and I'm getting wiser and stuff like that." The following year she echoes these thoughts: "She is more open to me now because I am more mature, and she looks at me as like someone that she can talk to and get some response back."

By the third interview, Amanda feels that something has come between her and her mother and that fighting has had negative effects on their relationship:

> I mainly saw it [change] this summer. We went on a family trip, vacation, and it was so incredible; my mother and I have always gotten along. We have been so close, and then this summer, I hadn't been home more than a week and we got in this huge argument. . . . [The fights] really were violent; I mean we screamed and yelled. . . . We are still going to be close, but there is going to be that little block or something that makes it difficult for us to resolve our conflicts and see each's opinions as important. . . . I think it's my mother's dealing with me growing up and I am not her little girl anymore basically, but I am beginning to make important decisions and they are not all irrational. . . . And so maybe the contest is, I don't see it as a contest, but maybe my mother does, is that I am trying to impose my will on her. *(What is the prize in the contest?)* I guess it would be whose . . . decision is most important, that would be the winner probably, self-satisfaction. . . . I probably will never change, until I am older and until she accepts me as a woman.

Amanda describes a connection between herself and her mother during all three interviews. In the final interview, she describes a change in the relationship as she fights to be heard and recognized as an adult, "a woman." She reports that her mother does not see the change ("I am not her little girl anymore"), and this puts a strain on the relationship ("a little block"). Yet, Amanda can envision a time when this block will be gone and the connection will be stronger—"when she accepts me as a woman."

Conclusion

This limited group of interviews suggests the importance of looking at adolescent development in terms of changes with connection as well as in terms of differentiation,[3] which does not necessarily come about at the expense of mother-daughter relationships. Developmental theory long held that an important developmental task for adolescents was to separate from their parents, especially mothers. This study of girls offers a new perspective on this question. By listening to the voices of the girls in this sample as they describe their relationships with their mothers, the dimensions of differentiation in relationships between adolescent daughters and their mothers becomes clearer.

Notes

1. This chapter summarizes research findings of the dissertation by the same author. See, S. Rich, "Change within Connection: A Study of Adolescent Daughters' Views of Their Relationships with Their Mothers," unpublished dissertation, Harvard Graduate School of Education (1986).

Because daughters may have a restricted view of mother-daughter relationships, it is important to note that this study presents girls' perceptions and explanations of their experience of their relationships with their mothers. The study also explores how these views shift across three years.

The data consists of self-reports from adolescent girls and were not observations of actual mother-daughter relationships. Sixteen of the twenty-two girls were boarding students who do not have daily face-to-face interchanges with their mothers. Although it has been possible to draw a composite picture of mother–adolescent daughter relationships based on the descriptions of these twenty-two girls, each relationship follows a distinct pattern. The findings generated by this study can be used as the basis for future research with a broader sample of both mothers and daughters of various socioeconomic backgrounds, using nonboarding school and coeducational settings and lasting over decades, allowing for a comparison of the views of pre-adolescents, adolescents, young adults, and older women.

Twenty-two girls were questioned with open-ended interviews, annually for three years. This sub-sample of the larger study consisted of all of the girls for whom three years of complete interviews were available.

During the first interview, they were asked to describe a relationship with a parent, and during the second and third interviews, they were asked about their relationships with their mothers.

The analysis of mother-daughter relationships began after the first interviews when I read fourteen of the first cases to be transcribed and noticed some consistent themes in the data. For the second and third interviews, we revised a question about describing a parental relationship and asked directly about the girls' perceptions of their mothers and their relationships with their mothers. After three years of data collection, I began reading the data with the goal of discovering what themes and patterns were represented. I first read forty-eight cases of thirty girls and then narrowed down the total sample by focusing on all of the girls for whom longitudinal data for all three years were available.

Initially, I did in-depth readings of eight girls' cases for all three years. These eight were chosen randomly by pulling case numbers out of a hat. After reading each case, I marked in the margins approximately twenty-eight themes that came up frequently. I then made separate files of every quotation relating to a theme. Each file was systematically read, and extensive notes were taken summarizing the themes (both modal and unusual responses). Along with gathering descriptive data, I also began a simplified quantitative analysis of the data by coding the themes for absence/presence. I then read the remaining fourteen cases of this sub-sample, noting the themes in the margins and coding each case. Also, new or illuminating information was added to the original notes on the themes. Following the reading of all the data, I took a step back to look at patterns and trends arising from the descriptions in order to come up with hypotheses about mother–adolescent daughter relationships from daughters' perspectives. Finally, the results from this study, composed of descriptive responses, were organized around three major themes: attachment/connection; increasing differentiation and independence; and change over time.

2. Differentiation will be explored in the following sections. Individuation is another term that has been used by researchers to describe the process of adolescent development, yet this term often implies "separation." I hope to avoid the association of separating from the mother-daughter relationship. (also see Josselson 1980, 188–210, and Sabatelli and Major 1985, 619–33).

3. There are important limitations about generalizations from this study. Most girls attending the school were white, intelligent, verbal, and from middle- to upper-class homes. A high percentage, half of the girls, came from single-parent homes or reconstructed families. Because of the limited range of socioeconomic and educational backgrounds, the study is limited in its applicability. Another bias in this study is in using a single-sex boarding school; the absence of boys may have influenced daughters' experience or perceptions of the mother-daughter relationships. Using a high percentage of boarding students (sixteen of the twenty-two girls, or,

seventy-three percent), in a study of mother–adolescent daughter relationships may well affect the hypotheses generated. Generalizations about
nonboarding school samples will not be made in this study. The relationship of boarding students to their mothers certainly may differ from
the relationship of nonboarders with their mothers. A benefit of using a
predominantly boarding school sample to look at mother-daughter relationships is that, by having gone through the process of leaving home
and by being at a distance from their mothers, the girls were more likely
to have confronted and reflected on issues of differentiation and connection.

Sources

Arcana, J. 1979. *Our Mothers' Daughters*. Berkeley: Shameless Hussy
Press.

Chodorow, N. 1974. "Family Structure and Feminine Personality" in
Women, Culture and Society, edited by M. Rosaldo and L. Lamphere. Stanford: Stanford University Press.

———. 1978. *The Reproduction of Mothering*. Berkeley: University of
California Press.

Cooper. C. H., H. Grotevant and S. Condon. 1983. "Individuality and
Connectedness in the Family as a Context for Adolescent Identity
Formation and Role-Taking Skill." In *Adolescent Development in
the Family*, edited by H. Grotevant and C. Cooper. San Francisco:
Jossey-Bass.

Crastnopol, M. 1980. Separation-individuation in woman's identity vis-
a-vis mother. Unpublished dissertation, University of Cincinnati.

Douvan, E., and J. Adelson. 1966. *The Adolescent Experience*. New
York: John Wiley & Sons.

Flax, J. 1978. The conflict between nurturance and autonomy in mother-
daughter relationships and within feminism. *Feminist Studies* 4:
171–189.

Friedman, G. 1980. The mother-daughter bond. *Contemporary Psychoanalysis* 16: 90–97.

Gilligan, C. 1982. *In A Different Voice*. Cambridge, Mass.: Harvard
University Press.

————. 1984. New perspectives on female adolescent development. Unpublished manuscript, Harvard University.

Greenberg, M., J. Siegel, and C. Leitch. 1983. The nature and importance of attachment relationships to parents and peers during adolescence. *Journal of Youth and Adolescence.* 12: No. 5, 373–86.

Josselson, R. 1980. "Ego Development in Adolsecence." In *Handbook of Adolescent Psychology,* edited by J. Adelson. New York: John Wiley and Sons.

Kandel, D. and G. Lesser. 1969. Parent-adolescent relationships and adolescent independence in the United States and Denmark. *Journal of Marriage and the Family* 31: 348–358.

Miller, J. 1976. *Toward A New Psychology of Women.* Boston: Beacon Press.

Murphy, W., E. Silber, G. Coelho, D. Hamberg, and M. Greenberg. 1963. Development of autonomy and parent-child interactions in late adolescence. *American Journal of Orthopsychiatry* 33: 643–652.

Peplan, L., S. Cochran, K. Rook, and C. Padesky. 1978. Loving women: attachment and autonomy in lesbian relationships. *Journal of Social Issues* 34: 7–27.

Sabatelli, R., and A. Mazor. 1985. Differentiation, individuation, and identity formation: The integration of family system and individual perspectives. *Adolescence* 20: No. 79.

Taylor, C. 1982. An empirical investigation of mother/daughter relationships in early adolescence using Peebles Telophasic Theory. Unpublished Qualifying Paper, Harvard Graduate School of Education.

Youniss, J. and J. Smollar. 1985. *Adolescent Relations with Mothers, Fathers and Friends.* Chicago: University of Chicago Press.

Girls' Sexual Choices: Looking for What Is Right
The Intersection of Sexual and Moral Development

KATHLEEN HOLLAND BOLLERUD, SUSAN BOYNTON
CHRISTOPHERSON, AND EMILY SCHULTZ FRANK

Most investigators of adolescent sexuality have observed that boys and girls approach sexual choices differently. Central to this difference is the relative importance that they ascribe to the interpersonal relationship (Christensen and Carpenter 1960; Coles and Stokes 1985; Hass 1979; Kinsey 1953; Schofield 1965). A generation ago, Ehrmann (1959) noted that the connection between the partners had an opposite influence on the sexual decisions of males and females. In close relationships, males were more inclined to restrain themselves sexually, whereas females were more likely to become more active sexually. Ehrmann concluded that female sexual expression is primarily concerned with romanticism, whereas eroticism is more central to males. In the mid-sixties, Schofield noticed a similar phenomenon and commented, "Girls prefer a permanent type of relationship in their sexual behavior. Boys seem to want the opposite; they prefer diversity and so have more casual partners . . . the boy seeks adventure while the girl looks for security (1965, 2).

In the last few decades, at least until the early 1980s, both male and female adolescent sexual values have tended to become more permissive (Chilman, 1980; Diepold and Young, 1979). However, in spite of this trend, profound differences between the sexes continue to exist regarding the importance of the relationship in sexual interactions (Coles and Stokes 1985; Gagnon and Simon 1973; Hass 1979). Scrutiny of the literature reveals that these differences are reflected in every level of sexual involvement beyond light petting (Holland 1985). Increased permissiveness has not diminished the pivotal importance of attachment in the sexual behavior of girls.

Theoretical conceptions of moral development, however, have excluded love and sex from the moral realm (Kohlberg 1984). According to Kohlberg's (1958) theory of "justice reasoning," in which morality is defined in terms of rights and duties, there is a distinction between personal and moral dilemmas. Sexual decision making is relegated to the realm of personal choice (1984, 230).

In the early 1970s justice reasoning was used to understand the interaction of moral principles and sexual behavior (Gilligan et al. 1971). This research used the framework of an invariant developmental sequence of moral thought based on principles of justice to develop a model called the "hierarchy of reasoning about sex," which concerns how adolescents think about sexual decisions and what values they take into consideration when deciding about sexual behavior.

The hierarchy is comparable to stages two through five in Kohlberg's theory of moral development. In this model, sex at the lowest stages is seen as an instrumental exchange of physical pleasures without any notion that it involves a relationship. With development, the individual becomes oriented toward more conventional social expectations, such as seeing sex as an expression of love. At the higher stages, partners are guided in their sexual interactions by freely made contractual agreements. Sex is seen as an ethical issue only in the sense that it should involve equal partners, dealing with each other honestly and responsibly.

Four studies have used the "hierarchy of reasoning about sex" to investigate the interaction of moral reasoning and sexual behavior. All of these studies report significant sex differences (Gilligan et al. 1971; Stein 1973; Jurich and Jurich 1974; D'Augelli and Cross 1975). The findings indicate that male reasoning about sex follows the traditional path of justice reasoning, but female reasoning does not. As a result, no females reached the highest stage of reasoning. Girls refuse to separate feelings of love from their consideration of the rightness or wrongness of sex. This is apparently true even when girls have shown an ability to reason at the higher stages in other moral domains.

The study

It is possible that there is a connection between gender differences in moral reasoning about sexual decisions and girls' failure to achieve higher levels on the "hierarchy of reasoning about sex," and it is also possible that the problem lies in the model itself. This chapter examines the ways in which a group of Emma Willard girls think about sexual decisions as one exploration of these issues.

Many of the girls interviewed at Emma Willard spontaneously raised issues about sex when asked about morality. These responses were prompted primarily by questions about how the girls would describe themselves or what moral conflicts they faced. A sample of thirty girls discussed in some detail what they considered when making sexual choices. These responses yielded evidence of two characteristic modes of describing sexual decisions; related to the care and justice orientations, they are called attachment and contractual reasoning.

Contractual reasoning reflects justice principles in that moral decisions are based on fairness and equality. Sexual behavior is seen as a personal choice and contract between individual partners based on standards derived from each person's beliefs and sense of responsibility. This orientation encompasses a continuum of principles regarding sex. Standards can be derived from sources external to the couple, such as parents, the Ten Commandments, and social norms; or they may focus on the mutual consent of the partners. In either situation, the relationship itself is of *secondary* significance to the personal values of each partner. Guilt or shame in this mode is generally related to breaking the rules or abuse of power.

In contrast, sexual decisions in the attachment orientation reflecting care reasoning are based on notions of connection and interdependence. In this mode, the standard of moral judgment is a standard of *relationship*. Individuals make sexual decisions based on the quality of intimacy, affection, and engagement in the relationship. Sex may be seen as an expression of love and how it will maintain, enhance, or endanger the interaction is a key consideration. Rules in this orientation are often self-generated and concern the quality of relationship necessary for sex. Physical desire is described in terms of attachment to a particular person.

The distinction between these two patterns echoes Sullivan's (1953) differentiation between cooperative intimacy, based on notions of equal power between individuals, and collaborative intimacy, which is based on profound empathy and a sense of "we-ness" with one's partner. Gilligan (1982) makes a similar distinction between relationships of equality and relationships of interdependence. The key difference between these orientations centers on the ethical significance of the relationship between the partners.

The following excerpts from interviews exemplify the girls' discussions about sex and allow the reader to reflect on the interpretation of two "voices" of sexual morality: attachment and contractual reasoning. These responses suggest that attention to the moral reasoning of adolescent girls challenges the existing model of sexual morality, the "hierarchy of reasoning about sex." For the girls in this sample, rather than excluding sex from the moral realm, the emergence of sexuality seems to portend a heightened scrutiny of moral beliefs and a search for guiding principles.

Elizabeth's poignant reflections capture the intensity of this struggle:

I was in love with this guy too, it wasn't a question of did I love him or not. I loved him. And I still didn't know if it was right or wrong. I can't make that decision because with guys my age, It's cool, it's great, you should do it definitely. With my parents, No, don't do it. And like with my friends, some say yes and some no. So I have no one to really look at and ask. . . . Yet, he loves me, but I am not his special love, you know. I didn't think that was the case. I mean I could have been, but I just didn't think so. I thought okay, if this relationship does fall through, which it probably will, given my age and his age and given the localities. I had the feeling right there, I thought maybe if I do, I will regret it, but I didn't know if I would. I couldn't—I didn't know what was right. *And I didn't know the definition of right, either.* Because I had no one to give me an answer, I listed all the people in my life and no one could give me a clear answer.

As her comments make clear, Elizabeth's vision of "what is right" pivots around the issues of love and connection with her boyfriend. This perspective is in sharp contrast with the justice reasoning construction of the moral domain. This emphasis on the primacy of the relationship typifies the attachment orientation.

Resonating with a similar belief that caring is a moral prerequisite for sex, another student, Harriet, comments:

I think it is right, if it is the right time—I think then you should make your decision, but I think [only] if two people care about each other, regardless of age, unless you are very, very young or preadolescent. I think when you are sixteen or seventeen, I think you can make your own decisions and take responsibility for it. And I think if you choose to have a relationship that is going to be close and caring, I think that sex probably will have a major part in it. And I think it is important to both individuals if they care about each other. But just for the heck of it—I don't think it is right. But I think if two individuals really care about one another, I think that could be very nice and a valuable part of the relationship.

For Harriet, the pivotal moral factor in sexual decisions is the quality of caring in the relationship. In the context of love, sex is an important part of the interaction; without love, sex for the "heck of it" is not right.

Dolores describes how attachment concerns influence her sexuality:

I am very comfortable with Sam and I've never wanted to be with someone as much as I want to be with him. And before I've been kind of nervous when I'm with a boy and especially when you are kissing him and thinking, Oh God, what is he going to do next, I'm going to have to stop it. And I don't feel nervous with Sam because I know that he is going to talk to me before he does anything because we have talked about that, too; that's not what we want. And because we are both very inexperienced . . . we are just moving very slowly . . . in deciding what is the next step for us. It's not really a moral problem because I don't think we are doing anything wrong, but in some aspects that relates to morals just because you are dealing with another person and you are learning how to deal with them. We are really naive and we don't know exactly what we want. We just don't want to jump into bed . . . we are deciding to what extent we want it to go, which is nowhere right now, which is fine. When we observe other relationships and . . . we notice sex is maybe all it's geared to . . . and we know that's what we don't want. And when we both feel comfortable in the situation and when we both feel okay, then we know to keep going . . . but basically there's not much to guide us except to observe other relationships and say no, that's not what we want.

In this situation, in contrast to the other girls, sexual decisions are made in the context of a couple exploring together what they want their relationship to be like. Having established an emotional rapport, Sam and Dolores feel comfortable discussing both their relationship and their sexuality. Rather than managing emerging sexuality through reference to individual personal beliefs, their interaction can be characterized by a sense of togetherness. The strength of this collaboration is apparent in Dolores' choice of pronouns—*we* rather than *I* decide.

A second salient theme for Sam and Dolores is how sex will affect their friendship. "Knowing that someone else is there" and "helping each other with problems" are essential elements of their alliance. Having a connection in which "sex is maybe all it's geared to" would threaten this intimacy. Determining that intercourse might change the nature of the relationship, they decide it is too great a risk. They value each other as friends and confidants and don't want sex to interfere with this closeness. This couple believes that refraining from sex will help to maintain, and possibly enhance, their connection. This emphasis on relationship is the touchstone of the attachment orientation.

In contrast to this viewpoint, the girls who used the contractual orientation articulated a very different set of concerns. Relying on her personal belief system, Laura makes a very different choice:

I don't really remember very clearly, I think at one point everything sort of just said, well, you are pretty much mature enough where you can handle this without going through any major guilt complexes. I don't know, the whole thing where my peers, it is this heavy thing where you aren't supposed to have sex until you are at least seventeen years old. I figured I was mature enough in my own mind to handle it. And I don't know, why not now? Just the whole thing, where the possible guilt I could feel . . . if anything did happen, I would be able to think clearly. I think it is like drinking or something, where if . . . something . . . is held back from you for a long time . . . just the fact that you can't have it makes you want it more. And it wasn't so much that I couldn't have it but I made my own choice that I wanted to and it wasn't such a big thing as society built up to me and it isn't this great trauma.

The contractual mode emerges as Laura faces the complexity inherent in sexual decisions. She assesses her maturity and her ability to deal with possible "guilt complexes" or consequences that could arise from sexual activities. A second critical variable is Laura's responsiveness to the influence of third parties on her sexual decisions. She explores her ability to tolerate censure from her peers should she violate the age guideline of seventeen as the marker for coital maturity. Notably absent is any discussion of her partner as a significant factor in this decision.

A third theme embedded in Laura's deliberations is her experience of physical desire or curiosity as "drives" without reference to a particular partner. Describing how abstaining from sex can "make you want it more," she accepts these physical stirrings as influences on her behavior. Each of these themes combine to create an interweaving of contractual considerations.

While this research was directed toward empirically distinguishing and clarifying two voices, or moral orientations, it is clear that many girls bring both voices, or perspectives, to bear in thinking about sexual choices. In their search for "what is right," girls often engage in an inner dialectic in which they explore different and even contradictory approaches to solving sexual dilemmas.

Maria voices the tension she feels:

A difficult moral decision I will have to make will be when I find a man whom I love, and I am a very sexual person and I love people and I love to be with them and when, say, I am with that man and I do not believe in premarital sex, although once I get going, it is fairly difficult to stop. And so I think that I would have to make a very quick decision, and I know inside of me that it is wrong, but outwardly I want to do it. So I don't know what I would do. *(What would be the conflict for you in that situation?)* My knowing and my wanting.

Anticipating conflict between a rule, likely derived from childhood authorities, and her love of being with her partner, Maria ponders what she sees as a moral dilemma. She expects to be caught between "knowing" the rules and "wanting" to do it.

Jessica also struggles to sort through her priorities:

I considered going out . . . having fun and forget[ting] about to-morrow and all the consequences. But I tried that one time before and I got in a lot of trouble and it wasn't anything big, but I decided that I just, it wasn't worth it. And I finally concluded that if Bob valued any kind of relationship that he would understand it, too.

Desiring to explore the sexual realm with carefree abandon, Jessica considers ". . . having fun and forget[ting] about tomorrow and all the consequences." At the same time, she anticipates "trouble" from her actions. Stymied by opposing considerations, she resolves her dilemma by focusing on the relationship. In effect, her boyfriend, Bob, must understand that in this circumstance sex might be hurtful for her; in doing so he is demonstrating his care for her. If he is unable to empathize with her concerns, she determines that the relationship is not strong enough to sustain sexuality.

Discussion

This chapter suggests that it is likely for girls to voice both moral orientations in describing sexual choices as each highlights important concerns inherent in the emergence of sexuality for girls in this culture. Contractual reasoning provides the security and structure of a clear set of rules, or guidelines, within which adolescents can learn about intimate relationships and sexuality. This orientation protects their needs and rights as a separate individual. The use of contractual reasoning helps to guard against exploitation as it ensures that one engages in sex because of one's own physical desire and out of one's own free will.

The attachment perspective brings issues of relationship into the forefront. In this orientation, the moral prerequisites for engaging in sex concern the quality of the relationship. Adolescents using this orientation can develop standards or guidelines about the foundation of attachment essential to intimate relationships. This orientation provides a language to define the characteristics of caring that adolescents need to receive and want to give to a sexual partner. Further, the attachment mode can be used to explore how sex affects and changes relationships.

To rely on either of these perspectives exclusively may be problematic in decision making. The contractual construction of morality, while acknowledging the importance of personal rights, can be dangerous because of its separation of sex and intimacy. The danger inherent in using the attachment perspective exclusively is that in focusing primarily on the relationship, the self's desires and rights can be overlooked. In an effort to secure the couple relationship or to please the partner, the adolescent girl especially becomes vulnerable to losing sight of her self. In this circumstance, the intolerable is tolerated in the name of "love."

Educational implications

Morality, with regard to sex, has tended to be cast as a timeless set of forbidden behaviors: what you are not supposed to do. However, for the past generation, researchers (Kirkendall 1961; D'Augelli and D'Augelli 1977) have decried the absence of a positive value framework to guide choice. Some have argued for "sexuality education" that would include "not only discrete acts or behaviors but . . . an understanding of the motives for and meanings found in relationships. It includes our ability to be intimate and loving" (Scales 1983). Such a positive framework seeks to define "what *is* moral" rather than focussing on "what is *not* moral." Instead of equating morality with restraint and identifying what is bad in sexual relationships, a positive framework attempts to articulate standards of what is good. Such a framework attempts to describe an ideal for sexual relationships.

To date, the "hierarchy of sex" articulated the only model of sexual morality. The discussion in this chapter grew in part from a discomfort with a model in which females, because of their preoccupation with relationship, consistently appeared less morally developed than their sexual partners. A second disconcerting premise was that issues of sexuality are personal and not "moral."

The data collected from girls at Emma Willard draw attention to an untold story about morality and sex. Examination of the interview material demonstrates that the girls' most salient concerns about sex are inherently related to basic moral questions about relationships and that morality is not simply imposed on them by external authorities. An analysis of the moral issues voiced by the girls suggests that the wellsprings of a positive value framework for sex lie not just in a fair contract between freely consenting partners, but also in the caring between the partners. The organization of the girls' concerns into the contractual and attachment orientations provides a framework for teaching about a greater range of moral issues deemed relevant to adolescents' sexual choices. The assumptions implicit in each orientation bring attention to two foundations of moral concern in human relationships: equality and care.

Recently, the topic of adolescent sexual decision making has become a major public health concern because of the alarming increase in the rate of teenage pregnancy and the AIDS epidemic. Parents and educators are facing a significant challenge as they struggle to safeguard teenagers from pregnancy and exposure to disease. Because of the lack of consensus on sexual values and legal strictures regarding the separation of church and state, there is controversy about the discussion of moral and ethical principles in regard to sex. As a result, the trend in sex education has been toward the development of "value neutral" curricula in which students are taught the facts of reproduction and contraception. This stance unwittingly ignores relational issues, which the adolescent girls in this sample consider moral problems and deem relevant to their sexual decision making. By omission, it supports the view of sex as outside the moral domain. On the other hand, when morality has been incorporated into sex education curricula, it has tended to be equated with restraint and sanctions against sexual behavior. Such an approach implies that morality prohibits sex and that adolescents who are engaging in sexual activities are not being moral. This lack of a positive standard leaves adolescents without guidance in making decisions, beyond the injunction to "just say no" to sex.

The findings from this pilot study suggest an avenue for curriculum development that does not dictate or sidestep sexual behavior. Rather, by joining in what Kegan (1982) calls the students' "natural curriculum of making meaning of life experience," educators can aid in the evolution of adolescents' thinking about sex. The adolescents in this sample have demonstrated the ability to articulate a moral base for their sexual choices. Exploring these criteria, using the framework of attachment and contractual reasoning, provides a language to address moral dimensions of personal choice. This phenomenological approach defines equality and care as foundations for sexual morality.

Many questions have been stimulated by this work. Notably, are similar patterns of reasoning apparent in the sexual choices of boys or in adolescents who have a homosexual orientation? Further research is also needed to chart how contractual and attachment reasoning develop over time and in interaction with pubertal development and sexual experience.

Conclusion

This chapter highlights the intersection of moral and sexual development in adolescence by illuminating girls' quest for "the definition of what is right" in sexual choices. Attending to the experience of a group of girls at Emma Willard reveals the need to incorporate care and attachment into the vision of mature sexual relationships elaborated by psychological theory. This recognition leads to a reformulation of the predominant model of sexual morality to include two moral "voices," both care and justice.

Sources

Chilman, C. 1980. Social and psychological research concerning adolescent childbearing: 1970–1980. *Journal of Marriage and the Family* 42 (9), 793–805.

Christensen, H. and G. Carpenter. 1960. Value-behavior discrepancies regarding premarital coitus in three Western cultures. *American Sociological Review*, 66–74.

Coles, R., and G. Stokes. 1985. *Sex and the American Teenager*. New York: Harper & Row.

D'Augelli, J., and A. D'Augelli. 1977. Moral reasoning and premarital sexual behavior: Toward reasoning about relationships. *Journal of Social Issues* 33 (2), 46–67.

D'Augelli, J., and H. Cross. 1975. Relationship of sex guilt and moral reasoning to premarital sex in college women and in couples. *Journal of Consulting and Clinical Psychology* 45 (1), 40–47.

Diepold, J., and R. Young. 1979. Empirical studies of adolescent sexual behavior: A critical review. *Adolescence* 14 (53).

Ehrmann, W. 1959. *Premarital Dating Behavior.* New York: Bantam Books.

Gagnon, J., and W. Simon. 1973. *Sexual Conduct: The Sources of Human Sexuality.* Chicago: Aldine Publishing Company.

Gilligan, C. 1982. *In a Different Voice.* Cambridge, Mass.: Harvard University Press.

Gilligan, C., L. Kohlberg, J. Lerner, and M. Belenky. 1971. Moral reasoning about sexual dilemmas: The development of an interview and scoring system. *Technical Report of the Commission on Obscenity and Pornography.*

Hass, A. 1979. *Teenage Sexuality: A Survey of Teenage Sexual Behavior.* New York: Macmillan.

Holland, K. 1985. Gender differences in adolescent reasoning about sex: A review of the literature. Unpublished Qualifying Paper, Harvard Graduate School of Education.

Jurich, A., and J. Jurich. 1974. The effect of cognitive moral development upon the selection of premarital standards. *Journal of Marriage and the Family,* 736–41.

Kegan, R. 1982. *The Evolving Self: Problems and Processes in Human Development.* Cambridge, Mass.: Harvard University Press.

Kinsey, A., W. Pomeroy, C. Martin, and P. Gebhardt. 1953. *Sexual Behavior in the Human Female.* Philadelphia: W. B. Saunder.

Kirkendall, L. 1961. *Premarital Intercourse and Interpersonal Relationships.* Westport, Conn.: Greenwood Press.

Kohlberg, L. 1958. The development of modes of thinking and choice in years 10 to 16. Ph.D. Diss., University of Chicago.

———. 1984. *The Psychology of Moral Development: The Nature and Validity of Moral Stages.* Vol. 2 of Essays on Moral Development Series. San Francisco: Harper and Row.

Scales, P. 1983. "Adolescent Sexuality and Education: Principles, Approaches, and Resources." In *Adolescent Sexuality in a Changing American Society,* edited by C. Chilman. New York: Wiley and Sons.

Schofield, M. 1965. *The Sexual Behavior of Young People*. Boston: Little, Brown and Company.

Sullivan, H. S. 1953. *The Interpersonal Theory of Psychiatry*. New York: W. W. Norton.

Stein, J. 1973. Adolescent reasoning about moral and sex dilemmas: A longitudinal study. Ph.D. Diss., Harvard Graduate School of Education.

Reflections

Conversations with Emma Willard Teachers about Their Participation in the Dodge Study

Editors' Note: *This chapter presents the response of a group of Emma Willard teachers to the research conducted at their school. The chapter was prepared by Nona Lyons from conversations with the Dodge Study Faculty Committee Members: Judy Bridges, Nancy Cushman, Jack East-erling, Trudy Hanmer, Marilyn Hunter, Darby Johnson, Shirley Kiepper, Paul Lamar, Kurt Meyer, Robert Parker, Anne Riendeau, Donna Simms, Robert Simms, Gail Viamonte, Margery Whiteman, and Barbara Wiley.*

. . . that always struck me as such a profound mismatch, what one person was seeing as being the issue and what the other person was seeing as the issue. And actually I play out in my own mind the frustration that the girl must feel because she is saying exactly what she sees as the problem and, I guess by extrapolation, what it is like not to have your point of view validated and how frustrating that would be over the long haul, never to be taken seriously.

—Paul Lamar, member of the Emma Willard
Dodge Study Faculty Committee

Sitting in the comfort of knowing that the school year had ended, Emma Willard teachers and administrators paused to look back on their participation in the Dodge Study. The sixteen people who sat around the room in June 1985 were members of the Dodge Study Faculty Committee. Four years earlier they had volunteered to act as liaisons between their faculty and the Harvard research team. Each year in June they had gathered to hear preliminary reports of the research, to share in exploring the data, and at times to suggest questions for inclusion in the research project. But today they came together to be reflective, to examine what the study had meant to them. In conversations with each other, they articulated a series of ideas about themselves, their teaching, and their practices in working with and teaching young women at Emma Willard School. These ideas are presented here as informal "conversations" with the teachers and administrators who participated in this study—an opportunity to share their perspectives as people and professionals.

These responses reveal at least three things:

The faculty committee found the research project powerful first in a personal way: That is, ideas about different approaches to morality that led to the Dodge Study caught the faculty personally, illuminating some aspect of their own lives, leading to insights about themselves, their relations with husbands, wives, or children or the people with whom they most frequently interacted. Reaction to the Dodge research for the adults involved almost inevitably included a personal response.

Second, over time interaction with the research led the teachers and administrators to critical reexaminations of their practice, that is, to reexaminations of their assumptions about learning and knowing and the construction of knowledge; about how girls learn; about how teachers foster learning; and, about the disciplines they themselves teach, how they were constructed and how they might be changed. These critical reappraisals developed only over time. They were encouraged by the research team, who suggested early in the project that the teachers follow their hunches in re-examining their practice. They were encouraged by the Emma Willard administration, who brought Peggy McIntosh, associate director of the Wellesley College Center for Research on Women, to Emma Willard and who, in turn, urged the faculty to examine the curriculum for the inclusion or exclusion of women and women's perspectives. And they were encouraged, too, when the Emma Willard faculty as a whole decided to embark on a major re-examination of its curriculum. Perhaps the re-appraisals were facilitated most by the Faculty Committee members themselves in what some describe as their "endless conversations" about this work.

Third, the responses of the Faculty Committee, while not representative of the Emma Willard faculty as a whole, are themselves diverse and complex. That diversity and complexity are presented here in the report of the Dodge Study Faculty Committee "conversations."

Because the Faculty Committee's response to the Emma Willard project was first a personal one, it seems useful to recall the context of the Dodge Study as the teachers first experienced and responded to it: that is, to talk briefly about the discoveries of the research prior to the study. That context will illuminate the meanings of certain "code words" used by the Faculty Committee throughout their conversations: two modes of morality—"response" and "rights"—and the autonomous self and the interdependent self.

Gilligan's initial research, described in her book *In a Different Voice*, set the context for the Faculty Committee and for the Emma Willard School's interest in the study. Gilligan's research in the field of psychological development highlighted and amplified women's conceptions of self and morality and called attention to the place of women within a life cycle that had been described and conceptualized largely by men (Gilligan 1977, 1982). Describing a self experienced as in connection with others and an overriding value placed on responsiveness in relationships, Gilligan explicated an ethic of responsibility or "response," which she contrasted with an ethic of justice and rights—the ethic psychologists had emphasized and one that presumed a separate self. *In a Different Voice* presents the different images of relationships and visions of maturity that define these two ethical standpoints or worldviews. Put simply, the ethic of justice focuses concern on respecting rights and maintaining fairness in relationships; the ethic of response presumes interdependence and focuses concern on responding with care and maintaining connections between people. It was by listening to people talk about their actual experiences of moral conflict that Gilligan first heard in women's conceptions of self and morality a different voice for psychological theory—a voice that resonated differently from the Western tradition and one that had implications for psychological development and for education.

And it was Gilligan's earliest research that was the substance of the initial presentation to the Emma Willard faculty and part of the lengthier conversations with the Dodge Study Faculty Committee. While the excitement of being part of a ground-breaking study of high school girls cannot be minimized, it is also clear from their own responses that the Faculty Committee found the research important in connecting with and touching their own lives.

It is interesting to speculate why this is so. It seems fair to say that it is not often that members of a faculty respond so personally to a research project outside of their professional interests. What seems plausible is that this work somehow touched a set of values and concerns not often acknowledged or given voice in our contemporary lives: ideas about morality, what constitutes people's moral values, and how these may cause them conflict; and ways of thinking about a person's connections with others, the significance of these attachments, and how individuals act on such concerns out of a sense of what is morally right or wrong. In this chapter, after presenting the response of the Faculty Committee, we will return to speculate on this observation and to relate it to a second observation: that is, that the study encouraged and supported some major reflections on and reevaluations of the teachers' own practices.

It seems important to say that these are not carefully constructed essays. The conversations presented here were taped at Emma Willard School in June 1984. In June of 1985 teachers and administrators met again to revise their comments and in some cases to elaborate their thoughts. These elaborations are presented here as conversations, a set of perspectives: the personal and professional reflections of a group of people who, as educators, participated in a study of adolescent high school girls—their students.

A *new perspective*

Paul Lamar, a teacher of English and the humanities at Emma Willard School, begins by telling how he usually introduced people to the Dodge Study by telling them a story. The story is of a young girl who is asked to resolve the classic Heinz dilemma—to respond to the question, Should Heinz steal the drug? The girl is asked to solve the hypothetical dilemma of a man, Heinz, who is trying to save his dying wife by obtaining a life-saving drug from a druggist. The girl in the story, an eleven-year-old, keeps trying to avoid an answer to the question, Should he steal? by looking instead for alternatives to the situation. Answering not *should* Heinz steal? she shifts the emphasis to Should Heinz *steal*? She seeks alternative ways to resolve the situation for all involved, but to the detriment of none.[1]

Paul Lamar talks about how he used the story of the young girl as a way of introducing people to the study and its meaning: "I think it is a very graphic story about what I think the basic differences are between the rights mode and the mode I call "connection," the mode of "response" and interdependence. It has been the easiest way for me to explain to someone in shorthand what the two ways of looking at things really are about . . . and what this means for teaching." He goes on to elaborate:

I usually expect all the response to come from the other person, and a kind of light to go on because when I heard that story for the first time, a light went on for me—particularly when the interviewer keeps saying to the girl, 'But you are not answering the question.' That always struck me as such a profound mismatch of what one person was seeing as being the issue and what the other person was seeing as the issue. And actually I play out in my own mind the frustration that the girl must feel because she is saying exactly what she sees as the problem and the solution and, I guess by extrapolation, what it is like not to have your point of view validated and how frustrating that would be over the long haul, never to be taken seriously. Frequently a light does go on in the other person.

Another English teacher, Gail Viamonte, comments on Paul's story:

The other interesting thing I think, though, is that, if I remember it correctly, the eleven-year-old is not frustrated by not being heard because she is so confident of what she knows. But a fifteen-year-old who was repeatedly questioned on her statements would not have that same confidence to keep coming back. She would start to look for what it is you want her to say—what you would want to hear.

Thus a conversation starts. Taking the point of view of the eleven-year-old girl, the teachers speculate on what it may mean if this view, found more predominantly in women and girls, is not acknowledged or valued in its own terms. What would that mean for girls? As reported, research to date indicates girls and boys, women and men can see problems both in terms of rights *and* in terms of responsiveness to others, although men and boys more frequently focus on "rights" and fairness, and girls and women—and Emma Willard girls—are more likely to focus on "response" (Gilligan, Langdale, Lyons, and Murphy 1982; Lyons 1982, 1983; Johnston 1988; Gilligan and Attanucci 1988). When the girl in the story turns away from one alternative the dilemma implies— that is, that there is a "fair" solution to the conflicting claims of Heinz, the druggist, and the wife of the story—the girl is seeking a different approa 1 to the problem. In effect she is saying: Is there a way around stealing? Is there another way to act to solve the problem? Couldn't the people involved just talk it out? This example forces the teachers to think about how their students approach problems and how a given student's orientation may not just imply an idiosyncratic style but a deep, structured logic for defining and resolving conflict that is grounded in a set of values.

But the conversation with the teachers goes on. Kurt Meyer, dean of students at the time, tells how understanding this logic—especially of the "response" mode, influenced his thinking:

> Listening to students is an important thing, emphasized for me by being involved in this study. I would be talking to a girl about her misbehavior, say, about her regard for the school and her regard for the rules of the school. Before hearing what this study had to say about the 'response' caring mode that places an emphasis on maintaining the connections between people, I think I was all too quick to think that a girl who 'had no regard for the rules of this school' was being sort of amoral, without standards. And I have come to learn that that is not the case at all. In fact she is working from a different place, a different set of standards, a different mechanism, but ones equally valid. And I have more sense of that . . . not that the rules of the school will therefore bend to take that into account, but my interpretation of her behavior and what she says about it, her feelings of her behavior, and I guess my response to what she is saying, will be able to change. It's really been very important. I can listen in a new way.

As individual teachers continue to explore the meaning to them of their participation in the study, they begin to weave a set of interconnections between their lives and their practice.

A rationale for understanding behavior in literature and in life

"Participation in this study has been the most stimulating event in my adult intellectual growth—bar none. Why this is true is very complex, but I think worth trying to articulate." Thus Donna Simms, teacher of English, begins:

> The study has allowed me to see myself and others in new and revealing ways. It has made me aware of my own assumptions. It has given me new tools for approaching literature, psychology, religion, pedagogy; and my insights continue to unfold or ripple forth and transform more and more of my world. But it has also released me from the limitations of my role as teacher and allowed me to be researcher and subject—allowed me to function as a true equal with students over whom I am accustomed to exercise au-

thority and with scholars whom I am accustomed to revere. The study itself has modeled a radical new approach to learning, and it has worked. I have never felt that I learned so much in such an intense way, and perhaps it is this experience that has the most powerful implications for education. When I think about the particular revelation that keeps coming back to me—one that I find I talk about in class or when I am just talking to people—is the finding, based on the TAT's (Thematic Apperception Tests), that men are more likely to fear intimacy and women to fear isolation (Pollak and Gilligan 1982).[2] That's just so revealing and it illuminates a lot of things that don't seem immediately explicit.

Nona Lyons, project director and discussion facilitator, interjects: "Could you say how you see that as illuminating?"

Well, it becomes the motivation or rationale for behavior that before seemed to have no particular rationale. You couldn't understand why so and so in the novel does this and somebody else does that. But when you take the fears as a possible premise, then you can begin to see different logics at work.

Think of Shakespeare's *Othello*. I have always been puzzled by the fact that Othello and Desdemona, who symbolize the power of love to transcend differences in race and age, have so much trouble communicating with each other. It seems so bizarre that these two people never talk to each other . . . that they are murdering each other. But what I think Shakespeare is showing us is that they cannot transcend certain differences. This warrior and his aristocratic housekeeper come to their marriage with radically different assumptions about reality. Upon reflection, they almost seem caricatures of the "rights" and "response" modes.

Othello does fear intimacy. He describes his marriage as putting his "unhoused free condition . . . into circumscription and confine" (I, ii, 28–30). For Othello love is a principled, all-or-nothing proposition, a "content so absolute that not another comfort like to this succeeds in unknown fate" (II, i, 220–22). Othello's devotion to the highest moral principles is also absolute. But his attachment to Desdemona is relative. When he has lost faith in Desdemona, he kills her in the name of justice, saying: "This sorrow's heavenly, it strikes where it doth love." Othello demonstrates the destructive consequences of being so absorbed in the principles and so fearful of the consequences and threats of intimacy that one cannot see the possibility of another vision of the same reality.

Desdemona, on the other hand, in just as exaggerated a way, reveals the strengths and weaknesses of the connected mode. The fact that she is willing to go to the Cyprus war with Othello argues strongly that she fears isolation, her separation from Othello. But rather than viewing their love as a static absolute, she sees it as something that will change and grow over time: "The heavens forbid but that our loves and comforts should increase even as our days do grow" (II, i, 223–25). For Desdemona, her attachment is absolute, but morality is relative. The two consequences of this are that she is willing to compromise herself by lying to both her father and Othello in attempts to protect Othello and that she is willing to endure the most unloving treatment (being slapped, insulted, neglected, and finally murdered) without blaming the man she loves.

It is a truism that opposites attract, and the love of these two characters seems to be based on their differences. But in their failure to see the full range of the differences between them and to value both moral stances, opposites also destroy; and the play suggests that it is the woman's voice that is silenced first.

(Is this what you meant when you said that this study makes you see your own assumptions differently?)

Yes—in part. And I guess on a very personal level it has helped me to acknowledge a certain part of myself. In the self-analysis that has accompanied my participation in this study, I have become aware of the connected side of my personality, and I can see my behavior in the classroom, in friendships, in my marriage, with my children, in new ways. I feel as though in my education and in my professional experiences I have been taught to see reality through the lens of the rights mode—to value rules, justice, fairness. The other side of my personality and of issues I have been dealing with has simply not been recognized or validated. *When something doesn't exist in the eyes of others, it is difficult to know whether it exists at all* [emphasis added]. Involvement in the study has liberated me to see my own wholeness and to acknowledge the connected mode in myself and in others.

Anne Riendeau, a math teacher, responds to Donna Simms by recalling how she first came to think about being a math teacher:

I agree with Donna. The study first affected me, almost immediately, on a personal level. It validated feelings I had, that I thought were perhaps wrong or odd. It made me feel good about myself. It made me more tolerant of others and it opened up conversations. I am now more confident talking to men and women who might more characteristically emphasize a "rights" approach. I have a security now that I didn't have before because I have a better sense of where my feelings are coming from and where others' feelings are coming from. It has made me more observant.

As a mathematician, also, I view the subject with a renewed personal approach. I first enjoyed math because my grandmother, whose opinions and love I valued above all others, kept telling me I'd have fun with math because she did. It now seems all right to say that I first tried and stayed with mathematics because it was something I could share with my grandmother and would make her happy, and because I valued her judgment that it was fun.

The biggest single change in my life as a mathematician is that I *no longer make a distinction between the real 'me' and the intellectual 'me.' In the past I think I needed a mask, a costume to become the mathematician. I was so alone as the only girl in a mathematics class in high school* [emphasis added]. It was a little odd to be the only female, often the first female, in the mathematics department of the colleges in which I first taught. I had to assume that lonely, self-sufficient role of the mathematician, I thought.

As a teacher I will never again teach mathematics the way I taught. I teach what is viewed as a men's topic. Parents and other adults often express the fear, or confirmation, that Susie will not do well in mathematics because her mother never understood it or because she's only a girl. Sometimes it is that Johnny will not do well in math because it runs in the family. Dad never did find a use for calculus. Some of this stems from the notion of mathematics as an absolute and not relevant to the female life or the life of a certain young man headed for a career in the humanities. Another part of this stems from the way mathematics is so often taught.

All my life I have known that I learned math by doing homework with my friends, comparing answers on the telephone, in the dorms, or on the way to school. This included male and female friends in high school and classmates in an all-female college. It was never something we would admit. If anyone ever found out we hadn't 'done our own work,' we felt wrong and accused of having cheated.

Yet all real intellectual pursuits and learning take place with exchanges of information and ideas. We do not learn in a vacuum. There is as much learning that takes place in the small groups of two or three as there is that takes place at the individual desk.

It is important at Emma Willard in teaching a subject that can be stressful for young women that we find a way to make the subject fun and that we recognize what is actually happening. These girls value their connections to others, and they may need or want to work together to learn mathematics. I don't necessarily mean to substitute math games for a rigorous proof, but I do think a rigorous proof or difficult problem can be worked out by a group of students reasoning together. One student may pick out a nuance of a problem that triggers the key to the next step for another. Students can also learn there are different methods of approaching the same problem by working together. There is more than one way to skin the cat. There are no absolutes. Students will try to find time to work together anyway. I think it is useful to recognize it, validate it, and use it to the best advantage.

"As for Anne and so many, the Dodge Study has for me proved a key to understanding the adolescent girls I teach and advise, but it has opened some personal vistas as well," comments Bob Simms, teacher of history, the humanities, and classical languages. Bob continues, emphasizing how he came to a new way of seeing collaboration in his own work:

The study immediately changed my attitude toward research. Myself a 'lone wolf' scholar, I had come to glorify the notion of autonomous investigation and had made the individual paper a fixture of my history classes. With the study in hand, however, I recalled the continual chatting and consultation in which my colleagues and I used to indulge at another institution and began to realize that, far from idle chatter, all this was the very flesh and blood of scholarship. The truly lonely scholar, in fact, is all too likely to be found the truly dotty scholar. Armed with this insight, I have become almost pitifully eager to mend my own links with distant colleagues in the profession; and in my classes, have striven to make collaborative research the rule. In both cases, the results have been gratifying.

'Collaborative work' can also be extended to include me, the teacher, and thus erase that line between leader and led, which can prove so destructive in education. If the teacher should take a research topic along with the class and participate with the students in the reporting of findings, a real change could take place in the classroom atmosphere. It would also be very good for the teacher. I used this sort of collaboration in a mini-term course some years ago and still treasure the good feelings of that experience. Now I think I can see their source.

For Margery Whiteman, Emma Willard's director of development, "It was difficult to think about my reflections about the Dodge Study because it seemed to me that the *only* insights I might have to contribute were personal in nature. The truth is, though, that the Dodge Study has been a wondrous journey in time, into myself, into the potential of relationships, into the ethos of an institution, and into psychology, a long preferred field of inquiry for me."

When it became clear that Emma Willard would be undertaking the study, Margery reveals that she sought energetically to be a part of the Faculty Committee, even though her job as development officer did not directly affect students. She says, "I knew I did not want to miss out on the adventure."

Then came the first meeting with Carol Gilligan. I found her insights riveting. Why did the boy and the girl see Heinz's dilemma so differently? Why did the women at a medical school experience increasing anxiety as they progressed in their professional training and tried to deal with the needs of their personal lives? The conclusions the research pointed to were compelling: Many women bring to the considerations of a problem a different set of priorities for its resolution than do men.

Suddenly certain fierce arguments with my husband over our years of marriage, especially the early years, came into focus with a sense of discovery and relief. He, very much a lawyer and logical thinker, tended to function in the 'rights' mode. I was more apt to look at issues through their connections. We were like the proverbial ships passing in the dark, too strong-willed to listen very carefully and try to figure out where the other was coming from. In those early years, we clung to our separate approaches as essential to our identity. As we've grown older, we have each developed some parts of the opposite approach and so have grown together. The consciousness raising encouraged by participation in the Dodge Study has even fostered that growth.

There have, of course, been many insights into points of classroom practice. One such moment came for me during our first session in evaluating the significance of the data at the end of the study's first year. We were discussing the answers given to a particular question by two Emma Willard girls. The group began to label one answer as articulate, the other as inarticulate; the first as clear, the second as meandering and disjointed, a 'muddled thinker.' It suddenly occurred to me that, within the context of a classroom assignment, the first would get an A, the second, about a C +. The student whose mind naturally focused on the development of an explanation as a hierarchy or 'logical' sequence would be rewarded. The one for whom an argument was not as neat, but rather more searching in its approach, would be marked down.

In thinking about this problem, it seemed to me that teachers might bring to the evaluation of student work an inherent bias in favor of the person who functions more in the rights mode than in the connected mode. After all, so much of our schooling is designed to teach us the logical sequencing of ideas. While there clearly is a place for that skill, it would seem that some females might have particular trouble in using only that logical approach—not only in writing, but in all kinds of problem solving. This problem should, in turn, have implications for our pedagogy.

The Dodge Study has ultimately been a process through which an institution has explored in some profound ways the purposes for which it exists. It has been an adventure to be a part of charting how some people, in this case, young women, understand why they do what they do. That's a very complex issue, at the heart of our humanity.

Reconsidering the education of young women

Judy Bridges, athletic director at the time, and now Emma Willard's dean of students, returns to Anne Riendeau's remarks, opening a discussion on "competition" and how she has come to think about winning and losing.

When I listen to Anne talk about math and what has traditionally been thought of as a male realm, probably some of the first things that hit me are similar to hers. I think back to my early childhood when I first realized that being active, playing different games, was really a special thing for me, realizing early-on that there were rules by which I had to play. I realized, too, that to play, I had to do it that way. For years, really probably up until three years ago, there was some uneasiness. There was more that I wanted to do with sports, but I could not dare to figure out what that was.

In the four years of this study, I have enjoyed the chance to look at my profession of physical education and at myself and who I am in that profession. I had been taught that, indeed, there are winners and losers and that the struggle is not only against others, but also against yourself, your own abilities. All of this was supposed to make up the wonderfulness of sport. What it asked of me was to put myself and those on my team in a secondary role to the need of the team to win.

As I heard my students making comments to belittle the opponents, I realized their dilemma and mine. *To compete against another person, my students felt they needed to separate from that person. To beat you in a competition meant that I could not know you or care about you.* The connections, the team spirit, that our team felt among its own members, were not shared with the individuals on the other team.

As coaches at Emma Willard, we began to experiment, to watch, as we set up intersquad games, where everyone knew each other. The skill level seemed just as high as in games with other schools, but the enjoyment level was much higher. The more I learned through the study and the more I watched and talked with my players, the more able I was to understand what I had felt in my childhood and what I was seeing and hearing from my students now. These young women are asking for and living a new definition of competition. This definition includes the acknowledgment of the relationships between those agreeing to compete. Competition truly is an agreed upon, shared experience. In this particularly human definition of competition, there is room for young women to develop skills, to value winning, and to enjoy the spirit and company of those they choose to compete *with* rather than against.

I will never be able to approach competition of any kind in the same fragmented way I used to. When I include my 'opponent' as a partner rather than an adversary, I become whole in the competitive experience. That I now can share this revelation with my students makes me a better person and a much better and more effective teacher. I am also a better listener. I am able to appreciate what a student is saying in a much more complete way than I could before.

The playing fields are not the only place where students feel a sense of competition. In the dormitories competition is felt for friends, between roommates, and for attention from adults living in the dorms. Again, if the definition of this kind of competition is an agreed upon, shared experience, students will not be threatened with losing part of themselves within the competition.

(But what are you saying about competition? There are many who would think that you are against competition, against competitive games. Are you?) I see competition as a positive force in our lives. But young women thrive in competition that validates, as well, their need for relationships and sharing. I believe if we as educators can value women's definition of competition and see it as being in the flow of a woman's life, then we really will be responsive to those we teach.

Shirley Kiepper, Emma Willard's associate director of admissions, remarks:

The question of competition is complex. And I see another aspect. Young adolescent girls are often quick to sacrifice their real fantasies and goals because they've been told their choices or ideas are inappropriate or too competitive for women. When I talk to prospective students in an admissions interview, I try to be very careful not to be another voice adding to the number who have already told them what they *cannot* do.

For instance, I ask them to tell me what some of their fantasies are about, what they'd like to do in later years, what crazy things they would love to do? And I'm careful that the question is conversational and light, that it does not say to the girl, You ought to know what you want to do with the rest of your life. Sometimes they say, 'Well, I'd really like to be a lawyer, go to Yale Law

School—that's what I'd like to do. But it's kind of crazy. I couldn't do that.'

And my response is, 'Well why couldn't you? Anything's possible. If that's what you are really thinking about and fantasizing, keep your goal in mind. Don't let people tell you, "No, that's too tough. You couldn't possibly do that!" ' I tell them to be aware of many possibilities, and to be open and aware that there are things in the world they haven't known or thought about yet.

As an interviewer, one has to keep things in perspective. I always hope the girls I talk to are not thinking about being a lawyer and Yale Law School because Dad is pressing them hard and they hope to make him happy. I want them to pursue an idea because it springs from within them. Other girls have told me they'd like to be veterinarians, but they'll add, 'A lot of people have told me it's not a job for a woman, so I don't think I'm going to do that.'

And then I ask, 'Why not? If this is of interest to you, look into it as a career. Think more about it. Consider exploring the field as an independent study. Find out what it's all about and don't echo what you hear. It may be tough training and a hard career, but if you want to be a vet, you probably could fulfill the requirements.'

"I agree with Judy about competition," begins Barbara Wiley, the Emma Willard librarian, "especially as it can be part of a model we hold up not just to our students but for ourselves." She goes on:

Too often, the people whose opinions I most valued were men. It was the male model of success—the 'climb the corporate ladder' model—that was held up to me as the only model worth considering if one wanted to 'be someone.' Women who wanted to succeed had to emulate men to do so. Over the years I have grown increasingly uncomfortable with that but have lacked the self-assurance to believe in my perceptions and feelings. The Dodge Study, in conjunction with speakers like Peggy McIntosh and with reading I have done, has made me absolutely certain that not only is the response mode an equally valuable and important mode, but the world desperately needs response-mode leaders in all fields of endeavor.

I now know that the time I and others spend 'making and mending the social fabric,' as Peggy McIntosh says, is vital to society. I have been laughed at in the past for the time I spend in corresponding with friends and in keeping up friendships that go back in some cases to kindergarten, for 'never losing a friend.' I used to feel self-conscious about this obviously—to my critics—silly waste of time. I am now very comfortable in saying that I highly value those friendships, that I need them, and that my friends need me. We give each other help and caring in times of difficulty and we make fun times and triumphs more meaningful because they are shared. My friends are my link with my pleasurable, memorable past and my link with the unknown future. They are my assurance that although our lives change daily, our friendships will continue and will grow and change as we do.

"Barbara reminds me that this study has made me much more aware of adolescent girls' development, especially aware of the importance to each of them of their relationships with their friends," comments Shirley Kiepper. "Girls tell me frankly, and I hear it often, 'I spend a lot of time talking with my friends and this is important to me.' Many of them will confess that this part of their lives is more important to them than studying and getting their school work done. They worry about this, and that's often why they think about boarding school. They hope that if they're with their friends all day, on a twenty-four-hour basis, they'll be able to put the needs of friendship and studying in perspective."

Nancy Cushman, Emma Willard counselor and teacher of psychology, recalling her own experience as an adolescent, reveals how her thinking about adolescent development has changed and what this has meant for her teaching:

I can remember as an adolescent girl questioning my ability to think, to reason, and to take a moral stand on issues. No matter how long I puzzled over my own thoughts, I never seemed to emerge with a set of principles that I could claim were my morals. Just when I would think I had found a principle to live by, I would find that I had made decisions that did not seem to indicate that I truly believed in my own values.

As I look back on those decisions from the vantage point of one who has heard Carol Gilligan and Nona Lyons articulate the thinking of the response mode, I realize that my decisions were made only after a consideration of the thoughts and especially the feelings of the various people involved in my dilemma. My resolution rested on what I can now call a principle of interdependence. Having this principle validated as a legitimate strength has given me a confidence in myself as a decision-maker that I never before possessed. Another important revelation was learning that the language of our culture articulates the rights mode but does not provide an adequate vocabulary for the response mode. When I was misunderstood, I assumed it was my inability to explain and not a lack of perception on the part of my listener. I now know that words such as 'dependence,' 'fairness,' and 'objectivity' have a different meaning for me and evoke different feelings than they do for others. I now have a psychological and theoretical basis for seeing what had been missing in my formal developmental psychology courses.

I am now able to listen for the different voice of each person with whom I have contact. I find myself asking Emma Willard girls who seek counseling to elaborate more fully their perceptions of relationships, to define for me just what it means to them that a teacher has given them a poor grade or a parent is angry.

I also have come to respect this connected voice that has not yet learned to incorporate herself into her network of caring. As I listen, I am awed rather than frustrated by the lengths girls go to, as Peggy McIntosh says, 'to make and mend the social fabric,' often at their own expense. I seek ways to help them see that this fabric can be preserved even though the initial response may be anger and withdrawal. Yet I comfort myself with the knowledge that each of these girls must make her own way toward a realization that she can include herself in the network of care.

I find that I must redefine the definition of independence given by traditional adolescent psychology texts when listening to our girls struggle for a new relationship within the family, based not on autonomy but on interdependence. In cases of child abuse or parental neglect, I no longer spend time helping a young woman separate from her parents. Rather, we look to other relationships in her life to fill the vital sense of connectedness. These cases have become increasingly tragic to me since recognizing this need for attachment that Gilligan has identified in both the rights and response mode. This banishing of the myth of autonomy so long perpetrated by developmental psychologists has confirmed my own long-held sense that this was not true.

Darby Johnson, whose own education has taken place in both single-sex and coed settings, reconsiders the value of an all-girls' school and Emma Willard:

This is my second year at Emma Willard. Although I taught a history course for one trimester last year, I am an admissions officer and not a teaching member of the faculty. Therefore, my reactions to the Dodge Study come from what this research has taught me about my education in coeducational and single-sex institutions.

After attending an all-girls' elementary school from 4th to 8th grade, I entered a private coed school that had recently started enrolling girls. Overall, my experience there was positive. I earned good grades, played three varsity sports, and made my share of good friends. Yet, something was missing, and it was not until I read what the Emma Willard girls had to say about dependence and leadership that I was able to put my finger on what those pieces were.

In their interviews, Emma Willard students have said that they definitely feel that the school opens up myriad leadership opportunities for them and that one does not have to assume that she cannot claim to be a leader until she has been elected to a particular position. At my school, girls were vice presidents, not presidents. Even in the classroom, one felt uncomfortable speaking up too much or too loudly. As a result, we never had enough of an opportunity to develop our leadership qualities or to learn how to lead. I was willing to take risks as an adolescent, but my faculty and peers were not so anxious to see this happen. My decision to attend a women's college was, in part, a response to this missed opportunity.

If I had to go to high school again, I would go to a girls' school. The Dodge Study has shown me that I did not make the 'connections' with my friends and teachers that many Emma Willard girls have made. I am still in touch with a few of my high school friends, but it is my Wellesley friends whom I will turn to first for advice, and it is their friendship that I value most.

The Dodge Study has made me realize that what I didn't like about my high school experience is exactly what makes me so enthusiastic about Emma Willard. As a result, I am an effective admissions officer because I believe in and understand what I am 'selling.'

Seeing your subject, your students, and your colleagues in a new way

(*Nancy, you mentioned that you have experimented with new ways to teach psychology. How did you happen to do that?*)

As I began to teach Introduction to Psychology from a text which seemed little changed since my college years, I was immediately struck by the different approaches to learning that girls in my class seemed to adopt. Young women whom I would characterize in the rights mode seemed interested in the theoretical concepts in and of themselves. They were eager to learn the vocabulary and master the theory. Girls in the response mode were delighted to find that the concepts explained a dear friend or relative and eager to spend class time relating specific personal experiences as examples of various theories. Had I not had this approach validated by the Gilligan research, I would have enjoyed these stories yet harbored an uneasy feeling that these were diversions. With a new sensitivity, I realized I was faced with the challenge of making the material available to each student in a way that was meaningful to her.

I have tried to vary the type of assignments and the structure of the class. While I demand that students master the vocabulary and concepts, I always provide time for work in small groups where students teach each other or relate the material directly to their own lives. I have added literature to the course and increased the use of movies that show real people rather than animated examples of concepts, such as perception and sensation. I encourage students to study together and require at least one group project allowing class-time for planning and research.

I have also begun to teach the hypotheses of Gilligan's work and the Dodge Study hoping that students will be validated as I was. Interestingly enough, I find both in my classroom and among educators participating in the Dodge Study, a reluctance to identify oneself as operating in the rights mode. While the society at large validates this mode, we seem reluctant to see its strengths and to acknowledge that we all use it, even those of us that predominate in the response mode.

I have come to recognize that the concepts we are developing are sophisticated, and the distinctions subtle. The need to listen and remain open to ideas that we have not considered is paramount. The process of working with a group of educators who represent different disciplines and different modes has become an integral part of the study. In a sense, we are all simultaneously teachers and learners, researchers and subjects. We are both pioneers and the first to caution against drawing conclusions based on data from a limited sample of students.

Bob Simms responds to Nancy Cushman's remarks:

This notion of different entry points to the acquisition of knowledge really throws some light on something which has bothered me for years. My predecessor in the teaching of ancient history occasionally used historical novels, such as those by Mary Renault. To say the least, I neither understood nor approved the use of this 'unhistorical' stuff! Now, however, I think I see what my predecessor was doing. A good historical novel, after all, is not really unhistorical: It merely takes the bare bones of historical evidence and fleshes these out with 'human interest'—yearnings, doubts, illicit thoughts, and so on. These vignettes have very much to do with human relationships and thus ought to be a congenial entry point for the response mode to the bare facts of history in which humanity is entangled.

"I'd like to respond to something you said about students learning in your psychology class." commented Margery Whiteman to Nancy Cushman. "Your point about the two quite different approaches to understanding and mastering the material puts me in mind of problems I faced as a learner in college when I took too many science courses. I think that one thing the Dodge Study has shown us is that material in many classrooms has tended to be approached in only one way, through rule and example. Maybe a reason why girls have tended not to excel in science and math in the past stems from the way the material of such courses has been presented to them. Your discussion of your psychology class seems to me to demonstrate that people can come at material from two quite different directions and yet end up learning the same fundamental points. Their experience of the material, and therefore their "knowledge," will be somewhat different, however.

(Anne, you started to talk about your responses to the need for a new approach in mathematics and you, I know, experimented with one. How did that go? Could you describe what you did? Maybe it would be helpful to be very detailed.)

It took me four years to see that we simply needed to begin searching for the best way to make good use of collaborative learning in mathematics. At first I needed to verify that it was useful. I chose a class of students who had been selected as a particularly able group for one of our problem-solving sections, now called Precalculus I. It seemed that any experiments I tried would damage the more able students the least. I had noticed all along that if time was given for work on homework in class that they automatically worked together. There were some exceptions. It became very clear as the year progressed that these 'loners' were uncomfortable working with others, that they felt it wrong to work with someone. This simply verified that some young women are more autonomous in their approach to learning. In this particular class, I felt these students suffered. That may have been my own interpretation. They did write nearly perfect final examinations.

The experiment with this class was a dismal failure. I tried too many things. I was more roundabout in encouraging collaborators. I think the experiment failed, too, because I videotaped the class and the camera intimidated most of the students.

The next year, and following, I was more direct. I openly encouraged students to work together when I thought it was especially needed. At least once each term or semester, I had the students group themselves at random in three's and designed tests with similarly worded but different questions for each group, that were to be answered by the group as a group. In addition, each individual student had to write out the answer to hand in for her grade, but she also received a group grade. I have used this approach for tests on quadratic functions with emphasis on graphing and finding zeros, axis of symmetry, domain, range, as well as applied problems with maximum or minimum and on tests in trigonometry, including solutions of equations, proofs of identities, and graphing. The comments from the students have been positive. They like having a test with their friends, especially when the test is on a topic they find difficult. The students who are in the autonomous mode and are uncomfortable may opt not to contribute to the group but they must contribute the individual paper. In some way then I satisfied both modes of thinking. The results weren't vastly different from those on routine tests. In following through to the final examination I can say from the data I have, although it certainly isn't scientific, that although the collaborative testing and grading didn't necessarily improve the overall grades on these topics, it didn't make them any poorer either.

But while there was little change in performance and learning, there was a lessening of the tension, particularly on a difficult topic that was new. What may be more important, however, is that this was a new way of working out problems and, I hope, a new way of feeling about mathematics. I have since progressed to ask the students to teach review sessions for the final examinations, and in one Precalculus II class to teach the Law of Sines, Law of Cosines, and the area of a triangle formula to the Algebra II and Trigonometry classes. In each case the students were asked to work in small groups and to plan which topic each would teach. These have been enormously successful. The students were enthusiastic about the work. They sought assistance and did research they never would have considered before, and they worked out together, with no help from me, the best way to present the material. Even the weakest students had good presentations. As one of them put it when asked how she would learn the materials that was not part of her presentation, 'I get a little help from my friends.'

During these past four years with all the discussions and awareness of the Dodge Study, the mathematics division at Emma Willard validated some of the activity that has always taken place in the Learning Center. The Learning Center is a mathematics office, staffed by a member of the mathematics faculty for as many periods as there are mathematics teachers and open to anyone in need of a boost for homework and study. Often, when there is frantic activity before major tests, there are more students than one teacher can accommodate in a period. The students seem to take over and teach each other and answer each other's questions. We have now dubbed the Learning Center as the Seat of Collaborative Learning in mathematics. We used to be concerned when we heard an admissions guide tell a prospective student that the Learning Center was the place where you could 'get all your questions answered' if you didn't understand your math. Now I think I understand what the guides meant. The Learning Center is viewed as the place where students help students as well as where teachers do. It may be the place where students feel good about mathematics.

The changes in approach to teaching mathematics are not very drastic or different from what are used in many other disciplines. The change for me is in the awareness of the two modes of thinking and in how I view my students. I must be aware of the two modes of thinking and sensitive to both. I must not judge either on the basis of approach but rather try to implement the learning process within each mode. I also want to try to make the students aware of each other's differences in approach and thinking. To me this is the strongest message from the study and one that is always present: be aware that there are different modes of thinking and try to learn more about them.

"While participation in this study has helped us see our students differently, I think it has also made me think about course materials we need to include," interjects Paul Lamar.

For example, from *Women's Diaries of the Westward Journey,* which we read in my autobiography course, we get a different perspective on the trip west, different from the standard one we've always gotten: There were opportunities for everyone out there, and everyone went with great enthusiasm. Not so. In this book we learn what it meant for women to leave friends behind. The emotional cost was great. We learn, too, about isolation and separation from a couple of terrifying passages about having to bury someone on the lonely plains. The women's diaries record these intense feelings, and we are thus able to look at the historical experience in a new light. I remember asking my students about moves their families had had to make and whose decisions had been involved. I think back to my own family's moves and my mother's very strong desire not to move to Washington, D.C., about twelve years ago. She had friends here. But at that time I don't know that I would have thought that a compelling enough reason to stay in Albany.

But even in thinking about hiring new faculty, for Marilyn Hunter, chair of the language division, new perspectives derive from the study:

As a teacher of adolescents for thirteen years, I feel that I have developed a kind of 'sixth sense.' It became apparent to me as I interviewed candidates last year for a teaching position in my division. Before participating in the study, I was unable to identify this other criterion that I was evaluating subconsciously in each interview. It had to do with the person's ability to be sensitive to both the rights mode and the response mode. This had to be true not only in their relations with students but also in their relations with colleagues.

The students operate in both modes and the teachers need to be able to respond in either. Regardless of a candidate's credentials or his/her fluency in the language he/she wishes to teach, he/she must demonstrate 'connectedness' as well. If, in an interview situation, a candidate speaks only of his/her ability to teach students to be fluent, or to pass standardized tests without mentioning their need to experience success in other ways, I immediately see a red flag. On the other hand, if he/she also takes pride in the student who manages to communicate in the language, even with gross mistakes in grammar and pronunciations, this tells me that he/she possesses a certain desirable sensitivity.

Likewise, a candidate needs to demonstrate an interest in sharing methodologies with his/her colleagues. Our approach in the language division is constantly being fine-tuned by exposure to updated and sometimes radical new directions. Through discussions and demonstrations we re-evaluate and incorporate, always being aware that one approach will not be the panacea for any given class. Because we are aware of different learning styles, we know that our teaching must be flexible. Now, because of what I've learned through the Dodge Study, it is apparent that the rights and response modes also play a significant role. Together as teachers we share and learn from each other. A candidate who believes otherwise would be unacceptable.

Cautions

While it is clear that the Dodge Study has entered the professional lives of members of the Emma Willard faculty, shaping new ideas for pedagogy and for curriculum materials, it has also raised some cautions.

Although acknowledging that "my participation in the Dodge Study at Emma Willard School has involved me in a succession of 'recognitions,' which extend from an awareness of my own personal choices to an evaluation of those choices as I apply them in my roles as educator," Gail Viamonte goes on to talk about both the "recognitions" and some "cautions".

Participation in the Dodge Study has helped me to articulate at least two modes of moral decision making. And thus to recognize that there may be even more. Through it, I can affirm the equal validity of these two different modes.

But I find myself being insistently cautious. I shudder when I hear phrases such as 'the special needs of young women' or envision this study and work being seen as justification versus objectification, as prescription rather than description. I see the goal of applying this study as helping others and myself to articulate the very factors which are taken into account when any form or mode of moral decision making takes place. I believe that to recognize and to explore these modes is to examine, not only adolescent women at Emma Willard School, but modes of humanness. I know many forty- to fifty-year-old males who have made the response mode a cornerstone of their professional lives. I wish us to recognize that, while for some educators, participation in the Dodge Study has been an entree into 'collaborative learning,' or the issues of different 'learning styles,' the value of either of these is not dependent upon 'the findings of the study.' Rather, 'collaborative learning' or 'learning styles' are valid as educational and pedagogical means; the study allows insight into how they function with some individuals [students] and allows other individuals [teachers] comfortably to approach these via another cogent academic study in educational psychology.

I see a danger in 'using' the study to confirm or to justify a previously existing agenda. I get nervous when someone claims that 'this work corroborates what we've said about' a set of institutional rules or dictates. I would hate to think that a study which asks us to listen to the *questions* and self-talk which reflect complexities of *ways* of thinking might be reduced to prescriptive 'givens' concerning *the way* all young women think; or the way we, as educators, *should* teach all of our subject matter; or the reasons why stereotyping of any sort should be fostered, though in an altered form.

I imagine an excited colleague talking about what he has gained from the study. Now, he says, he understands why, instead of running over the goalie in order to score, his female team members stop to pick their opponent up. His conclusion is that women need to learn 'to play the game.' He does not question whether or not 'the game' is meant to test ferocity or skill. He does not seem to recognize that this situation could lead us to question in at least three directions. Certainly, we might question what kind of 'education' would teach women to trample a goalie in order to gain the point. We might also ask if a more skillful team might not be able to both pick up the goalie and gain the point. Or we might ask— as we need to of our school grading systems—if the scoring system and rules validate those abilities and behaviors we wish to award. We need to consider the possibility that any situation which frames a conflict in these terms ought, itself, to be questioned. If we assume that structures—institutions, pedagogies, grading systems, whatever—precede rather than embody a particular perspective, we miss what has been, for me, one of the most significant aspects of this study.

Conclusions

Recently Robert Bellah, a sociologist, and his associates completed a study of individualism and commitment in American life. From this research Bellah draws a stark conclusion: "Americans today lack a common language to discuss the serious dilemmas of their lives." From their interviews with Americans, Bellah suggests that people today are confused "about how to define for themselves such things as the nature of success, the meaning of freedom, and the requirements of justice." Bellah points to the necessity to "find a moral language that will transcend their radical individualism" (Bellah et al. 1985).

It may be that Bellah's findings offer one perspective on the responses of Emma Willard teachers to the Dodge research project. If Bellah is correct in arguing that Americans lack a language through which to discuss important values and relationships of their lives, it may be that this research project in its larger context provides a new vocabulary, as well as a way of thinking about one's attachments to others—a new grammar of relationships. In connecting ideas about relationships to ideas about morality, this work offers a way to connect people's ideas to their actions, actions they might judge "right" or "wrong." That in turn gives a new interpretive lens to bring to one's everyday interactions.

Through their involvement in this project, teachers of Emma Willard School not only could see a way to validate their often unspoken concerns about values they held, but were also led to new appraisals of their practice. The research project provided a medium for self-validation and renewal as it connected the personal and professional lives of teachers. Paul Lamar says it best:

> It's made the school a much livelier, more stimulating place to be. And when too many people come in we may lose our steam and then we get fired up again, you know, and go off and expand and elaborate on something else. As you discovered, we knew this and with positive questions and input—you go in one direction for a little while and you realize that there are ten more questions and you start. . . . But I think for the community here, it's just been a wonderful thing, and, as [another teacher] said, it has created a kind of network here and special relationships—not that we just work together but a kind of excitement . . . and you really don't have a feeling that this is a school full of teachers doing the same old thing every year and . . . it just isn't. We are killing ourselves by doing it so differently every time we walk into the classroom, but nonetheless, you know, you can't help loving it.
>
> *(How are you doing something different every time you walk into the classroom?)* Well, you start by saying, Why am I using these books, let's rewrite the syllabus. And then you look at a particular work and you say; 'What if I had taught it this way?'— and all the other questions we ask, and you walk into the classroom and say why am I teaching this at all? Kids should be teaching this, you know, and it goes on and on.
>
> Once you get going with this, what happens is you can never hear in the same way you heard before. So when you walk into the classroom, you do it differently every day. You don't even know as you go in that door, how it is going to be different sometimes. So it depends on what's coming from the kids and what you now are able to hear that you couldn't hear before and what you do with that. I am still listening, going okay, I think I got that and, no, there might be another angle to it. So that, for me, has been something and has made every day exciting.

Notes

1. Asking people to resolve the Heinz dilemma is the method developed by Lawrence Kohlberg to map and measure the development of people's "justice" reasoning (Kohlberg 1984). Carol Gilligan, in her book *In a*

Different Voice, uses the example of eleven-year-old Amy to demonstrate the logic of an ethic of "response" or care and to show the relationship between Amy's approach to solving the Heinz dilemma and her description of herself in relation to others. Amy's thinking about self and morality differs from the justice or fairness response Kohlberg has described (Gilligan, 1982), the one the interviewer was listening for.

2. The TAT finding refers to results from a study by Pollack and Gilligan. Through stories written in response to pictures—thus called Thematic Apperception Tests (TAT's)—the study revealed different patterns of responses for males and females (Pollack and Gilligan, 1982). Males tended to see danger in intimacy and females to see danger in isolation.

Sources

Bellah, R., R. Madsen, W. M. Sullivan, A. Swidler, and S. M. Tipton, 1985. *Habits of the Heart.* New York: Harper and Row.

Gilligan, C. 1977. In a different voice: Women's conceptions of self and of morality. *Harvard Educational Review* 47:481–517.

Gilligan, C. 1982. *In a Different Voice.* Cambridge, Mass. Harvard University Press.

Gilligan, C., S. Langdale, N. Lyons, and M. Murphy, 1982. The contribution of women's thought to developmental theory: The elimination of sex bias in moral development research and education. Final report to the National Institute of Education. Unpublished.

Gilligan, C., and J. Attanucci. 1988. Two moral orientations: Gender differences and similarities. *Merrill-Palmer Quarterly.*

Johnston, D. K. 1985. Two moral orientations—two problem-solving strategies: Adolescents' solutions and dilemmas in fables. Ph.D. diss. Harvard University.

Kohlberg, L. 1984. *The Psychology of Moral Development: Essays on Moral Development* 2. San Francisco: Harper and Row.

Lyons, N. 1982. Conceptions of self and morality and modes of moral choice. Ed.D. diss. Harvard University.

Lyons, N. 1983. Two perspectives: On self, relationships and morality. *Harvard Educational Review* 55:125–45.

Pollak, S. and C. Gilligan. 1982. Images of violence in thematic apperception test stories. *Journal of Personality and Social Psychology* 42:159–67.

Epilogue
Soundings into Development

CAROL GILLIGAN, ANNIE ROGERS, AND
LYN MIKEL BROWN

Editors' Note: *This essay which draws on the Emma Willard Study originally appeared as Section IV of* Psyche Embedded: A Place for Body, Relationships, and Culture in Personality Theory.

Soundings has many meanings: measuring the depth or examining the bottom of a body of water, making or giving forth sound, and sound that is resonant, sonorous. In all these senses of the word, we are taking soundings into psychological development. And we are arranging these soundings in musical terms, because by drawing a language for psychology from music rather than from the visual arts, the idea of development enters time. Psyche, or self, rather than being placed at stages, steps, or positions and marked off by borders and boundaries, can be represented as *in* relationship—relationships that exist in the medium of time or change. The experience of self can then be compared with the unity of a musical composition, where meaning at any one moment is indeterminate, since it can only be apprehended in time. Then, in speaking about development, one can speak about themes that develop, change key, recur, drop out; of discrete movements characterized by changes in rhythm and tempo; of harmonic sequences that change the sound of individual notes and intervals; of leitmotifs that convey character and dramatize the ways in which people affect or move one another. In addition, the shift away from a visual imagery that depicts Psyche or self as fixed, still, stopped in time and from positional metaphors to a musical language makes it possible to speak about differences in terms other than hierarchical arrangement or invidious comparison.

If we imagine a child as visually positioned in relation to others (smaller and immature in relation to a standard of what we call human), we can talk about the child's progression toward an ideal of equality or to a position of domination. But if we imagine a child engaged in responsive relationships, we can also talk about the transformations or changes in the experience of those relationships, the changing sounds of human connection over time and the different tonalities that tend to characterize particular relationships. For example, mother-daughter relationships or relationships between fathers and daughters characteristically differ in tone from relationships between mothers and sons and fathers and sons, and extend differently through time. During the period of adolescence, for instance, the harmonic pattern and the discordant notes of these various relationships tend to differ so that one would rarely mistake one for the other. Similarly the rhythms of male and female sexuality are not the same, and sexual relationships have different implications for males and females in adolescence, so that boys and girls when speaking of sexuality, all tell a story recognizably sexual but tell it in different terms.

As we listen to people speaking and imagine different ways of speaking, which in turn imply different ways of seeing, feeling, and thinking, male and female development may be characterized in terms of a particular way of arranging themes that pertain to the experience of one's body and relationships with others, and to living within a family and a culture.

Beginning at Emma Willard and then continuing in a variety of schools and after-school settings, we have listened to girls and to boys who have been interviewed annually over a period of years (Gilligan, Johnston, and Miller 1988; Gilligan, Ward, and Taylor 1988). We have asked them to describe themselves, to talk about important relationships in their lives, including their relationships with their parents and friends; to describe experiences of conflict and choice; to discuss their lives in school, how they learn, and their hopes and expectations for the future.

Metaphors of voice and vision: Themes of connection and separation

Themes familiar from traditional accounts of adolescent psychology appear in these teenagers' descriptions, connected to a visual imagery of self and denoting separation, individuation, and concerns about autonomy and freedom. This psychological framework is aligned with American tradition with its emphasis on individual rights and independence from others—the tradition fostered by formal education. Within this framework, femininity is either idealized (associated with altruistic self-sacrifice) or appears suspect, disturbing. Girls reflecting back on their childhood from this perspective, speak of growing apart from their parents and of their wish to lead their own lives, a wish often coupled with the wish that their mothers would do the same. "I have grown," Rebecca explains. "I have kind of grown apart from my parents. I don't think we have become less close, it's just that now I am beginning to see more, you know, me myself, not me and Mom and Dad. In the past," she says, in a passage filled with visual images,

> ... I really had no notion of myself, of *just me* and not *me in relation* to my friends or me in relation to my parents or anything. *I see* myself ... *I see,* I feel a lot less scared about myself, because when you associate yourself so much with others that you can't kind of *separate yourself* from a group, you feel there are times when you feel all alone and have to think, Wow! I remember, this is really strange, but at moments kind of being stricken with fright. *I would look into the mirror* and say, This is me, X. These are my hands, and *I am all alone,* and *I am not glued to any other person.*

The following year, when as a senior in high school Rebecca talks about her mother, a visual language continues to mark her discourse of separation.

> *I see* her as a middle-aged woman with her own life, and her own problems, *very separate* from mine. And it is fascinating to me *to see her* as a person, a real, whole, complete person who makes bad judgments and who yells when she is upset and who really doesn't function rationally all the time. So she is important to me. *She* doesn't really influence me anymore, but she is important to me.

This quintessentially adolescent description is so in line with the language and imagery of contemporary psychology, with its emphasis on separation and on the adolescent deflation of idealized images of parents, the perception of parents as "real people," that it is surprising when Rebecca, after speaking about the similarity between herself and her mother ("My mother and I are basically caring people and outgoing people. I see a lot of her in me, but it doesn't scare me; it used to terrify me, because I used to think, Oh God, I am going to end up like her."), suddenly observes, "I don't think anybody is self-sufficient, and no woman is an island."

With this statement, the talk of separation with its imagery of seeing and of mirrors suddenly yields to a different language for describing connection and closeness with others, a language of talking, of listening, of being with, of being touched. "I can't imagine going through a rough time," Rebecca says, "without somebody there *to talk to* or somebody *to be with* or *hold my hand.*"

When we speak about growth in visual metaphors of separation and signify what we mean by development in a positional language, Rebecca's unexpected statement may appear as a "regression" to a less separate, less independent, less developed position. Or we might simply gloss over her words. But if we think of our language and how it shapes her understanding of her experience, of our interpretation as one that obscures or recognizes her meanings, then we may feel compelled to wonder about the meaning of development, the very words we have used to describe her development.

Twelve years ago the specification of a voice that differed from the voices that have guided and been amplified by developmental psychologists immediately raised questions about development, which were linked to questions about women (Gilligan 1977). Listening to women's conceptions of self and morality drew attention to a different voice and to the extent to which developmental theories had been drawn from studies of men. Variations in women's ways of speaking about morality and about themselves suggested patterns—distinctions between different women and changes in a woman's thinking in the face of crisis and over time. These changes could be framed in terms of the vocabulary commonly used by developmental psychologists: that is, in terms of stages, positions, levels, and the transitions between them. Women's concerns about their own survival in the face of what they perceived to be abandonment by others, their concerns about their appearance or "goodness" in the eyes of others, and their concerns about truth—specifically truths about relationship and about violence—suggested a pattern of increasingly sophisticated thinking about the nature of relationships between people. This pattern more or less conformed to the progression from an egocentric, through a normative or conventional, to an autonomous or reflective or critical position: the progression that most developmental psychologists have traced.

The two transitions in this process—from "selfishness" to responsibility and from "goodness" to truth—however seemed reparative, repairing a loss or correcting an error or undoing an exclusion. While women tended to label the exclusion of others as "selfish" and as cause for being considered "bad women," they tended—following the norms of conventions of feminine virtue—to label their exclusion of themselves as "good." Yet the "selfless" position that has been valorized in Western culture, and associated with idealized images of mothers, seemed so pain-ful for women and was often accompanied by signs of psychological distress—symptoms of eating disorders and depression (Jack 1987; Stei-ner-Adair 1986). The fact that women were, in conventional terms, "doing good and feeling bad"—as Jean Baker Miller (1976) put it, began to focus a number of questions: about women's activities and cultural values and about problems of inclusion and exclusion on a societal and cultural as well as on a personal scale. Asked to speak about conflicts and choices, women spoke about problems of inclusion and exclusion in a way that suggested a growing understanding of the psychological logic of rela-tionships and an awareness of problems in relationship, having to do with the inclusion and exclusion of women in a larger framework of relationships—in the family, in the society, and in the transgenerational cultural world. Women's concerns about inclusion and exclusion were not simply interpersonal concerns, and the representation of women's relational concerns as "interpersonal" or "conventional" seemed to con-tribute to women's confusion—to augment the problems of growing up female within a tradition where "human" often meant male.

Attention to this confusion—to the tension between psychological theories of human development and the experience and situation of women—suggested that what had been represented as steps in a devel-opmental progression might be better conceived as an interplay of voices, creating a "contrapuntal theme, woven into the cycle of life and recurring in varying forms in people's judgments, fantasies and thoughts" (Gilligan 1982, 1). This interplay of voices seemed particularly intense in the lives of both women and men at times of crisis and change. Thus insights gained by studying women's conceptions of self, relationship, and mo-rality taken together with the recurrent problems psychologists had en-countered in understanding or interpreting women's experience raised the question of whether there was a need for new language—a shift from a visual imagery of stages, steps, positions, levels to a musical language of counterpoint and theme.

Development: an etymology

We turn now to questions about development like etymologists, by studying the origin and historical meanings of words. This may seem at first like an esoteric choice, but to know the history of words is to recover the full meaning of their present form and sense. Worn and altered within a particular discipline, words may take on peculiarly narrow meanings.

In order to understand the many possible meanings of the word "develop," to wash our language of the layers of theory collected upon it, and to restore root meanings of ideas, we turn to the *Oxford English Dictionary* (OED hereafter). The oldest meanings of the word develop are "apart" (*dis*) and "to wrap" (*voloper*) from the Latin and French. In Italy in the fourteenth century *suiluppara* meant "to unwrap, disentangle, to rid free." In modern Italian, this word means to "enwrap, to bundle, to roll up, to entangle." The OED gives four major meanings to the word develop: (1) to unfold, unroll, to flatten out a curved surface, to cut out of its enfolding cover; (2) to lay open by removal of that which enfolds, to unveil, to unfold (as a tale, the meaning of a thing); to disclose, to reveal; (3) to unfold more fully, bring out all that is potentially contained in; and (4) to change a mathematical function, to expand into the form of a series, (a) to cause to grow, (b) said of a series and sharing progression from a simple or lower to a higher or more complex type.

Developmental psychologists have taken on the fourth meaning and elaborated this notion into stages of cognitive, moral, social, and emotional growth. We are now recovering the first three meanings of development, particularly the third meaning: to unfold more fully, bring out all that is potentially contained within. Among the uses of this meaning, is the musical use (Stainer, Composition ix, 1880) "of a melody or theme developed by frequent changes of key, or harmony. . . . A fragment of melody is said to be developed when its outline is altered and expanded so as to create new interest." Of course, all these meanings do not exclude the meaning of development as growth or expansion, with the connotation that what develops becomes gradually fuller, larger, and better. When this meaning is put in context beside other meanings of development—and stripped of the notion of linear progress that currently undergirds hierarchical stage models of development—it, too, can become a new way to comprehend the process of development. The infant who is exquisitely responsive experiences attachment differently from the adult. The mother or father or caretaker who serves as the interpreter and nurturer of the infant's new attachment becomes attached to the infant in the process of that care, but the attachment is not the same. The young child who fails to control an impulse and breaks a rule is not the same as the teenager who breaks a law to protest the making of nuclear arms, knowing and accepting the consequences he or she risks to do this. Development implies a telos—and the telos is a fuller and, in some ways, more adequate way to understand the world and to live one's life. But to organize this growth into stages, and call some stages higher, or more complex, misses the point. Development is fraught with vulnerabilities; it entails both losses and gains, and it is open to the world beyond the individual's personal control, including changes in relationships critical to growth.

Models of development: development as a double fugue

What model, or models, of development capture this kind of complexity? Lacking a language, and unable to speak clearly within the constraints of the language of current developmental theory, we turn back to the OED. The meaning of development in its musical sense, of altering or expanding a basic melody, picking up different voices and a recurrent contrapuntal theme, suggests the musical form of the fugue, or of a double fugue.[1] The OED tells us that the fugue (from the Latin *fuga*, flight) is a "a polyphonic composition on one or more short subjects or themes, which are harmonized according to the laws of counterpoint, and introduced from time to time with various contrapuntal devices" (Stainer and Barrett 1880). Other dictionaries describe a fugue as a musical form or composition design for a definite number of instruments or voices in which a subject is announced in one voice and then developed contrapuntally by each of the other voices. A double fugue is the common term for a fugue on two subjects or themes, in which the two begin together. This musical form is sensitive to development in its many meanings, and in a plurality of voices.

An additional note, from Samuel Pepys' *Diary*, cited in the OED, clarifies the fine fit of the fugue as a musical form with the notion of listening to many voices. Pepys wrote, "The sense of the words being lost by not being heard, [is corrected] especially as they set them with Fuges [sic] of words, one after another." The fugue, then, offers a way to listen to many voices, as themes and variations on themes, and to correct for not listening to particular voices. Fugue also comes from the Latin word *fuga*, flight, and in modern psychiatry means a temporary flight from conscious experience, or a state of amnesia. During the process of development, human beings compose a fugue and are sometimes seemingly subject to fugue states. In other words, we might ask what becomes lost, forgotten, or silenced as development occurs, and in what contexts do certain kinds of losses occur?

The plainsong of justice and care

Let us look more closely at the key terms of musical notation. The theme, the OED says, "in music, [is] the principle melody, plainsong, or canto fermo in a contrapuntal piece; also a simple tune on which variations are constructed." A themester is one who labors at a theme, or one can be themeless, without a theme, and then a theme-maker furnishes a theme or subject. This language of labor and loss is sensitive to the active, constructive nature of development. We are all, fundamentally, themesters.

Listening to themes allows us to hear differences in voices. For example, the plainsong of care—its themes of connection and response to others—beginning with great clarity and simplicity, can be heard clearly in the words of thirteen-year-old girls and boys who wrote responses to sentence stems on the Washington University Sentence Completion Test, Loevinger's measure of ego development:

> The thing I like about myself is—I can make good friends.
>
> When people are helpless—I try to help them.
>
> A good father—is caring and he has fun with you.
>
> My conscience bothers me if—I have hurt someone's feelings.

And the plainsong of justice—its themes of fairness, respect for rights, and independence—can be heard just as clearly in their responses:

> My conscience bothers me if—I am unfair or betray a friend.
>
> When a child will not join in group activities—the poor kid has a right to be alone!
>
> The thing I like about myself is—I do things my own way.

The counterpoint of justice and care

Using the musical form of the fugue, a composer develops one or more short subjects or themes, "harmonized according to the laws of counterpoint." Webster defines counterpoint as "a melody accompanying another melody, the art of adding a related, but independent, melody, with fixed rules of harmony, to make a harmonic whole, a thing set up in contrast or interaction with another." Themes within the basic melody of the care voice may be enriched by adding themes of the justice voice, in counterpoint, through discernible rules of English grammar: that is, conjunctions, independent and dependent clauses, and the like. Such an example, written by a teenage girl, is "My mother and I—love and confide in one another but I am also quite independent." Or themes within either voice alone may become resonant and become rich in tone as they are contrapuntally placed together in a single sentence. A teenage boy writes: "A good father—gives his children a set of rules to live by and plays an important role in raising them."

The form of the fugue, understood in this way, reflects the very process of development. Loevinger and her colleagues discern high ego levels partially by examining how ideas are contrasted and combined, and we mark the orchestration of justice and care voices as a sign of moral maturity.

But the words counterpoint and contrapuntal have older meanings. Counterpoint, the OED says, comes from the French word *contrepointe* (against, or meeting of points). This is not the imagery of opposition and war, however, but of the process of quilting. The term meant "to quilt, or quilt stabbed or stitched through." A counterpoint-maker is a quilt-maker. And contrapuntal meant "a back-stitch in sewing, elaborating a quilt or tapestry" and only later as "the harmonic treatment of melodies as a counterpoint in a musical composition." So the terms counterpoint and contrapuntal meant to elaborate a design, in a quilt, tapestry, and later, in a musical composition.

What does the elaboration, the fine counterpoint of justice and care voices, sound like? In what ways does it differ when the plainsong of justice and care is developed contrapuntally, or when the basic melody of care and justice is developed contrapuntally? When we listen carefully to male and female voices, what does the fugue of development sound like played, as it were, as a double fugue? What are the contrapuntal devices of language that, when used by a speaker or writer to wrap themes and variations on themes together, result in a rich harmony?

At sixteen, the clear plainsong of justice and care is not so easy to discern in sentence completions. Instead the variations on themes suggest a more complex fugue of voices. To listen to boys and girls now requires more effort. It is necessary to attune one's ear to contrapuntal variations within and across the voices of justice and care.

Within care, this sounds like:

My mother and I—get along well though we sometimes run into tension.

Attention to the quality of relationship leads to a description of tension in relationship, which contains an implicit acknowledgment of difference, lending new meaning to "getting along."

Across justice and care, this variation sounds like:

My conscience bothers me if—I did not follow through on something I promised or said something mean about someone else.

Two themes are introduced, a commitment to keeping promises and a concern with not hurting others. These themes are joined by the word "or," laying out alternative causes of regret.

A method for identifying content themes of justice and care

Sentence stems are a well-established way to take soundings of psychic processes. The method of reading sentence stems for moral voice or relational theme (Rogers 1988b) makes it possible to ask how our analysis of voice and our exploration of development in terms of a musical notation relates to a standard measure of development. This method also brings together the musical meanings of development with the positional stages of Loevinger's theory of ego development.[2]

By attending closely to the language of the writer, and by observing grammatical constructions as a manifestation of self or Psyche and a source of developmental understanding, one can hear changes in the way themes of justice and care sound at different times for different individuals. Putting the themes back together, like chords, for an entire set of written responses to sentence stems (which cue thoughts and feelings about self, relationships, and morality) makes it possible to describe what one hears as a fugue of voices. Joining the themes of voice to the meaning of development as a process of laying open, unfolding, or revealing (a tale, the meaning of something), allows us to write character sketches of people. Loevinger and her colleagues originally wrote character descriptions of the people they studied by asking what sort of person would have written the test protocol they were examining. Similarly, we listen closely to sentence completions, looking for sets of themes, repetitions, overlaps, logical gaps, inconsistencies, erasures, and changes in tone to guide our sketches of the character or personality of the writer.

What do our sentence-stem soundings into development—listening for relational themes or moral voice—add to the understanding of character and development?

The case of Tanya

Twelve-year-old Tanya is a seventh grader, a participant in a longitudinal study of girls' development across the elementary and secondary school years. In addition to being interviewed, she also filled out the

Washington University Sentence Completion Test. Her ego development level is "conscientious-conventional."

What this tells us about Tanya is that, according to Loevinger's theory (1976), she is in the transition between the conformist and conscientious stages, a time in development marked by a heightened consciousness of oneself and one's feelings. As Loevinger's theory would predict, Tanya sees multiple possibilities and alternatives in situations. She is able to think about what is appropriate and to talk about exceptions and contingencies in relationships. She has a conception of striving, of goals, purposes, and expectations. She is aware of differences in feelings and can express concern for others with this awareness.

After reading Tanya's responses for themes of moral voice, what can we add to this picture? When she speaks in the voice of care, Tanya talks in plain, uncompromising terms about what she believes in—a form of care rooted in listening to and caring for herself—she believes that she can count on herself, that she knows and follows her own desires, that she knows what is right, and that she values the capacity to speak up. In the following statements, we hear the tone of a twelve-year-old girl who can speak directly about her own needs and wants, of what she knows without a doubt, and even of what she shouldn't know.

> The thing I like about myself is—I can usually count on myself for doing the things I want to do.
> A girl has a right to—be whatever she wants to be.
> A girl feels good when—she knows she did something right.
> A woman should always—speak up for what she feels.
> My conscience bothers me if—I know something I shouldn't know.

When Tanya talks about relationships, she is sensitive to differences in perception and to differences in human beings that can't be collapsed into general norms. These ideas underlie a capacity to know others in their own terms, one characteristic of the care voice.

> My mother and I—look the same, but never feel the same way about things.
> A good mother—will never be, all mothers are different and have different qualities.

This child is capable of reaching out to others in a gracious, non-threatening way and of expressing empathy in a way that reveals the interdependence of her happiness with her mother's well-being. She also describes her own vulnerability to loss, her own longing to matter to others.

> When a child will not join in group activities—no special attention should be given, but she should be nicely questioned and urged on.
>
> If my mother—relaxed and had a good time, I would be happy. I have empathy for her.
>
> When they avoided me—I felt left out.
>
> Sometimes she wished that—she could mean more to other people.

In her statements about men and women, we hear themes of justice (her concerns with a potential for oppression and with equality) and we see a disparity between Tanya's ideals of equality and her perceptions of women's inferior status. The tone of her remarks (only in these statements) becomes argumentative and somewhat defensive.

> A wife should—have as much power as the husband and she should be working.
>
> For a woman a career is—the same thing as it is for a man.
>
> Women are lucky because—they can prove many things.
>
> The worst thing about being a woman—is being spit on by men.

The fugue of voices we hear in Tanya's responses is the clear plainsong of care and a quieter plainsong of justice, with very little conscious contrast or conflict between the themes of these two voices.[3]

The case of Laura

If we turn now to Laura, a sixteen-year-old and a sophomore in high school, we find that, according to Loevinger's theory of ego development, she is more advanced in ego development than Tanya; her fugue of voices also sounds different. Laura's ego level is the conscientious stage. This implies that she can describe inner states and individual differences in vivid terms, that she is capable of articulating long-term goals and ideals; that she can think not only in terms of interpersonal differences, but also in terms of how people affect one another. Laura spontaneously refers to psychological development in herself, something that, Loevinger observes, almost never occurs at previous levels.

Listen to her sentence completions:

> The thing I like about myself is—that I can apply myself to any situation and, with effort, succeed.
>
> What gets me into trouble is—when I don't plan ahead and act impulsively in a given time.
>
> If I can't get what I want—I sometimes throw a fit. I'm going to try to outgrow that soon.

These capacities, however, come into conflict with what Laura expects of herself as a girl growing into a woman in Western culture. How she defines herself seems conflicted and difficult. As if to say that to achieve her goals and to know how to trust are incompatible, she erases one part of her response.

> Women are lucky because—they have a lot of choices open to them and people don't expect as much from them, so it's easier to be impressive.
>
> Men are lucky because—they are given expectations to achieve and are also given more encouragement.
>
> At times she worried about—loosing [sic] interest and becoming an underachiever.
>
> I am—happiest when [I have achieved my goals. This was erased] I know I can trust people.

Laura speaks in terms of themes of care as she describes her relationships with her parents: her capacity to disagree with her mother (although she seems to doubt herself), and her appreciation of her father's attention and willingness to accept her as she is.

> My mother and I—don't always agree, but she is usually right, and I love her.
>
> My father—comes to my field hockey and lacrosse games, and he is always really proud of me when I do something well. And if I don't do anything well, he just smiles and doesn't worry about it.

Laura's understanding of relationships includes ideas that people should be able to be themselves, that honesty and trust are necessary, that love feels good, and that one should be able to set limits in relationships. Yet for all of this clarity, she seems unable to trust others, to find people who are trustworthy, and feels dishonest in her relationships.

I feel sorry—for anyone who is intimidated and can't be themselves.

A girl has a right to—ask people to back off and expect them to do so.

I just can't stand people—who are backbiting and two-faced.

A woman feels good when—she is loved.

At times she wished that—he could be honest and really trust her.

Usually she felt that sex—would be all right if it was with the right person and she could really trust him with anything. That is very, very rare, though.

My conscience bothers me if—I feel dishonest with others and I feel this way often.

Her confusion seems compounded by the themes of her moral vision. The ability of women, wives and mothers, to care is linked with notions of selfless love and self-sacrifice and to cultural prescriptions for how women should behave.

A wife should—take care of her husband (they usually don't know much about cooking, etc.).

A husband has a right to—expect his wife to be willing to listen and understand.

A good mother—is there for her children and husband regardless of all other things.

The fugue of voices we hear in Laura's responses is the counterpoint of themes of both care and justice, sung now and then in a clear way, but more often in a confused and wavering voice.

Soundings: through character, into development

These character sketches are soundings into development that reveal not only the emerging psychological strengths of adolescents, but also the conflicts that girls face coming of age in a culture the conventions of which are not the same for women and men. The close analysis of themes is a method for unwrapping the complexities of development by listening closely to language; this allows us to differentiate the clear voice from the wavering voice, to mark passages of certainty and passages of confusion, and to note how and when it becomes difficult to speak. Although Laura, at sixteen, is more sophisticated in her thinking and at a more advanced level in Loevinger's scale of ego development than twelve-year-old Tanya, something is different by mid-adolescence. From listening to her responses to the above sentence stems, it appears that Laura does not have Tanya's clear way of speaking nor Tanya's knowledge of relationships—a knowledge that does not exclude herself. And these differences are not captured by a linear model of development. At sixteen, Laura faces a major conflict in becoming at once an adult and a woman in Western culture, the deeply knotted dilemma of how to listen both to herself and to the tradition, how to care for herself as well as for others. Girls' and women's solutions to this dilemma have often been either to deny difference in the name of equality, or to deny self in the name of morality, as if Psyche were not affected in significant ways by gender. This dilemma is frequently so difficult for adolescent girls and adult women that it can confound belief in their own perception and experience, leading to equivocation and contradiction, such as we started to see in Laura's sentence stems.

Listening to a fugue of voices that can be traced over time and tied to the development of self, we have taken soundings of development. The shift to a musical language marks us a way out of the deadlocked paradox of self and relationship that continues to plague the fields of personality and developmental psychology: that one can only experience self in the context of relationship with others and that one can only experience relationship if one differentiates other from self. Because music is a language of movement and time—notes are heard in relation to other notes, and become part of themes, leitmotifs, melodies—a musical notation gives us a way to capture people speaking in relationship and living in a body and in a culture.[4]

Notes

1. Dianne Argyris suggested the idea of a fugue to Annie Rogers in a discussion about development.

2. The method alluded to here is described in detail in *Two developmental voices: A method for identifying a fugue of justice and care themes in sentence completions* (Rogers 1988b). In brief, sentence stem responses to items of the Washington University Sentence Completion Test are coded for ego development using empirical scoring manuals constructed by Loevinger (1970a, 1970b), and then read for sixteen different content themes of moral voice. Character sketches, written for each individual, are based on ego development stage descriptions as well as themes of moral voice.

3. The plainsong of justice and care themes we discern in Tanya's sentence-stem responses echoes the clarity and candidness of her statements about care and justice in our analysis of her interview narrative using the Reader's Guide. Preliminary evidence of the validity of the moral voices of justice and care on Washington University Sentence Completion Test responses and the real-life conflict and choice interview (Rogers 1988b) point to promising directions for validating developmental themes of moral voice revealed by these two different measures.

4 The change in the order of the authors (see Gilligan, Brown, and Rogers below) reflects Rogers' work on the etymology of development and on the musical language of the fugue in this excerpted section of the longer paper.

Appendix

Tanya's Sentence Completion Test
(Girls' form 2-77a)

1. If I had more money—I would be no more happier, but I would be more content to spend when I do.

2. A wife should—have as much power as the husband and she should be working.

3. When a child will not join in group activities—no special attention should be given but she should be nicely questioned and urged on.

4. My mother and I—look the same, but never feel the same way about things.

5. The thing I like about myself is—I can usually count on myself for doing the things I want to do.

6. Being with other people—I enjoy very much, but when I'm wrong I need to concentrate.

7. If my mother—relaxed and had a good time I would be happy. I have empathy for her.

8. Education—is on almost the top of my list when I think of the future.

9. What gets me into trouble is—when I do bad in school or don't do what I'm told to do.

10. A good mother—will never be, all mothers are different and have different qualities.

11. I feel sorry—for anyone who can't get to where they want to go.

12. The worst thing about being a woman—is being spit on by men.

13. Women are lucky because—they can prove many things.

14. At times she worried about—letting people down.

15. She felt proud that she—had gotten where she was so far.

16. Rules are—do things right.

17. When she thought of her mother, she—fell silent with a grin on her face.

18. When I get mad—all I want is to be left alone.

19. When they avoided me—I felt left out.

20. Raising a family—is probably one of the toughest jobs there is.

21. I am—sitting at a table.

22. A girl has a right to—be whatever she wants to be.

23. I just can't stand people who—don't take things seriously when they should.

24. My father—is the perfect example of what and how I want to be when I grow up.

25. If I can't get what I want—I try to forget about it and think about the things I already have.

26. A girl feels good when—she knows she did something right.

27. My main problem is—that I worry with my imagination.

28. Crime and delinquency could be halted if—the world halted.

29. Sometimes she wished that—she could mean more to other people.

30. When I am criticized—I take it personally and always think about it, but try to fix it.

31. For a woman a career is—the same thing it is for a man.

32. When people are helpless—they are in the ditch of morality.

33. When my mother spanked me, I—spanked her back.

34. Men are lucky because—they don't get pregnant.

35. My conscience bothers me if—I know something I shouldn't know.

36. A woman should always—speak up for what she feels.

37. A good father—is my father.

Note: Item 37 is added to the 36 items of this form of the test.

Laura's Sentence Completion Test
(Women's form 81)

1. When a child will not join in group activities—his friends should go see what is wrong.

2. Raising a family—is really important and shouldn't be under-rated.

3. When I am criticized—I should try to accept what I am told, but I usually don't too well.

4. A man's job—can be done by a woman if she chooses.

5. Being with other people—is usually more fun than being alone, but not necessarily more fun than being with just a few.

6. The thing I like about myself is—that I can apply myself to any situation, and with effort, succeed.

7. My mother and I—don't always agree, but she is usually right, and I love her.

8. What get me into trouble is—when I don't plan ahead, and act impulsively too often in a given time.

9. Education—is necessary to survive in the world.

10. When people are helpless—you should try to help them if you can in any way.

11. Women are lucky because—they have a lot of choices open to them and people don't expect as much from them so it's easier to be impressive.

12. A good father—takes time to [come to. This was erased] spend with his children when he is home.

13. A girl has a right to—ask people to back off and expect them to do so.

14. When they talked about sex, I—was convinced to become a nun.

15. A wife should—take care of her husband (they usually don't know much about cooking etc.).

16. I feel sorry—for anyone who is intimidated and can't be themselves.

17. A man feels good when—he knows who his friends are and has good friends.

18. Rules are—important, but should be always able to modify to fit the situation.

19. Crime and delinquency could be halted if—education and morality could be put into culture of poorer educated.

20. Men are lucky because—they are given expectations to achieve so are often given more encouragement.

21. I just can't stand people who—are back-biting or two-faced.

22. At times she worried about—what she would do after college.

23. I am—happiest when [I have achieved my goals. This was erased] I know I can trust people.

24. A woman feels good when—she is loved.

25. My main problem is—losing interest and becoming "an underachiever."

26. A husband has a right to—expect his wife is willing to listen and understand.

27. The worst thing about being a woman—is [no response]

28. A good mother—is there for her children and her husband regardless of all other things.

29. When I am with a man—I don't think I can generalize about this—everyone is different.

30. Sometimes she wished that—he could be honest and trust her.

31. My father—comes to my field hockey and lacrosse games and he's always really proud of me when I do something well, and if I don't do anything well he just smiles and doesn't worry about it.

32. If I can't get what I want—I sometimes have a fit, but I'm going to try to outgrow that soon.

33. Usually she felt that sex—was all right if it was with the right person and she really could trust him with anything. That is very, very rare, though.

34. For a woman a career is—good if she can handle it plus everything else.

35. My conscience bothers me if—I feel dishonest with others and I feel this way often.

36. A woman should always—be able to smile, if you can't keep things in perspective, you are in trouble.

Sources

Gilligan, C. 1977. In a different voice: Women's conceptions of the self and of morality. *Harvard Educational Review* 47:481–517.

———. 1982. *In a Different Voice.* Cambridge, Mass.: Harvard University Press.

Gilligan, C., L.M. Brown, and A. Rogers. 1989. "Psyche Embedded: A Place for Body, Relationships, and Culture in Personality Theory." In *Studying Persons and Lives,* edited by A. Rabin et al. New York: Springer Publishing Company.

Gilligan, C., J. Ward, and J. Taylor, eds. 1988. *Mapping the Moral Domain: A Contribution of Women's Thinking to Psychology and Education.* Cambridge, Mass.: Harvard University Graduate School of Education.

Gilligan, C., D. K. Johnston, and B. Miller. 1988. *Moral Voice, Adolescent Development, and Secondary Education: A Study of the Green River School.* Report of the Project on Adolescence, Monograph #3, from the Center for the Study of Gender, Education, and Human Development. Cambridge, Mass.: Harvard University.

Jack, D. 1987. "Silencing the Self: The Power of Social Imperatives in Female Depression." In *Women and Depression: A Lifespan Perspective,* edited by R. Formanek and A. Gurian. New York: Springer Publishing.

Loevinger, J. 1957. Objective tests as instruments of psychological theory. *Psychological Reports* 3:635–94.

———. 1976. *Ego Development: Conceptions and Theories.* San Francisco: Jossey-Bass.

———. 1979. "Theory and Data in the Measurement of Ego Development." In *Scientific Ways in the Study of Ego Development,* edited by J. Loevinger, 1–24. Worcester, Mass.: Clark University Press.

Loevinger, J., and R. Wessler. 1970a. *Measuring Ego Development I: Construction and Use of a Sentence Completion Test.* San Francisco: Jossey-Bass.

Loevinger, J., R. Wessler, and C. Redmore. 1970b. *Measuring Ego Development II: Scoring Manual for Women and Girls.* San Francisco: Jossey-Bass.

Miller, J. 1976. *Toward a New Psychology of Women.* Boston: Beacon Press.

Rogers, A. 1988b. Two developmental voices: A method for identifying a fugue of justice and care themes in sentence completions. Unpublished manuscript, Harvard University.

Steiner-Adair, C. 1986. The body-politic: Normal female adolescent development and the development of eating disorders. *Journal of the American Academy of Psychoanalysis* 14:95–114.

DATE DUE			
MAY 1 4 1991			
DEC 2			
AUG 1 8 1994			
MAY 0 9 1997			